*Slavery
in the Caribbean
Francophone World*

Slavery
in the Caribbean
Francophone World

DISTANT VOICES,
FORGOTTEN ACTS,
FORGED IDENTITIES

Edited by Doris Y. Kadish

THE UNIVERSITY OF GEORGIA PRESS

ATHENS AND LONDON

© 2000 by the University of Georgia Press

Athens, Georgia 30602

All rights reserved

Designed by Betty Palmer McDaniel

Set in 11/13 Fournier

by G&S Typesetters, Inc.

Printed and bound by Maple-Vail

The paper in this book meets the guidelines for

permanence and durability of the Committee on

Production Guidelines for Book Longevity of the

Council on Library Resources.

Printed in the United States of America

04   03   02   01   00   C   5   4   3   2   1

Library of Congress Cataloging-in-Publication Data

Slavery in the Caribbean Francophone world : distant voices,

forgotten acts, forged identities / edited by Doris Y. Kadish.

p.   cm.

Based on a conference held at the University of Georgia in Oct. 1997.

Includes bibliographical references (p.   ) and index.

ISBN 0-8203-2166-4 (alk. paper)

1. Slavery—West Indies, French—History—Congresses.

2. Slave insurrections—West Indies, French—History—

Congresses.   3. Slaves—West Indies, French—Social

conditions—Congresses.   I. Kadish, Doris Y.

II. University of Georgia.

HT1107.S58   2000

306.3'62'0972976—dc21   99-37913

British Library Cataloging-in-Publication Data available

Contents

Acknowledgments

This book grew out of a conference on "Slavery in the Francophone World" that was held at the University of Georgia in October 1997. I wish to express my gratitude to all those who provided papers, responses, and comments on that occasion and to the many other faculty, students, and members of the public whose active participation gave new meaning in the 1990s to the tragic events that occurred in France, the United States, and the Caribbean two centuries earlier.

Special thanks are due to those colleagues who graciously offered me their literary and historical expertise (Carrol Coates, John Inscoe, and Lester Langley) and to those other colleagues (Freda Scott Giles and Jean-Pierre Piriou) who helped me to realize my dream of producing Maryse Condé's *In the Time of the Revolution*. The production of that play was an integral part of my project, as I explain in the closing chapter of this book. Finally, I wish to express my appreciation for the moral support and assistance with details that I received from Myrna Becker, Leara Rhodes, and Raymond Woller and for the wonderful advice I received at all steps along the way from Karen Orchard of the University of Georgia Press.

Preface

DORIS Y. KADISH

This book includes three parts dealing with three geographical areas: France, the United States, and the French West Indies. Part 1 begins in France in 1789 and closes with an episode from 1847, a year before abolition brought an end to direct French involvement in slavery in 1848. Part 2 dwells on the United States, beginning in Georgia with the participation by some of the future leaders of the Haitian revolt in the American Revolution and going on to consider the impact of the waves of immigration to the United States starting in the 1790s and the repercussions of Francophone slavery in the states of Virginia, Louisiana, and Maryland. Part 3 looks at the Caribbean, beginning with Creole as the language of slavery in the colonial period and turning then to writers from Martinique and Guadeloupe in the contemporary period who are grappling with the meaning of their history under slavery. The book concludes with a fourth part containing two assessments of the legacy of Francophone slavery, one for the United States, the other for the Caribbean. Placing France first, the United States second, and the Caribbean last in the organization of this book in no way reflects the political or cultural importance of those locations but rather their chronological position in the unfolding of historical events.

The essays presented here, of course, cannot begin to cover the full range of literary and historical topics in Francophone slavery studies. The choice of topics here is of necessity limited and attributable to the circumstances of the interests of the participating scholars. The significance of these essays lies less in their comprehensiveness than in the variety of approaches they exemplify. One of the goals of this book is to make the point that different scholarly methods bear different but equally enlightening results. Within the pages of this book those methods include approaches within the fields of literature, social history, linguistics, and journalism.

Although the formal organization of this book is chronological and geo-graphical, its underlying structure consists of a series of interrelated and over-lapping themes that cross boundaries of time and place and that center on the participants rather than on the events as such. That is not to say that consider-able work does not remain to be done in unraveling the vast web of political, economic, and military acts that produced the system of Francophone slavery and led to the revolutionary events in the French Caribbean. Historians con-tinue to piece together the complex puzzle of the events surrounding the Hai-tian Revolution and its aftermath. But this volume has a different purpose. It contributes to the growing body of scholarship that focuses more on social and cultural issues than on political, military, or economic matters and that turns its attention to the lives of the participants: their struggles, their aspirations, their forms of expression, their legacy. All of the essays in this book aim to show, in short, who the participants were, what they said, and what they did. The essays all attempt to listen to the participants' distant voices, to re-create their forgot-ten acts, and to grasp the nature of their forged identities.

These essays share the underlying themes of voice, agency, and identity. The scarcity of primary source material providing access to the *voices* of the historical participants, especially persons of color, constitutes unquestionably one of the greatest challenges to Francophone scholars and writers. The rea-sons for the paucity of material are numerous: chaotic conditions in the places in which records would have been kept; illiteracy of many of the participants; absence in many Francophone locations of the necessary infrastructures to sup-port producing historical records, maintaining archives, or conducting histor-ical research; reluctance by the French to face up to their colonialist past; and silence by historians generally surrounding the Haitian Revolution.[1]

What is more, existing materials tend to be fragmented and difficult to lo-cate. Important works such as *Les Marrons du syllabaire*, which represents the fruits of the Haitian historian Jean Fouchard's access to often obscure archival material, have not been widely available. And even Fouchard's materials add up more to a tantalizing set of bits and pieces than a coherent picture: for example, instances of slaves who knew how to read and write Arabic before they came to the New World; of slaves who used various vegetal substances to fabricate ink and paper in order to inscribe prayers they knew from Africa; of a female slave writing in blood. Existing sources of information are only gradually gain-ing the attention and careful scrutiny they deserve. They include the speeches, petitions, pamphlets, and other political material published by literate persons of color who assumed a public role around the time of the French and Haitian

Revolutions; a few literary works by free persons of color; some songs and other texts in Creole; the judicial record from the large number of slaves living in France in the eighteenth century, some of whom won verdicts against their masters in the French courts by evoking the age-old principle that anyone setting foot on French soil was free; records from court cases in Saint-Domingue and the United States; journalistic records such as the *Affiches Américaines* published in Saint-Domingue from the 1760s to the 1790s, the *Revue des Colonies* founded in 1834 and published in France by free persons of color, and French-language newspapers published in the United States in the 1790s, such as the *Journal des Révolutions de la Partie Française de St. Domingue* in Philadelphia or the *Moniteur de la Louisiane* in New Orleans.[2] The paucity and fragmentation of Francophone material stands in sharp contrast to the rich supply of American slave narratives, for which there is no French-language equivalent for reasons that include the fact that literacy in the Francophone colonies was more strictly confined to members of an elite, mulatto class who were not eager to dwell on their connections with slavery even though they wrote pamphlets and other works demanding their rights; and the fact that many French abolitionists, unlike their American counterparts, focused their attention on obtaining rights for free persons of color, not on helping to record or make known the lives of slaves to help the cause of abolishing slavery.[3]

The scholars whose work is presented in this book draw on various sources to gain access to the voices of persons of color. Regardless of the sources, however, they share a willingness to listen to the participants themselves, to take seriously the recorded material that has been largely unnoticed and undervalued in the past, and to contextualize those voices in the specific locations and conditions in which they were produced. Catherine Reinhardt's "French Caribbean Slaves Forge Their Own Ideal of Liberty in 1789" breaks with an exclusively hegemonic perspective on colonial history by recording the competing voices of abolitionists, slaves, and planters. Looking closely at two letters from 1789 by Martinican slaves, she analyzes a broad range of rhetorical strategies, including their reappropriation of the discourses of religion, Enlightenment philosophy, and abolitionism. Kimberly S. Hanger's "Greedy French Masters and Color-Conscious, Legal-Minded Spaniards in Colonial Louisiana" looks at notarial and judicial documents in Louisiana from 1794, a time when the prospect of a shift from Spanish to French rule seemed imminent and when persons of color were weighing the competing advantages and disadvantages of the two colonial systems. Bringing to life real individuals and restoring their actual words, Hanger highlights the complexities of their political and racial views. In "Creole, the Language of Slavery," Albert Valdman looks at the ways in which the enslaved Africans who were brought to the New World processed their linguistic situation and participated in the creation of creole language. Creole, he concludes, was produced through a complex restructuring of African and European languages in which both slaves and masters were active participants. One of the few scholars who has scrutinized existing creole texts from the French colonial period, Valdman brings to our attention a play written in 1818 by Juste Chanlatte, Henry Christophe's secretary, in which Creole competes with the various registers of French language used in colonial times. Having read Valdman's demonstration of the significance of Creole in the formation of the slaves' identity during the period leading to independence, we are better able to understand the moving statement by the contemporary novelist Daniel Maximin: "Equality speaks French, but freedom speaks Creole."[4]

Other essays in this book provide further examples of what happens when scholars gain access to the distant voices of Francophone slaves by combing through journalistic accounts, scrutinizing church archives, and analyzing political and literary texts. All of these examples are instances of what Michel-Rolph Trouillot calls "the unearthing of silences" and "the historian's . . . emphasis on the retrospective significance of hitherto neglected events." As he points out, dealing with such material requires not only scholarly labor but also a commitment to delving beneath layers of often obfuscating historical interpretations of the events to produce subtle and insightful new readings of the past. Hearing the voice of the other is clearly not the simple, straightforward affair it was considered to be in earlier times. Hence, for example, the criticism leveled against the nineteenth-century abolitionist Victor Schoelcher by the Guadeloupian novelist Maryse Condé (whose views on slavery are discussed in the last chapter of this book) for having failed to pay attention to or listen to the slaves themselves and thus for having failed to grasp their true creativity and independent identity. Condé also underscores the limitations of other nineteenth-century Eurocentric accounts of slavery in which the oppression of slaves was to a significant extent an occasion for whites to talk about forms of oppression in their own lives.[5]

Francophone writers have increasingly felt the need to fill the void in documented records of their past by creating fictional accounts in which the past serves to create the present and an informed Caribbean identity grounded in its own, rather than French, history. In Maximin's *L'Isolé Soleil*, for example, an eighteenth-century free person of color and writer, Jonathan, produces his own account of the revolutionary events at the time of his death in the battle of 1802.

That document is then passed on to his half-sister, Ti-Carole, who, after using it as a bible of revolutionary messages for teaching mulatto children, transmits it to her descendant Louise in the twentieth century. Thus the need to reconstruct slavery and even invent archival records of the past motivates other reenactments of the past in contemporary French Caribbean literature. In those works, as in Maximin's, women are often the ones who pass on to the next generation the legacy of their past under slavery. In Patrick Chamoiseau's novel *Texaco*, for example, Marie-Sophie Laborieux serves as the narrator who reconstructs Martinican history as told by her father, Esternome Laborieux, a slave on a plantation near Saint-Pierre.

The second of the underlying themes of this book is *agency*, the actions that whites and blacks performed in response to Francophone slavery and the effects that their actions had at the time. Few of those actions are well known; indeed, most have been forgotten, for such reasons as the paucity of documented material, the lack of attention to uneducated or semi-literate historical subjects, and the silence that generally surrounds the Haitian Revolution. Acts of opposition to slavery by whites did exist, although the nature and efficacy of those acts are subject to considerable debate. Abolitionism occurred in France during the short period from 1788 to 1793, when the abolitionist *Société des Amis des Noirs* was in existence. Formed upon the urging of British Quakers, the *Amis des Noirs* was from the start less systematic, less organized, and less effective than its counterparts in England and the United States. Meetings were held irregularly; membership was small and costly; members were drawn from a narrow group of the Parisian upper or upper-middle classes; little active participation or networking was expected of members. Most members had little or no firsthand familiarity with the French colonies or the slave trade—that is, with real slaves. Unlike English abolitionists such as Thomas Clarkson and William Wilberforce, who visited ports and documented the egregious abuses encountered by slaves in captivity, the *Amis des Noirs* adopted a more abstract, literary approach to the subject of slavery that relied more on the printed word—newspapers, pamphlets, literature—as opposed to the documented evidence that could be obtained from oral accounts of slaves' lives.[6]

Too often, however, historical considerations of abolitionism in France have focused narrowly on the *Amis des Noirs* and have overlooked the variety of other abolitionist activities that existed during and after the years of that movement's existence. A broader perspective in which to view French abolitionist activity is provided in "Voices Lost? Staël and Slavery, 1786–1830" by John Claiborne Isbell. This essay documents the varied and extensive contributions

to ending the slave trade and to emancipation by one of the leading French abolitionists, Germaine de Staël, as well as by the members of her family and her
close circle of friends and fellow writers during a period that spans close to half
a century. This lifetime of abolitionist activity has regrettably been overshad-
owed by the contributions of male abolitionists such as the marquis de Condorcet and the abbé Raynal or male Romantic writers such as Alphonse de
Lamartine and Victor Hugo.[7] Isbell's essay documents the literary and political
features of Staël's writings on slavery as well as placing them in the social and
political contexts of abolitionist activity throughout Europe in the eighteenth
and nineteenth centuries. Unlike the *Amis des Noirs*, she took a pragmatic,
political approach that put her in touch with the realities of slavery and individual persons of color: her dealings with William Wilberforce and her intervention in behalf of Magloire Pélage are two illustrative examples. As Isbell
states, Staël's abolitionist activities were "anchored in the particular." His
analysis compliments Reinhardt's, which contrasts the *Amis des Noirs'* abstract,
future-oriented discourse of pity with the concrete, immediate demands of the
slaves. Notwithstanding the good intentions of the *Amis des Noirs*, they spoke
to and for the privileged, whereas women and blacks left a legacy of a different,
more direct opposition to slavery based on their own experiences or firsthand
knowledge.

Gabriel Moyal also dwells on white participants in "Transmitting the Sense
of Property: Reporting on a Slave Massacre in 1847." His essay highlights the
inability of Europeans to conceive of blacks as possessing agency, which for
whites was strictly a function of property: hence, for example, the fact that
property was a requirement at the time for status as an "active," voting citizen.
In contrast with the Spanish, who, as Hanger's essay explains, had liberal practices allowing persons of color to initiate self-purchase without any involvement by their masters, the French considered self-purchase a radical threat to
property owners, and despite a law requiring its institution as a social policy to
prepare for the eventual abolition of slavery, it was inconsistently enforced.
Moyal shows that even liberal legislators and journalists who called for enforcement were motivated by political, not humanitarian, concerns. His essay
thus echoes Reinhardt's and Isbell's in showing that among the most serious
limitations of abolitionism in France was the legacy of privilege that the *Amis
des Noirs* left behind. That legacy resurfaced on January 1, 1847, when a massacre of two thousand slaves occurred on the west coast of Africa, allegedly because the British naval blockade made it impossible for the slave owners to ship
their slaves, whom they couldn't afford to keep. By analyzing the way in which

a leading French newspaper rushed to deny that this inhuman act could have been committed by European slave traders, Moyal demonstrates the extent to which the French suffered from a deep-seated and pernicious blindness regarding the nature of European agency.

In turning now to black opposition to slavery, *marronage* assumes special importance, especially from a Caribbean perspective. The practice of escaping the plantation slave system by running away to the hills existed from the earliest years of colonial rule. In Haiti, it also extended to the practice of escaping across an unguarded border to the eastern, Spanish side of the island, where there was far less control, little chance of extradition, and a general mixing of races and classes. Fouchard maintains that it was a form of extra-legal self-emancipation, creating a class between free persons of color and slaves that was also increased by many masters who did not want to go through administrative channels to recover runaway slaves. Practices of *marronage* intensified and became increasingly collective and political during the revolutionary period. Many issues surrounding *marronage* are debated among scholars: Were the maroons motivated by a desire for freedom or just material conditions of mistreatment? Would the slave revolts in Haiti have occurred without *marronage*? To what extent were the maroons guilty of complicity with white plantation owners, exchanging their own freedom for an agreement to deliver runaway slaves? In grappling with these and other questions relating to *marronage*, a number of writers have attempted to provide fictional accounts of the maroon mentality. One such attempt by Chamoiseau is described by Marie-José N'Zengou-Tayo in "Exorcising Painful Memories: Raphaël Confiant and Patrick Chamoiseau." Another contested issue in studies of *marronage* concerns gender. Since more than two-thirds of the maroons were men, and since their role as rebels has been associated with the success of the Haitian Revolution, considerable debate has centered on what some see as the overly romanticized, male-centered myth of the maroon. This issue is at the heart of A. James Arnold's "From the Problematic Maroon to a Woman-Centered Creole Project in the Literature of the French West Indies."[8]

On American soil, blacks from Saint-Domingue exercised agency in other ways, including their direct participation as soldiers and their influence as models of heroism for American slaves. In "Haitian Contributions to American History: A Journalistic Record," Leara Rhodes looks at the contingent of free blacks who fought in the Siege of Savannah in 1779. That troop included several future leaders of the revolts in Saint-Domingue: André Rigaud and reportedly Henry Christophe as well. Although American troops were forced to retreat, the free blacks are credited with having protected American and French troops and enabled the embarkment of further reinforcements. Regarding the issue of the silence surrounding the Haitian Revolution noted earlier, Rhodes questions the silence in France and the United States concerning this particular instance of black heroism, both at the time of the battle and still today. She argues that the Savannah battle serves as an inspiring example of black agency for Haitians today, in the United States and in the Caribbean, where ironically their own stories of heroism often remain unknown or uncelebrated: until recently the story of Delgrès's rebellion did not even appear in the official textbooks of Guadeloupian schoolchildren.[9] A far different but related story of black heroism emerges in Douglas R. Egerton's "The Tricolor in Black and White: The French Revolution in Gabriel's Virginia." Looking at social and political developments in Virginia during the 1790s, Egerton records the shift away from pro-French sentiments among whites, in large part as fear grew that the slave revolts in the French colonies would spread to the United States.[10] But from a black perspective at the time, France came to stand as a model of freedom for oppressed people, for whom Toussaint Louverture represented a "symbol of militant success."

The third of the underlying themes of this book is *identity*, bearing on questions of how the various white, mulatto, and black participants in the drama of Francophone slavery forged a racial, ethnic, collective, or personal sense of self. During the colonial period, issues of race were inextricably linked in the French colonies to issues of ethnicity and class, as they are still today. Among other things, identity was a function of retaining African or European ties while forging a new Caribbean identity that combined those diverse ethnic components. Valdman shows the importance for slaves of retaining speech rhythms, intonation, and ways of using language to guard against total acculturation and retain their "African soul." He also shows the role that creole language played in forging white identities at the time. He notes that Creole became the language of whites as well as blacks in the French Caribbean, unlike in the English-speaking colonies; indeed, he observes that Creole is still used in private among white Louisianans as a part of their French Caribbean legacy.

In "Francophone Residents of Antebellum Baltimore and the Origins of the Oblate Sisters of Providence," Diane Batts Morrow makes a closely related point about ethnic identity, which in this case intersects with both class and race. Her essay looks at the important contribution of several educated women of color who left Saint-Domingue to found the first religious order for women and the first school devoted to educating black women in the United States.

Their order was created in 1829 in Baltimore, Maryland, the center of the American Catholic Church. Regarding identity, she observes that these women experienced a consistent loss of privilege and status in the American two-tiered racial system as opposed to the three-tiered system of the French colonies. Accordingly, their assertion of French ethnicity, which occurred in part through retaining their ties with the French language, represented an assertion of an anti-American identity, as they came to identify the United States with racism. Similarly, for the French priest who cofounded their order, maintaining a conservative, Catholic, non-Americanized theological position was tantamount to asserting advocacy for black women and legitimizing their role in the church and society. For him, too, asserting French identity meant rejecting American racism.

Some of the same issues of identity resurface in the French Caribbean world today as writers try to negotiate intersecting ethnicities and develop complex formulations of hybrid identity rather than asserting an exclusively African identity, as in the earlier "negritude" movement. The goals of negritude included celebrating black achievement, acknowledging common African roots unifying black experience worldwide, and raising black consciousness about past and present forms of victimization and oppression. Originally conceived in Paris in the 1930s by the African poet Léopold Senghor, the Guianese poet Léon Damas, and the Martinican poet and playwright Aimé Césaire, who was the first to use the term, the concept of negritude gained international attention through writings by such popular French writers as André Breton, whose essay "Un Grand poète noir" served as the preface to Césaire's *Cahier d'un retour au pays natal* (1947); Jean-Paul Sartre, who similarly wrote an essay, "Orphée noir," to introduce Senghor's *Anthologie de la nouvelle poésie nègre et malgache de langue française* (1948); and Jean Genet, in his widely performed play "Les Nègres" (1958). Frantz Fanon's *Peau noire, masques blancs* (1952) argues that blacks have interiorized white cultural notions and have the same collective unconscious as whites; and although not an affirmation of negritude, Fanon's work represented a related and highly influential effort to bring about liberation through its probing analysis of the psychological bases of black inferiority. Negritude in France closely paralleled such related movements elsewhere as the Harlem Renaissance in the United States, *La Revue indigène* in Haiti, and Negrismo in Cuba.[11]

The shift from negritude to more complex forms of hybrid identity has moved through a number of stages and has provoked debates that find expression in the Caribbean section of this book. From the 1960s to the present time,

Edouard Glissant has effectively worked to deconstruct negritude's presumed search for "authentic" African roots, for which he substitutes a more nuanced literary and creative search for origins. In *Poétique de la relation* and other works he has articulated in the place of negritude a relational Caribbean identity in which diverse cultural traditions come together in a fluid process of constantly changing social, racial, and ethnic interactions. In contrast with Glissant's deconstruction of negritude's "essentialist" African identity, which is often expressed in highly theoretical and obscure terms, the Martinican writers Patrick Chamoiseau and Raphaël Confiant have formulated the notion of *créolité*, which has assumed growing importance in discussions of Francophone identity over the past decade. *Créolité* posits an identity formed by the coming together of African, European, and Caribbean components in much the same way that those components come together in creole language, which these writers promote and consistently incorporate into their use of the French language. This book contains two essays that reflect the debates surrounding the competing theories of Glissant versus the Creolists Confiant and Chamoiseau. In "Exorcising Painful Memories," N'Zengou-Tayo presents the Creolists' position as compatible with Glissant's, casting their treatment of the literature and history of Francophone slavery in a largely positive light. In contrast, in "From the Problematic Maroon to a Woman-Centered Creole Project," Arnold views the Creolists as essentialists whose concepts of ethnoclasses exclude women and newer ethnic minorities in the French West Indies. Arnold also levels charges of class superiority against the Creolists: as males in relation to females, as mulattoes to blacks, and as writers from Martinique to writers from Guadeloupe, where black and women writers have been more successful in asserting their competing versions of creole identity. By thus providing a theoretical analysis of gender, Arnold's essay gives added depth to the important subtheme of gender in this book, which Morrow looks at from the standpoint of women educators and Isbell and I treat in the context of specific women writers.

The conviction that the story of Francophone slavery did not end with the independence of Haiti in 1804 or emancipation in the French colonies in 1848 is a recurring theme in the writings of Francophone writers and scholars, and it is this conviction that receives consideration in Legacies, the final part of this book. The idea that slavery lives on in the Francophone world arises in part, as N'Zengou-Tayo explains, from the status of Martinique and Guadeloupe, which as French Overseas Departments are nevertheless considered by many as "neocolonies" rather than islands having acquired equal status with the departments in France proper. Writers from those islands return to their past under slavery to discover models and inspiration in their search for contemporary social, cultural, and political change. More broadly, some would argue that the legacy of slavery lives on throughout the Americas and that we would be turning our backs on our own past to conceive of slavery as a bad moment from an earlier time that has happily ceased to exist without a trace.

In "From the Plantation to the Penitentiary: Chain, Classification, and Codes of Deterrence," Joan Dayan follows along the path traced in her recent book about the Haitian revolution, *Haiti, History, and the Gods*. In that work she provided an in-depth analysis of the French *Code Noir* as a discourse of dispossession, in which slaves become things and are divested of selfhood; and she showed how dispossession continued after emancipation through a legal and judicial system that maintained continued mastery over the former slaves. Although Dayan's contribution here does not deal directly with Haiti, her analysis of modern structures of containment and dispossession goes to the heart of the enduring legacy of the slavery that existed in the Caribbean Francophone world and that persists still today in the Western hemisphere. In her essay, Dayan argues compellingly that without realizing it we are duplicating the mental structures inherited from the *Code Noir* and Francophone slave owners. The example she provides involves the specific instance of the Arizona prison system and the practice of chain gangs, which were used in the state of Georgia into the 1960s; but the relevance of her essay extends beyond this example to other unjust and coercive forms of labor and confinement. Then and now, she argues, the prisoner is a slave to the state, experiencing a form of "civil" or "social" death. The result is a loss of rights in the eyes of those who hold property and who feel justified in resorting to practices of containment and incapacitation that parallel earlier practices of control and classification. According to Dayan, today's practices not only parallel the earlier ones but derive from them: our familiarity with codes of containment from the past under slavery resurfaces and draws on images deep in our psyches. Dwelling on the Thirteenth Amendment of 1865, which abolished slavery except as punishment for crime, Dayan argues that plantations became prisons instituting systematic practices of racial subordination.

The key issue that Dayan raises and that the second essay in Legacies also addresses is our relation today to slavery. A participant at the conference on "Slavery in the Francophone World," Maryse Condé has on numerous occasions addressed issues related to the subject of slavery. One of her most extended and insightful treatments of that subject is the play *In the Time of the*

Revolution, originally written and performed for the bicentennial of the French Revolution in Guadeloupe in 1989 and performed for the first time in English during the conference at the University of Georgia. In my closing essay, "Maryse Condé and Slavery," which includes Condé's observations at the conference and her reactions to the play, I give her the last word by examining her views on slavery and recording her strong conviction, which echoes Dayan's, that it is a problem of the present, not the past. It seems appropriate to close this volume with the words of Maryse Condé, not only because she stands as one of the foremost Francophone writers in the world today, but also because she has emerged as one of the most important French women writers of the twentieth century. By looking at her views on women and the role of Francophone women under slavery, the last chapter thus links her views to the insights gleaned elsewhere in this book from the lives and writings of other women: the eighteenth-century French writer Germaine de Staël, the nineteenth-century Caribbean emigrants and educators Elizabeth Clarisse Lange and Therese Duchemin, the twentieth-century Guadeloupian sociologist and writer Dany Bébel-Gisler, and others. It is to be hoped that as other studies continue to pursue the complex and multifaceted story of slavery in the Francophone world, these and other women will occupy a significant place.

NOTES

1. Michel-Rolph Trouillot, *Silencing the Past: Power and the Production of History* (Boston: Beacon Press, 1995), 47–58, 88–107.

2. Jean Fouchard, *Les Marrons du syllabaire* (Paris: Edition de l'Ecole, 1972). For political materials, see the twelve-volume edition of *Traite des noirs et esclavage* (Paris: Editions d'histoire sociale, 1968). For literary writings by free persons of color, see Shelby McCloy, *The Negro in France* (Lexington: U of Kentucky P, 1961). For creole material, see Médéric Louis Elie Moreau de Saint-Méry, *Description topographique, physique, civile, politique et historique de la partie française de l'isle de Saint-Domingue* (Paris: Société de l'histoire des colonies françaises, 1958). For court cases, see Pierre Pluchon, *Nègres et juifs au 18e siècle: Le Racisme au siècle des lumières* (Paris: Tallendier, 1984); Carolyn Fick, *The Making of Haiti: The Saint-Domingue Revolution from Below* (Knoxville: U of Tennessee P, 1990), 251–59, and Sue Peabody, *"There Are No Slaves in France": The Political Culture of Race and Slavery in the Ancien Régime* (Oxford: Oxford UP, 1996). For the *Revue des colonies*, see Chris Bongie, *Islands and Exiles: The Creole Identities of Post/Colonial Literature* (Stanford: Stanford UP, 1998).

3. Martha K. Cobb provides two French examples, neither of which really qualifies as a slave narrative: prose texts by Julien Raimond, a free person of color who distanced

himself strongly from slaves and did not favor the abolition of slavery; and recollections written by a white woman, Hannah Farnham Lee, about Pierre Toussaint, a slave born in Haiti but brought as a young boy to New York, where he lived for over sixty years. See Martha K. Cobb, "The Slave Narrative and the Black Literary Tradition," in *The Art of Slave Narrative: Original Essays in Criticism and Theory,* ed. John Sekora and Darwin T. Turner (Macomb: Western Illinois University, 1982), 36−44.

4. Daniel Maximin, *L'Isolé Soleil* (Paris: Seuil, 1981), 252.

5. Trouillot, *Silencing the Past,* 58; Maryse Condé, *La Civilisation du bossale* (Paris: L'Harmattan, 1978), 48; Condé, "Contes antillais," in *Notre librairie* 42, 43 (1978): 99; Condé, *La Parole des femmes: Essai sur des romancières des Antilles de langue française* (Paris: L'Harmattan, 1979), 26.

6. Daniel P. Resnick, "The *Société des Amis des Noirs* and the Abolition of Slavery," *French Historical Studies* 7, 4 (1972): 558−69; David Brion Davis, *The Problem of Slavery in the Age of Revolution* (Ithaca: Cornell UP, 1975), 94−112.

7. Staël's contributions are discussed in Doris Y. Kadish and Françoise Massardier-Kenney, eds., *Translating Slavery: Gender and Race in French Women's Writing, 1783−1823* (Kent, Ohio: Kent State UP, 1994), chapters 2 and 6. *Translating Slavery* also provides English and French versions of Staël's abolitionist texts.

8. Fick, *Making of Haiti,* 49−57; Jean Fouchard, *Les Marrons de la liberté* (Paris: Editions de l'Ecole, 1972), 148−49, 336−48. For a recent attempt to render the maroon point of view by an American novelist, see Madison Smart Bell, *All Souls' Rising* (New York: Pantheon, 1995).

9. Clarisse Zimra makes this observation in the introduction to the translation of Daniel Maximin's *L'Isolé Soleil: Lone Sun* (Charlottesville: UP of Virginia, 1989), xl.

10. See Paul Finkelman, *Slavery and the Founders: Race and Liberty in the Age of Jefferson* (Armonk, N.Y.: M. E. Sharpe, 1996), 8off.

11. Aimé Césaire, *Discourse on Colonialism,* trans. Joan Pinkham (New York: Monthly Review Press, 1972); Clarisse Zimra, "Négritude in the Feminine Mode: The Case of Martinique and Guadeloupe," *Journal of Ethnic Studies* 12, 1 (1984): 53−77.

Introduction

DORIS Y. KADISH

This book presents an interdisciplinary perspective on slavery in the Caribbean Francophone world, with special focus on the ramifications of the dramatic series of events surrounding the slave revolts that occurred in the French Caribbean colonies of Saint-Domingue, Guadeloupe, and Martinique, beginning at the time of the French Revolution in 1789 and culminating in the declaration of the independent state of Haiti in 1804. Among the effects of those revolts was the influx of thousands of white, slave, and free black or mulatto refugees from the French islands into the southern port cities of New Orleans, Savannah, Charleston, Norfolk, and Baltimore.[1] Not surprisingly, the lower United States is said to have been seen at the time as "the extremity of Caribbean culture" because of its large black population, slave plantation economy, and French and Catholic flavor.[2]

What do we know of the stories of the French colonial events that led to the influx of refugees to the United States? How have the stories of those events and their aftermath been passed on to us? What is the legacy of the slave revolts for the Caribbean and the United States today? These questions were addressed by a group of scholars from a variety of disciplines and cultural perspectives at a conference on "Slavery in the Francophone World" that was held at the University of Georgia in October 1997. The resulting essays included in this book provide a diversity of topics, methods, and attitudes that goes beyond and enhances the exclusive viewpoint of American, African-American, Caribbean, or Francophone studies, to name a few of the scholarly areas that are represented in this volume. Too often those areas remain neatly enclosed within their disciplinary boundaries, thus regrettably cut off from contact with the concerns of other related fields, even though all may dwell on the same historical topics.

Since readers may not be thoroughly familiar with the historical background with which the essays in this book deal, an overview of the events relating to Caribbean Francophone slavery in the decades preceding and following 1789 is needed. Following the initial French settlements in the West Indies in the first half of the seventeenth century, slavery increased steadily. So, too, did a variety of inhuman practices of containment and control, notwithstanding the *Code Noir*, instituted in 1685 under Louis XIV to assure humane treatment of slaves but never strictly observed. Slavery was harsher in the French colonies than in the United States for a number of reasons, including the disproportion of slaves to whites and the consequent danger of insurrection, the arduous labor involved in producing sugar, and the preponderance of absentee masters with little feeling or concern for the slaves. As a result of these harsh conditions, mortality rates were higher than in the United States for both physical and psychological reasons. Economic, political, and social conditions were chaotic.[3]

During the eighteenth century, the slave trade increased dramatically—some 864,000 Africans were imported into Saint-Domingue alone during that century—and had begun to arouse considerable consternation and concern in France: "Let the colonies be destroyed rather than be the cause of so much evil," said the Encyclopaedia in its article on the slave trade.[4] Popular philosophical works of the Enlightenment such as the baron de Montesquieu's *L'Esprit des lois* (1748), the abbé Raynal's *Histoire des deux Indes* (1770), Louis-Sébastien Mercier's *L'An 2440* (1771), and the marquis de Condorcet's *Réflexions sur l'esclavage des nègres* (1781) made slavery one of the most significant social and literary topics of the time. Those works highlighted the cruelty and injustice of slavery, warned of *marronage* and slave revolts, and pleaded for more enlightened colonial policies and enforcement of the *Code Noir*. Although Raynal's work does on occasion address the need for the eventual abolition of slavery and even, in later editions, calls for violent revolt led by a black leader, for the most part his and other works of this period take a moderate, reformist position adhered to by Germaine de Staël and other liberal writers and political figures whereby an amelioration of the slaves' lot and preservation of European commercial interests were viewed as feasible and compatible goals. That moderate position was also espoused by the abolitionist *Société des Amis des Noirs*, founded in 1788, which was opposed to slavery in principle but soon turned its attention to other goals, such as rights for free persons of color. The position of the *Amis des Noirs* was forcefully opposed by the right-wing proponents of the *ancien régime* and owners of colonialist property who gathered at the Club Massiac.[5]

For whites living in the three main Caribbean colonies, the events of the French Revolution gave rise to hopes for changes in their political, economic, and social status. Having attained a heightened prosperity and commercial importance for the French economy, the planters sought representation for their colonies in the Estates General. Colonial planters looked to the example of independence achieved in North America and the political freedom promised in 1789 by the French Declaration of the Rights of Man and the Citizen, which declared that all men are born free and equal in rights. They proceeded to seek greater control of the island without interference from France, notably an end to the Exclusive, which allowed France exclusive rights to all commercial dealings with its colonies, thereby preventing the development of free trade and closing most French colonial ports to other countries. The planters' cause provoked considerable opposition, however. In France, liberal legislators and abolitionists like Honoré-Gabriel Mirabeau opposed strengthening the control exercised by slave owners and by those who refused to recognize the rights of free persons of color, many of whom lived in Paris and who as a group were also seeking representation in the Estates General. Talk of independence and colonial representation also provoked fear among the French maritime bourgeoisie and absentee proprietors residing in France, who had major economic interests at stake and wanted to retain their considerable power over the colonies.[6]

In the colonies, conflicts became increasingly marked among the various social and racial groups, each of which interpreted freedom in a different way. For wealthy white planters residing in the colonies (*grands blancs*), who remained monarchists, it meant the kind of autonomy vis-à-vis metropolitan France that American colonists fought for and obtained in the Revolutionary War, notwithstanding their different political positions regarding monarchism. For shopkeepers, artisans, soldiers-of-fortune, and other members of the white lower and middle classes (*petits blancs*), who favored the revolutionary agenda of abolishing privilege and extending rights to the bourgeoisie, it meant freedom from the privileges and abuses of the upper classes, as it did for the middle class generally in France. For persons of color, many of them elitist mulattoes who wanted to extend to themselves the privileges of the *grands blancs,* it meant reconceiving colonial society as a meritocracy in which their talents and education would be recognized. (At the time of the French Revolution, free men of color in Saint-Domingue, many of whom had been educated in France, owned a third of the plantations, largely in the West Province, and a quarter of the slaves.) For slaves, it meant freedom from bondage, oppression, and suffering. Not surprisingly, tensions and conflicts in the colonies soon became apparent. As early as August 1789, a slave uprising occurred in Martinique.[7] The likelihood of conflict increased with the return to the island of persons of color who, having lived in France and having been exposed there to the ideas of French abolitionists, formed another group with expectations about freedom. Violence was instigated by the *petits blancs* against the mulattoes; and, as the colonists refused to acknowledge mulatto rights called for by the *Amis des Noirs*, mulattoes, too, became increasingly militant. White colonists not only resisted granting rights to mulattoes: they defied the proposal passed by the French Assembly on March 8, 1790, granting the right to vote to "every citizen," which was taken by many to include persons of color. As historian C. L. R. James has stated, "It was the quarrel between bourgeoisie and monarchy that brought the Paris masses on the political stage. It was the quarrel between whites and Mulattoes that woke the sleeping slaves." Saint-Domingue was soon divided between royalist *pompons blancs*, who opposed the social and political changes brought about by the revolution, and patriot *pompons rouges*, who saw those changes as a way to gain greater autonomy.[8]

The Ogé affair exemplifies the conflicts at the time between French metropolitan and colonial societies as well as among competing social groups within Saint-Domingue. In October 1790, Vincent Ogé returned from France to Saint-Domingue, passing through England, where the aid he received from the English abolitionist Thomas Clarkson enabled him to purchase arms. His goal was to obtain the voting rights for mulattoes that he and others argued had been granted to them by the National Assembly. Unable to win those rights by legal means, he joined together with his brother Jacques and the mulatto leader Jean-Baptiste Chavannes to lead an armed attack against Cap François, the center of European trade commonly known as Le Cap. Although initially successful, their revolt ended in defeat; Ogé and the other leaders were subjected to torture and executed. He became a martyr and a hero in France and among mulattoes in Saint-Domingue. In reaction, the Assembly granted full political rights to four hundred mulattoes born of free parents, an act that enraged the white colonists, whose authority was further undermined when in March 1791 troops of French soldiers arrived spreading the revolutionary message of freedom and equality and refusing to support the royalist colonialists.[9]

Conditions were ripe for revolt in the French colonies. One reason was the sheer size of the slave population, estimated in Saint-Domingue in 1788 at 452,000, which was greater than the combined slave population of the British

West Indies at the time. In contrast, the white population numbered only 40,000 with the number of free colored estimated at 28,000.[10] Also, because of dynamic immigration after 1750 and because the harsh conditions made it necessary to replenish the work force constantly, slaves in Saint-Domingue were closer to their African roots than in other slave economies at the time—two-thirds had been born in Africa—and were far more resentful and intractable than their creole counterparts. In addition, as a result of the events surrounding the French Revolution and their repercussions in the colonies, from 1789 to 1791 slaves had occasion to observe and learn about the revolts by both whites and mulattoes, giving them a certain awareness of the principles and tactics of revolution.[11]

In 1791 the events in the French colonies moved into a phase marked by mass destruction of life and property. On August 22, a well-planned and carefully executed uprising occurred led by the slave leaders Boukman, Jean-François, and Biassou. Plans for the uprising were finalized at a vodun ceremony held at Bois-Caïman on Saint-Domingue, presided over by Boukman and a vodun priestess. The slaves, who began their planning in July and succeeded in keeping their plans secret, rose up en masse to set fire to the city of Le Cap with its surrounding plantations and to massacre the white plantation owners. Within a few weeks, it is estimated that as many as 80,000 blacks and mulattoes had joined the rebellion. As a result, large numbers of whites and their slaves fled Saint-Domingue to the United States. Unlike Guadeloupe, where later uprisings were led by mulatto military figures from Martinique, from the start the leaders of the uprising in Saint-Domingue were from that island and with few exceptions were slaves themselves or had been slaves. And unlike in the United States, plantations were not widely spread out. More opportunity thus existed for communication among slaves, who attended vodun ceremonies at which the message of revolt spread effectively from one plantation to the next.[12] At this time, the future leader Toussaint emerged on the scene. Commonly referred to as Toussaint Bréda during his years on the Bréda plantation as a slave, albeit one who enjoyed the freedom to come and go as he pleased (*liberté de savane*), he assumed the name of Toussaint Louverture when he emerged as a military leader in 1793.[13]

One finds a variety of responses to the revolutionary events in the French colonies according to changing American social, political, and economic conditions. The reception received by the streams of exiles who arrived on American soil ranged from welcome by Thomas Jefferson and his Republican supporters to rejection by Federalists, who considered them dangerous aliens, although responses by these parties to French and French colonial politics would shift considerably over the following years. As reports of violence and slave uprisings became known, growing fear developed in the United States. News spread quickly in southern port cities, centers of revolutionary ferment at the time; such news meant an increased demand for provisions and arms, which furthered the interests of American merchants. French consular agents in Charleston played an active role in promoting the French revolutionary cause, which was especially well received by sailors and artisans who, like their counterparts in Caribbean port cities, bore great animosity toward planters and rich merchants. American ships flew the tricolor flag and bore such French revolutionary and French colonial names as *Ça ira, Carmagnole, L'Ami-de-Pointe-à-Pitre,* and *La Guadeloupéenne.* There would be repercussions for years to come from the close contact between North American and French Caribbean patriots, especially at this explosive time when slave uprisings were occurring in the Caribbean.[14]

The years immediately following the revolts in 1791 were marked by the acceleration and growing radicalism of revolutionary activity, both in France and the French colonies, where loyalist planters became more and more intractably pitted against pro-revolutionary "patriots." In 1792 there were incessant insurrections and shifting compromises and alliances among whites, mulattoes, and slaves, each group trying unsuccessfully to strengthen its own position and gain control through association with other groups. Unwisely for their cause, whites decided to arm and train the slaves in the fight against the mulattoes, thereby providing the slaves with the expertise and the means that considerably strengthened their military and political power in the years to come. In response to the upheavals in Saint-Domingue, Léger Félicité Sonthonax and two other revolutionary commissioners from Paris were sent to the island in September 1792 with six thousand troops: Sonthonax for the north, Etienne Polverel for the west, and Jean Antoine Ailhaud for the south. With Ailhaud's departure a month later, Polverel was left in control of both the west and the south. By the beginning of 1793, loyalist planters, who opposed Sonthonax's Jacobin politics and his appointment of mulattoes to official positions, increasingly turned for support to the English and the Spanish, both at war with revolutionary France as of February 1793. Instead of putting down slave revolts, as he had initially been sent to do, Sonthonax found himself fighting against loyalist interests supported by the English and the Spanish. Toussaint, Biassou, and Jean-François, leading an increasingly militant army of black soldiers and officers, including the future leader Dessalines, joined the Spanish against the

French. In May 1793, the new governor, Thomas François Galbaud, arrived and leagued together with white counterrevolutionaries. A major military schism occurred, with French troops split between those loyal to Sonthonax and those supporting Galbaud. On June 20, 1793, armed battle between the forces of Galbaud and Sonthonax resulted in massive destruction in the city of Le Cap. Desperate to assure victory against increasingly powerful foreign military forces, Sonthonax decreed on June 21 that all slaves in the north fighting on the side of the French would be granted freedom and full rights as French citizens. With the danger from internal and external forces increasing, Sonthonax went further and declared emancipation of all slaves in the north on August 29, 1793. As a result of Sonthonax's action and similar measures enacted by Polverel in the south, many slaves rallied to the French cause.[15]

Historical interpretations of the intent and results of the emancipation decrees in Saint-Domingue during this period differ. One issue is the role played by the French, both in the colonies and in France, where the National Convention decreed universal emancipation on February 4, 1794: the abbé Grégoire called that decree "a great new clearing in the forest of abuses."[16] Some have argued that Sonthonax and the Convention were motivated by necessity and military expediency, while others contend that he was profoundly opposed to colonial ideology and convinced that slavery violated the laws of nature.[17] It has also been claimed that the blacks are the ones who gained their own freedom by showing that they alone could save the colonies from English conquest. Ironically, because of the delays in conveying information from France to the colonies, news of the French decree did not reach Saint-Domingue until May, too late to affect the rapidly changing and worsening course of military and political events. By that time, Toussaint had gained considerable control of the slaves and had shifted to the French side with his four thousand well-armed, disciplined troops, including Henry Christophe and Dessalines. On May 6 he defeated Jean-François, who still retained his allegiance to Spain.[18]

The events in Guadeloupe parallel those in Saint-Domingue. The cause of the patriots gained ground with the arrival of Captain Jean-Baptiste de Lacrosse in January 1793. Lacrosse's mission was to proclaim the end of monarchy and the institution of the republic; when he left on April 4 of that year, he declared himself satisfied at having provoked the hatred of the aristocratic planter class. Although born noble, Lacrosse embraced the fall of the monarchy and enthusiastically endorsed the principles and goals of the revolution. After his departure, however, the situation worsened, with the island beset from within by the threat of upheaval from counterrevolutionaries and slaves and from outside by war with the English. Committees of surveillance were mandated in each commune to maintain law and order, leading over the following months to a reign of terror not unlike that which existed in France. Slaves suspected of rebellion were put to death; planters suspected of loyalist sentiments were denounced and condemned.

Although the terror was well under way in 1793, it intensified considerably with the arrival of the revolutionary commissioner Victor Hugues in 1794. Because of the delays in conveying information from the colonies to France, Hugues arrived in Guadeloupe to announce abolition without realizing that the island had been occupied by the English since April 21, 1794, following their occupation of Martinique on March 22 of that year. Also as a result of the time lag, many of the colonists had joined the side of the English, believing in a viable allied British and French monarchist cause and preferring allegiance to the English to the threat of annihilation by the slaves. Many French supporters of monarchism and allies of the English were executed following Hugues's reconquest of Guadeloupe as a French island, although the exact number remains unclear.[19] Also, rigorous work codes were enforced after the emancipation decree, with the result that former slaves were forced to work under conditions that according to some historians differed little from what they endured under slavery; others argue that work conditions were purposely kept at a tolerable level for fear of pushing the former slaves to insurrection. The work codes were perhaps necessary in a period of transition from a slave to a wage labor system, but a serious question remains regarding how much freedom resulted from emancipation at this time. Freedom and appropriate levels of productivity after slavery were defined, after all, in terms that made sense to the leaders of the colonial society, not to the slaves themselves.[20]

As on other occasions during the French revolutionary period, repercussions of the events in the French colonies were felt in the United States. Many loyalist Saint-Domingans fled at this time to port cities in the United States, where outpourings of philanthropic aid were provided. Relief was voted by many states including South Carolina and Virginia and by the federal Congress.[21] For many property-owning whites or persons of color forced to flee the upheavals in Saint-Domingue, slaves were the chief possession and only means of support in their new location. For southern plantation owners, however, the prospect of contamination of their slaves by slaves from the French colonies who had directly experienced, if not participated in, slave revolts provoked great alarm. Many Americans feared poisoning, having heard of the 1757

Mackandal conspiracy in Saint-Domingue, in which slaves attempted to poison all whites. In Louisiana, measures were taken early on to prevent the entry of slaves from the French colonies, and other southern states began to enact similar measures. Ships were routinely inspected; masters were required to register their slaves and show proof of their good conduct; and slaves were banned altogether in some cases, although such bans never proved thoroughly effective.[22] Some slave revolts did occur in the United States, and they were inevitably linked with French or Saint-Domingan conspirators: in the German Coast district of Louisiana in 1793; in the isolated, overwhelmingly black parish of Pointe Coupée north of New Orleans in Louisiana in 1795; in Virginia in 1800.[23] Whereas in those cases real links with French Caribbean slaves or persons spreading French revolutionary messages have been established, in many other cases it is likely that no such links existed. It has indeed been observed that "the most spectacular effect on the United States of the Santo-Domingan revolt was that for thirty years every slave revolt was attributed to blacks from that island."[24]

The decade following 1794 marks the culmination and conclusion of the search for freedom and independence in the French colonies. In France, the climate had changed considerably under the Directory, which sought to restore order and regain control of the French colonies. Hopes for freedom and independence took a further backward turn under the Consulate, when Napoleon Bonaparte took control of the French government in a *coup d'état* on November 9, 1799 (18 Brumaire, Year 8). The changed political climate in France had profound implications for the history of Guadeloupe, which in turn played a decisive role in the history of Haitian independence.

In Guadeloupe, Victor Hugues was now considered too revolutionary and was replaced by a group of leaders led by General Laveaux and including two Martinican officers of color: Magloire Pélage and Louis Delgrès. Despite Laveaux's sympathetic treatment of the black population, he was replaced in 1801 by General Jean-Baptiste de Lacrosse, who had treated the black population with compassion and respect in 1793 but who now returned to Guadeloupe with a decidedly harsher and more repressive program to carry out. Attempts to arrest officers of color, who represented two-thirds of the military leaders in Guadeloupe at the time, led to rebellion. Lacrosse was forced to flee to the nearby island of Dominique, with Pélage functioning as the provisional leader of the administration in his place. During this period, Pélage met with considerable economic success, leading to developing trade relations with the United

States. Edward Jones, whom President Jefferson sent as his commercial agent to Guadeloupe in 1801, reported favorably on the economic prosperity and political stability under Pélage's administration.[25]

Despite Pélage's success, on May 6, 1802, General Antoine Richepance arrived with 3,470 men to take control of Guadeloupe and get rid of the officers of color. Delgrès soon concluded that accommodation with Richepance was impossible and that open rebellion was the only choice for those opposed to slavery: his rallying cry was "Live free or die." He then joined forces with the radical soldier Ignace—the only Guadeloupian among the major participants in the revolutionary events on that island—to rise up in military opposition to Richepance's army. The resulting conflict occurred at Fort Saint-Charles from May 11 to May 20, 1802. With the likelihood of victory diminishing steadily, Delgrès and 400 men, women, and children escaped from Fort Saint-Charles and withdrew to the fortified position at the Danglemont plantation at Matouba, a mile or two above the city of Basse-Terre. Having reportedly told his followers that they would not survive, he then commanded the final battle on May 28, which resulted in death for him, his followers, and an equivalent number of enemy soldiers. Ignace and his troops had proceeded to Grande Terre to divert attention from Delgrès's troops and spread resistance elsewhere in the island. They ultimately took up their position at the Baimbridge fortress at Pointe-à-Pitre, where more than 650 men, including Ignace, died.[26]

The last chapter of the revolutionary events in Guadeloupe is indelibly marked by defeat and tragedy. On May 20, 1802, a law was passed that restored "the system that existed prior to 1789" in the islands returned to France under the Treaty of Amiens (Martinique, Sainte-Lucie, and Tobago), without explicitly stating that slavery was part of that system. On July 16, that law was extended to the other French islands including Guadeloupe. The law explicitly stated that only whites could be citizens. Within several days of Delgrès's defeat, a system of reprisals that lasted for over a year was instituted by Lacrosse, who returned on August 5, and by Richepance, who died on September 3 of yellow fever. Pélage was arrested and deported to France, where he was imprisoned but eventually freed. In all, thousands of persons of color were killed, deported, or tortured. Black soldiers and officers of color who had served in the army, many of whom supported Richepance, were considered suspect and brought to trial. Those who fled to the countryside were hunted down and in many cases executed. Women were not spared: notable among them was the woman designated variously in the historical record as Delgrès's mistress or wife, Marthe-Rose (also known as Toto), who is reported to have been exe-

cuted on October 5, 1802; and the mulatto revolutionary heroine known as
Solitude, who was put to death after the birth of her child. White planters who
had emigrated were called back and their property restored. Thousands of formerly emancipated slaves were reenslaved or forced to pay for their freedom.
The class of white planters increasingly formed economic and political ties
with the English, who invaded the island in 1808 and took control of it from
1810 to 1814. Slavery was only definitively abolished in Guadeloupe and the
other French colonies on April 27, 1848.[27]

In Saint-Domingue, political and military conflicts surrounded Toussaint,
appointed by Sonthonax as commander-in-chief of the army in May 1797.
There was civil war, in which the black-dominated north led by Toussaint ultimately won out over the mulatto-dominated south led by Rigaud. Rigaud was
forced to leave Saint-Domingue, and Toussaint authorized harsh reprisals
against his army. On January 4, 1801, Toussaint invaded and took control of the
eastern side of the island controlled by the Spanish, thereby placing the whole
island under his control and posing an ever greater threat to the French. He
provoked Napoleon's anger and exacerbated relations with France when he and
a group of influential whites and mulattoes issued a constitution in July 1801,
which made him governor for life and which was viewed by Napoleon as con-
stituting a de facto declaration of independence. Toussaint's relations were also
deteriorating with the slaves, who resented his imposition of high levels of
agricultural productivity and his lack of sympathy toward their demands for
land distribution. Toussaint's adopted nephew, Moïse, who gave voice to the
slaves' demands, was executed upon Toussaint's orders. Increasingly Toussaint
came to be seen more as a member of the black elite than as a former slave. Indeed, his desire to promote the return of white émigrés, who possessed agricultural knowledge that he valued, and to import African workers to work the
land have led some to allege that he himself wanted to restore slavery. However, historian Lester Langley observes that his vision consisted of creating a
modern economic system based on a stable labor force, which necessitated
forced plantation labor, but not slavery, the abuses of which he systematically
attempted to prevent through such measures as outlawing use of the whip, requiring that planters work in the fields with blacks and share the profits with
them, and providing guns to black laborers.[28]

Napoleon's response to the situation in Saint-Domingue was harsh and ultimately ill-fated. On February 2, 1802, General Charles Leclerc, Napoleon's
brother-in-law, arrived in Saint-Domingue at the head of a massive contingent
of ships and troops carrying out orders from Napoleon to regain control of the

island, disarm the black army, and reestablish slavery. The result was open warfare and the virtual destruction of Le Cap, but not immediate victory for the black army, which, after an initial succession of military victories, gradually began to disintegrate, desert, or defect to the French. Leclerc's good fortunes did not last, however. By June he had suffered tremendous losses due both to the initial military victories gained by the black army and the yellow fever that spread through the army and would claim his life later that year, on November 2, 1802. Also in June, Leclerc succeeded in arresting Toussaint and having him shipped to France. The news of Toussaint's arrest heightened already existing resistance among the slaves, which had been exacerbated by Leclerc's move to disarm them and which was further intensified by the news the following month of Richepance's decision to restore slavery in Guadeloupe. By November 1802, Dessalines was commander-in-chief of a united black and mulatto army, which gained increasing strength in the early months of 1803, as mulatto officers of the south came over to the side of the rebels and the blacks became increasingly militant. By March 1803 insurrection was widespread and violent. The French cause was weakened by the resumption on May 16, 1803, of France's war with England, which supported Dessalines by supplying his black army with arms. From July onward the British naval blockade prevented the French from receiving reinforcements, thereby giving Dessalines's army a significant military advantage. By the end of November 1803, the French general Rochambeau capitulated to the British at Le Cap and left the island. Toussaint died in prison in France on April 7, 1803. In all, sixty thousand soldiers and sailors had been sent from France, and nearly all had perished. The independence of Saint-Domingue as the new nation of Haiti was declared on January 1, 1804, under Dessalines. After giving the whites the opportunity to leave, Dessalines eventually ordered the massacre of most of the two to three thousand remaining whites, against the wishes of Henry Christophe, who later became king of Haiti. Dessalines was coronated, as Napoleon would be in the same year, on October 8, 1804.[29]

Although some refugees emigrated to the United States at this time, the greatest migration was to neighboring Cuba, where they settled and contributed significantly to the economic development of the sugar and coffee industries. "There were reputedly 10,000 to 18,000 French in Santiago de Cuba in 1803," David Geggus observes.[30] They were forced to leave in 1809, when Napoleon invaded Spain during the Peninsular War, and the Spanish retaliated by expelling the Saint-Domingans from Cuba. Substantial numbers made their way to Louisiana. On June 28, 1809, Congress authorized the entry of those blacks accompanying Saint-Domingan refugees expelled from Cuba into the United States, both for humanitarian reasons and to promote the kind of agricultural development that the planters and their slaves had accomplished in Cuba. During a thirty-day period over thirty ships landed in New Orleans bringing some 10,000 white, free black, and slave refugees. That influx had a decisive impact in Louisiana, which at the time had a total population hardly any larger than the number of refugees. The result was not only a dramatic increase in the slave population but also an augmentation of French and French Caribbean social and cultural patterns such as the the three-caste racial system. In addition to Louisiana, emigrants arrived from Cuba in Baltimore, Charleston, and Norfolk; one ship brought 141 refugees from Cuba to Georgia in 1809. Although eventually assimilated into American life, these emigrants maintained their Francophone language and identity for several decades, thereby significantly influencing and enriching the culture of the American South.[31]

NOTES

1. I use *Francophone*, according to current academic usage, both to denote "French speaking" and to connote an emphasis on the formerly overlooked non-European areas of the world in which French is spoken. I use *free black*, *free person of color*, and *mulatto* interchangeably to refer to a class standing between slaves and whites, although there were in fact significant differences among the persons thus classified with respect to legal status, color, education, ownership of property, and other matters.

2. Alfred N. Hunt, *Haiti's Influence on Antebellum America* (Baton Rouge: Louisiana State UP, 1988), 1–7.

3. Joan Dayan, *Haiti, History, and the Gods* (Berkeley: U of California P, 1995), 199–212; Carolyn Fick, *The Making of Haiti: The Saint-Domingue Revolution from Below* (Knoxville: U of Tennessee P, 1990), 28–29, 33–39; Lester D. Langley, *The Americas in the Age of Revolution, 1750–1850* (New Haven: Yale UP, 1996), 104.

4. Hunt, *Haiti's Influence*, 14; C. L. R. James, *The Black Jacobins* (New York: Vintage, 1963), 48, 24.

5. Wylie Sypher, *Guinea's Captive Kings* (Chapel Hill: U of North Carolina P, 1942), 93–100; Doris Y. Kadish, "Translation in Context," in *Translating Slavery: Gender and Race in French Women's Writing, 1783–1823*, ed. Doris Y. Kadish and Françoise Massardier-Kenney (Kent, Ohio: Kent State UP, 1994), 35–46.

6. Fick, *Making of Haiti*, 76–81; Anne Pérotin-Dumon, *Être patriote sous les tropiques: La Guadeloupe, la colonisation et la révolution* (Basse-Terre: Société d'histoire de la Guadeloupe, 1985), 87–88.

7. For a comprehensive account of slave rebellions and conspiracies from 1789 to

1815, see David Patrick Geggus, "Slavery, War, and Revolution in the Greater Caribbean, 1789–1815," in *A Turbulent Time: The French Revolution and the Greater Caribbean*, ed. David Barry Gaspar and David Patrick Geggus (Bloomington: Indiana UP,
1997), 46–49.

8. Fick, *Making of Haiti*, 16–22; James, *Black Jacobins*, 33–44, 73.

9. David Brion Davis, *The Problem of Slavery in the Age of Revolution, 1770–1823*
(Ithaca: Cornell UP, 1975), 141; Fick, *Making of Haiti*, 82–83.

10. Yves Bénot points out that the number and importance of mulattoes was far
greater in Saint-Domingue than in either Martinique or Guadeloupe: in Martinique
in 1787 there were 81,978 slaves, 4,166 mulattoes, and 11,008 whites; in Guadeloupe,
82,978 slaves, 1,877 mulattoes, and 12,039 whites. Bénot, *La Révolution française et la
fin des colonies* (Paris: Editions la Découverte, 1988), 60.

11. Hunt, *Haiti's Influence on Antebellum America*, 9; Fick, *Making of Haiti*, 19, 25,
75; James, *Black Jacobins*, 55–56. Pierre Pluchon claims that census records are mis-
leading and that the free colored population in Saint-Domingue actually exceeded the
population of whites. Pluchon, Introduction to Général Pamphile de Lacroix, *La Révolution de Haïti* (Paris: Karthala, 1995), 9.

12. Fick, *Making of Haiti*, 91–117, 260–66; Dayan, *Haiti, History, and the Gods*,
29–30; James, *Black Jacobins*, 86–90.

13. *L'ouverture*, meaning "the opening," is a reference to his military victories or
openings, if not also to the gap in his teeth. He preferred that his name be written *Louverture*, without the apostrophe. James, *Black Jacobins*, 126; Hunt, *Haiti's Influence on
Antebellum America*, 3.

14. Winston C. Babb, "French Refugees from Saint-Domingue to the Southern
United States: 1791–1810" (Ph.D. diss., University of Virginia, 1954), 284–91; Win-
throp D. Jordan, *White over Black* (New York: Norton, 1968), 377; Pérotin-Dumon,
Etre patriote sous les tropiques, 211.

15. Fick, *Making of Haiti*, 157–82, 315; James, *Black Jacobins*, 121–37.

16. Germain Saint-Ruf, *L'Epopée Delgrès: La Guadeloupe sous la Révolution française*
(Paris: L'Harmattan, 1977), 47.

17. Davis, *Problem of Slavery*, 148; Pluchon, Introduction, 13.

18. Fick, *Making of Haiti*, 162–64.

19. Perotin-Dumon, *Etre patriote sous les tropiques*, 195; Jacques Adelaïde-Merlande,
Delgrès: La Guadeloupe en 1802 (Paris: Karthala, 1986), 7.

20. Perotin-Dumon, *Etre patriote sous les tropiques*, 170–221; Henri Bangou, *La
Révolution et l'esclavage à la Guadeloupe, 1789–1802: Épopée noire et génocide* (Paris:
Messidor/Editions Sociales, 1989), 69–87; Oruno Lara, *La Guadeloupe dans l'histoire*
(Paris: L'Harmattan, 1979), 89–99; Adelaïde-Merlande, *Delgrès*, 30–48.

21. Jordan, *White over Black*, 377–82; Babb, *French Refugees from Saint-Domingue*,
103.

22. Paul F. Lachance, "The Politics of Fear: French Louisianians and the Slave Trade, 1786–1809," *Plantation Society* 1, 2 (1979): 162–76.

23. For Pointe Coupée, see Gwendolyn Midlo Hall, *Africans in Colonial Louisiana: The Development of Afro-Creole Culture in the Eighteenth Century* (Baton Rouge: Louisiana State UP, 1992), 343–74; for Virginia, see Douglas R. Egerton, *Gabriel's Rebellion: The Virginia Slave Conspiracies of 1800 and 1802* (Chapel Hill: U of North Carolina P, 1993).

24. Babb, "French Refugees from Saint-Domingue," 242.

25. Adelaïde-Merlande, *Delgrès*, 49–112; Saint-Ruf, *L'Epopée Delgrès*, 75–76.

26. Bangou, *La Révolution et l'esclavage*, 109–37; Lara, *La Guadeloupe dans l'histoire*, 106–56; Adelaïde-Merlande, *Delgrès*, 113–49.

27. Bangou, *La Révolution et l'esclavage*, 133–43; Lara, *La Guadeloupe dans l'histoire*, 157–78; Adelaïde-Merlande, *Delgrès*, 151–70.

28. James, *Black Jacobins*, 181–240; Fick, *Making of Haiti*, 204–36; Aimé Césaire, *Toussaint Louverture: La Révolution française et le problème colonial* (Paris: Présence Africaine, 1962), 261–75; Langley, *Americas in the Age of Revolution*, 125–28.

29. James, *Black Jacobins*, 295–374; Fick, *Making of Haiti*, 204–36; Bangou, *La Révolution et l'esclavage*, 145–61.

30. Geggus, "Slavery, War, and Revolution," 25.

31. Lachance, "Politics of Fear," 186–97; Lachance, "The 1809 Immigration of Saint-Domingue Refugees to New Orleans: Reception, Integration and Impact," *Louisiana History* 29, 2 (1988): 109–41; Babb, "French Refugees from Saint-Domingue," 378–84.

ONE

French
Perspectives

French Caribbean Slaves Forge
Their Own Ideal of Liberty in 1789

CATHERINE REINHARDT

"They are intoxicated with freedom" write colonial deputies from France to their compatriots in Saint-Domingue on August 12, 1789.[1] The revolutionary ideals of liberty and equality that abounded around 1789 had far-reaching effects not only on society in France but also on colonial administration in the French colonies. Profoundly affected by these changes, the planters watched the increasing volume of philanthropic writings by the *Société des Amis des Noirs* in Paris as they worried about the fate of their plantations, entirely upheld by the labor of black slaves. In turn, the slaves and the people of color began speaking up for themselves, demanding that they be granted their inherent right to freedom and equality.[2]

   In 1789, the philosophical condemnation of slavery and the active resistance of slaves in the West Indian sugar plantations converged for the first time. The *Société des Amis des Noirs* engaged in widely publicized written attacks on the institution of slavery and the slave trade beginning in 1788.[3] At the same time, the August 1789 revolts of Martinican slaves initiated rebellion that went beyond the resistance of maroons, as it was aimed at changing the system in place.[4] Preceding their actions with several letters addressed to colonial authorities, the slaves made specific demands that slavery be ended. Though this particular revolt was unsuccessful, it was of paramount importance as an inspiration for further revolts on other Caribbean islands, in particular in Saint-Domingue.[5] Taking issue with both the philanthropic writings from the metropolis and the local insurgencies, the planters underscored the dangerous link between philosophical ideals and rebellious actions. For the first time in the history of slavery, philosophical debates were considered to have a historical impact, and slave actions were given a larger philosophical dimension.

This cluster of warring discourses, all clamoring for attention in the face of extensive political change, illustrates Edouard Glissant's view that the history of Caribbean nations is made up of transversal roots branching outward and forming what he calls "the Relation of histories."[6] He contrasts this perspective with the hegemonic vision of History written with a capital *H*, which until recently has been imposed by the West: "One of the most terrifying consequences of colonization will be this univocal conception of History and thus of power that the West imposed on other nations."[7] Glissant argues that the hegemonic perspective of colonial history does not allow for Caribbean nations to understand their past, as it has erased their participation in historical events, foreclosing the possibility of a collective memory. Even today, the people struggle with what Glissant calls their "non-history."[8] Unable to identify with colonial history, they are forced to find ways of recapturing bits and pieces of their past in order to construct their own historical identities. This task is consciously taken up by many Caribbean writers who "search" the historical memory of their people, using latent traces they have come across in the reality of their Caribbean existence.[9]

My approach to the question of liberty during the Enlightenment is inspired by Glissant's perspective on the relational quality of histories giving Caribbean nations a chance to "remember" their past as it was formed in relation to and in conjunction with that of European nations. By comparing three different discourses on slavery and freedom—texts written by the *Société des Amis des Noirs*, by Martinican slaves, and by white colonial planters from the French West Indies—I bring neglected eighteenth-century documents into relation with one another, retracing kaleidoscopic visions of liberty around 1789. Homi Bhabha underscores yet another advantage of bringing together contentious discourses when he points to the importance of negotiating "contradictory and antagonistic instances that open up hybrid sites and objectives of struggle, and destroy those negative polarities between knowledge and its objects."[10] The revolutionary ideal of the Enlightenment that advocates freedom, equality, and fraternity does not cause a singular opposition between those who have the power to "give" freedom and those who are the passive recipients of this humanitarian gift. Instead, the multiple discourses point to "disjunctive forms of representation," imbued with ambiguity and continually slipping from one position of enunciation to another.[11] None of these discourses is in a position of supremacy, as each one continually modifies and is modified by the others.

They do not add up to a monolithic whole but instead are "added to" one another, to function side-by-side in the transversal way described by Glissant.[12]
What is revealing for my study is to examine what happens "in between" these
discourses, in the interstices of their diverse enunciations, as they take a stand
on the question of liberty. By analyzing the discursive encounters between the
Société des Amis des Noirs, the slaves, and the planters during the late eighteenth
century, it becomes possible to recapture bits and pieces of the Caribbean past.

FROM THE PERSPECTIVE OF THE *SOCIÉTÉ DES AMIS DES NOIRS*

The *Société des Amis des Noirs* was founded in 1788 by Brissot de Warville, an
obscure public law specialist. It followed the model of the London Society for
the Abolition of the Slave Trade, founded in 1787 by Thomas Clarkson. Drawing most of its members from high society, the *Société des Amis des Noirs* was
rather short-lived, as the leading members—Brissot de Warville, Etienne
Clavière, the marquis de Condorcet, and Pétion de Villeneuve—were all
killed during the Reign of Terror.[13] The principal aim of the *Amis des Noirs*, expressed during its first meeting in February 1788, was to rally support for the
abolition of slavery and the slave trade in view of enlightening the slaves: "En-
lighten men and they will better themselves; but experience throughout the
centuries tells us: *Give men their freedom* and they will become necessarily and
rapidly *enlightened* and they will necessarily *better* themselves."[14] Conceding
the slaves a potential for morality, the *Amis des Noirs* revolutionize traditional
discourse on slaves that considers the Africans' vile nature as an impediment to
emancipation. Nonetheless, the *Amis* don't consistently hold such revolutionary discourse, and their specific plan of action, published in 1789 in the *Règlements*, is exceedingly moderate: "Only a Society of men united through the
principles of humanity and justice could gather all the *facts* . . . collect all the
plans . . . to change the actual system, *examine them and submit them to calculations* . . . finally propose a *plan for work*, execute it and *maybe even attempt some
experiments*."[15] Primarily focused on abstract calculations and only vaguely
suggesting the possibility of action, this discourse is far from the earlier call for
liberty. This moderation has been criticized by various historians, such as Yves
Bénot, David Brion Davis, and William B. Cohen.[16] All point to the discrep-
ancy between the *Amis des Noirs'* ideal of abolition and their very cautious approach toward this aim.

The *Amis des Noirs'* contradictory discourse, advocating emancipation while
continually postponing abolition to a distant future, can be better understood

from a different perspective. In *Essai sur la révolution,* Hannah Arendt proposes what she calls the "politics of pity" to explain the rising role of pity in political events since the middle of the eighteenth century. Identifying with the suffering of others through the experience of pity was central to the revolutionary struggle and created in people the capacity to lose themselves in the suffering of others.[17] However, the action that is implicit in this identification does not necessarily have to be realized, as the feeling of pity can be maintained through the elaboration of plans for future action, even if these plans are repeatedly postponed. In fact, one of the principal characteristics of the politics of pity is that its loquacity prevails over action—a loquacity that brings the suffering closer to the spectators and provides them with the verbal or visual means of identifying with those who suffer far away.[18]

The members of the *Société des Amis des Noirs* made it their aim to bring the question of slavery to the attention of the French public. To this end, they made use of the "politics of pity" precisely to lead their readership to lose themselves in the suffering of the black slaves in the colonies. Slaves had traditionally been viewed in terms of their race and color, their uncivilized African origins, their violent nature, and the economic importance of their labor force for France. Rarely were they conceded a human identity, and thus the problem of their suffering remained relatively unknown. The *Amis des Noirs* for the first time elaborated a discourse specifically focusing on the human aspect of the slaves' misery, calling for an emotional involvement of the French public in the cause of African slaves.

The *Amis des Noirs'* politics of pity is largely developed through a discursive strategy that brings the plight of the suffering slaves *visually* closer to the public: "In order to determine you [the *Assemblée Nationale*] to [abolish the slave trade], do we have to *put before your eyes the picture* of this horrible commerce? . . . You would be revolted, if we *exposed* the circumstances of this atrocious robbery *to your sight* . . . who can *contemplate this spectacle,* without shuddering in horror." [19] "Please follow me [readers], in the *rapid sketch* I will make for you of a slave ship, of the heaps of victims and of the bad treatment they are subjected to." [20] Visual representation brings the spectacle of suffering into proximity of the audience through the awakened imagination. The readers are led to imagine the spectacle they are called to witness and are told what their emotional reaction should be, through descriptive evocations of pity, such as "you would be revolted" and "shuddering in horror." The readers are further drawn into the discourse as they are repeatedly addressed as "you." Phrases such as "if *we* exposed to *your* sight" and "the sketch *I* will make for *you*" bring the readers into a direct relationship with the writer, who is sharing his knowledge of suffering. The feelings of pity thus take on a personal relevance for the audience. These experiences of suffering are further linked to the universal quality of such feelings: "*who* can contemplate this spectacle without shuddering in horror." The readers' experience of awakened sensitivity is universal and is given an authority that goes beyond the individual experience of pity. Although the readers find a confirmation of their own feelings in this statement, they are also released from the sense of responsibility as the possibility of personal commitment is lost in the universality of the question.

The readers are further led into the position of imagined observers through eyewitness accounts: "We will give an example here [of the conditions on the slave ships] reported by an *eyewitness*."[21] Invited to follow the eyewitness account in their imagination, just as Pétion de Villeneuve invites them to follow the discursive painting of a slave ship, the readers *see* and *visually* witness the spectacle of suffering as though they were physically present. Visual representation is further exploited in the actual painting of a slave ship published in the *Amis des Noirs' Description d'un navire négrier*. The painting and measurements of the slave ship *Brooks* allow readers to *see* for themselves the inhumane conditions in which the slaves are transported to the Americas. They can directly *see* the slaves through the text, as though the discourse replicated the original scene of suffering. Language disappears behind the spectacle that is brought to the foreground as readers focus on what they *see* in their imagination rather than on what they *read*.

While the *Amis des Noirs'* politics of pity is successfully elaborated through visual representation, bringing the spectacle of suffering closer to the French readers, the moment of action and relief of suffering is suspended and continually postponed to a distant time in the future: "*The moment is not favorable to emancipate the Negroes and to prohibit the slave trade:* it would augment the disorder and fears which already torment our existence too much. It would seem infinitely wiser to await a calmer time."[22] The formulations that "the moment is not favorable" and "it would seem wiser" disengage the readers from their emotional identification with the suffering slaves. The discourse moves away from feelings toward reasoned arguments based on political and economic considerations: "I won't conceal that the solutions [regarding slavery and the slave trade] will drag things out. . . . *But these delays, far from being useless or harmful will be very precious. They will give commerce time to prepare for the change without violent or deplorable commotion.*"[23] Political considerations of safety are not the only motivation behind these calculations. The economic factor plays an essential role, as slavery is still inextricably linked to France's commercial fortunes. Though abolitionist writings are fundamentally based on philanthropy, the commercial and political realities are not entirely forgotten.

Future philanthropic intention only gradually gives rise to abolitionary plans while carnage is perpetuated every day: pity has to be mediated through time, economic, and political calculations before it can lead to the implementation of change and the end of atrocities. The *Amis des Noirs'* politics of pity ambiguously combines emotional identification and plans of action tailored to France's economic and political needs. While readers are personally addressed to open their hearts, the implementation of change is rendered universal and distant: "*The day will doubtlessly come, when the African's chains will be broken, when liberty will spread its benefits over the whole earth.*"[24] The passive voice is used to describe the abolition of slavery, as no agent can yet be pinpointed to this end. While a utopian freedom will spread liberty in the world, human agency is denied, and the future day of freedom appears like a dream. In the meantime, on the road to French civilization, slaves will continue to be slaves, and the plantation economy will be protected from the financial burden of freedom.

FROM THE PERSPECTIVE OF THE SLAVES

In contrast to the ambiguous standpoint of the *Amis des Noirs,* the discourse of the slaves clearly and univocally demands immediate emancipation. To illustrate the slaves' position, I analyze two letters written by slaves from Martinique on August 28 and 29, 1789.[25] They were addressed to the governor of Martinique and the military commander of St. Pierre, respectively.[26] Even though scholars agree that these letters are authentic and were most likely written by educated slaves or free blacks, opinions are divided about the specific identity of their authors. One of the specialists on the question of literacy among Caribbean slaves, the Haitian historian Jean Fouchard, makes extensive use of archival sources to prove that a few slaves and especially emancipated blacks in the French colonies did know how to read and write during the eighteenth century. There were two types of literate slaves: those who were literate due to their previous Islamization in Africa and those who became literate through a great deal of perseverance as they somehow managed to thwart the colonial administration's policy of keeping slaves in a state of total ignorance. How they went about acquiring education is a question about which historians so far have only been able to speculate. Were they taught by members of the clergy, by philanthropic masters, or perhaps by the white children of the master? Another important question is the extent to which such documents were dictated to a scribe, such as an educated emancipated black person or even a white member of the clergy, since the author was not necessarily literate.

As far as the two letters from Martinique are concerned, one of the primary sources historians have used to ascertain the identity of the writers is Pierre Dessalles's *Historique des troubles survenus à la Martinique pendant la Révolution.* Written by the magistrate of the *Conseil souverain de la Martinique* between 1794 and 1800, this manuscript remained unpublished until 1982. According to Dessalles, though the negroes of the city of St. Pierre plotted the revolt in cooperation with the plantation slaves, it is the negroes who were the primary instigators and authors of the letters. They were in turn inspired to revolt by Father Jean-Baptiste, a Capuchin monk who was the negroes' parish priest and who allegedly encouraged them to rebel. As a result of his active involvement in the cause of freedom, he had to take refuge on the island of Dominica even before the slaves' August revolt in order to avoid arrest.[27] This influence may explain the direct references made to the Catholic Church in the two slave letters. However, Dessalles establishes no direct link between Father Jean-Baptiste and the writing of the slave letters. Rather, he cites another circumstance that supposedly gave the slaves their final push. Having replaced the former governor of Martinique, Vioménil—to whom one of the slave letters was addressed—had circulated a letter to all the military commanders of the parish of St. Pierre warning against the excessive cruelties committed against the slaves. Dessalles claims that the negroes of St. Pierre had obtained a copy of this letter and interpreted it as the proclamation of the freedom promised earlier by Father Jean-Baptiste. According to this viewpoint, it was their disappointment that led them to write the threatening letters and ultimately to revolt.[28]

In a recent historical analysis of these letters, David Geggus summarizes different perspectives on the authorship of the letters without privileging any particular viewpoint. Instead, he contends that the antislavery movement in France had a greater effect on these letters than did the French Revolution, the news of which did not reach Martinique until September 15th of the same year. Moreover, the traditionalist discourse of these letters, making reference to both church and king, does not echo the "secular libertarianism" of 1789. According to Geggus, the slaves' repeated use of the word *nation* in both letters does not reflect French revolutionary discourse but is instead indicative of the slaves' ethnic consciousness: they considered themselves an ethnic group separate from that of the whites and of the free coloreds.[29]

Even though the identity of the authors of the letters and the instigators of the revolts cannot be ascertained with certainty, the fact remains that during the eighteenth century these letters were interpreted not only as emanating from the negroes but also as reflecting the antislavery ideas coming from France. Dessalles's account of the events in Martinique is indicative in this regard. He notes that the *Amis des Noirs'* writings were widely available in the colony and circulated among the slaves who assembled together to read them aloud.[30]

Despite the probable influence of the European antislavery movement, the slave letters nonetheless retained their own originality and diverged from the *Amis des Noirs'* discourse in a variety of ways. One of the principle contrasts is that the slaves consider themselves as active agents in the abolitionary process whereas the members of the *Amis des Noirs* depict the slaves as "receptors" of Enlightenment, civilization, and freedom. The *Amis* members argue for abolition in view of its enlightening effect, but the slaves consider themselves to have already been enlightened by the amount of suffering they have experienced: "This is no longer a Nation blinded by ignorance and trembling before the lightest punishments, *its sufferings have enlightened it and determined it to shed its blood to the last drop* rather than continue to endure the shameful yoke of slavery, a dreadful yoke, condemned by the laws, by humanity, by nature, by the Divinity, and by our Good King Louis XVI."[31] Suffering has awakened the slaves to their determined fight for freedom even at the cost of their own lives. Borrowing the typical language of abolitionists, the slave discourse reappropriates this language to its own ends by confronting ideals of the Enlightenment with evocations of violent action. Unlike the abolitionists, who consider the inherently violent and uncivilized African character as an obstacle to emancipation, the slaves champion the free and willful use of violence as an ultimate tool in the concerted refusal of slavery.

The violent images of the first letter indicate the uncompromising position of the slaves' abolitionism: "Remember that we the Negroes . . . *we are ready to die for this freedom,* for we want to and *will obtain it at any price,* even with the help of mortars, canons, and rifles. . . . If this prejudice is not entirely eradicated before long, there will be *torrents of blood,* as powerful as our streams flowing in the streets."[32] As compared to the eternally postponed emancipation plans that prevail in the *Amis des Noirs'* abolitionist writings, the slaves' menacing description of imminent bloodshed entirely recasts the ideal of liberty.

In *The Location of Culture* Bhabha calls the conditions of enunciation that make possible multiple uses of the same words and phrases the "Third Space": "It is that Third Space, though unrepresentable in itself, which constitutes the discursive conditions of enunciation that ensure that *the meaning and symbols of culture have no primordial unity or fixity; that even the same signs can be appropriated, translated, rehistoricized and read anew.*[33] The slaves' reference to "liberty" and "slavery" is imbued with the urgency of attaining freedom "at any price" and thus stands in opposition to the *Amis des Noirs'* philosophical musings, which are aimed at raising the consciousness of the upper classes of French society. The discursive conditions of the slave letters, governed by the immediacy of enslavement, are underlined through the repeated use of "we." The slaves are united through their common experience and bring themselves to the direct attention of the readers: "remember that we the Negroes." The tension between writers and readers is heightened through the detailed warning of bloodshed that awaits the readers should they choose to disregard the cry for freedom.

Aside from threatening with violent means of self-liberation, the slaves also strengthen their abolitionary arguments by examining the possibility of pity: "Gentlemen, we must in fact believe you to be very *inhumane since you are not touched with commiseration for the suffering we are enduring.* Even the most barbarous nation would dissolve into tears if it knew of our sorrows; I leave it to you to imagine *how promptly it would seek to abolish such an odious law; anyway, it is in vain that we appeal to your feelings and humanity, for you have none.*"[34] Holding readers personally responsible for the action that needs to be taken, the slaves make an urgent appeal to pity that differs considerably from the *Amis des Noirs'* distinction between feelings and actions. By creating a tension between the writers/speakers "we" and the readers/listeners "you," the slaves directly confront the colonial administrators with their demands: "we must believe *you* to be very inhumane"; "I leave it to *you* to imagine"; and "it is in vain that we appeal to *your* feelings." Action is not, as with the *Amis'* discourse, mediated through a universal subject or through time. The feelings of pity and the relief of suffering are both expressed in the same enunciation and are inextricably linked to immediate abolition. In the writings of the *Amis*, on the other hand, the tension between writer and readers is only maintained in the context of pity, while it is released in that of abolition; emancipation becomes the problem of the universal subject requiring the passage of time and thus losing all urgency.

A further distinction between the slave letters and the writings of the *Amis des Noirs* is linked to the issue of distance and proximity, a fundamental aspect of the politics of pity. As Luc Boltanski points out, distance allows for the identification with suffering people. The first aim of the politics of pity is to awaken interest in a distant cause through sentimental identification with those who suffer. The *Amis des Noirs* extensively develop this aspect through the visual representation of suffering. In contrast, writing to colonial administrators who are confronted daily with the realities of slavery on the plantations, the slaves refer to pity not in order to awaken interest but as a justification for immediate action. In this case the sentiment called for is not so much pity but rather compassion. Hannah Arendt investigates the difference between the two sentiments, concluding that pity is marked by loquacity due to its methods of persuasion and negotiation that aim at political modifications of a particular situation. Compassion, on the other hand, lends its voice to suffering itself and demands direct, quick, and immediate action, often through violent means.[35] In their letters, the slaves are not referring to the same type of sentiment as the *Amis des Noirs*. As their primary concern is immediate freedom, their reference to commiseration enters into a logic of action and change. Furthermore, the accusations of inhumanity are tightly linked to the threat of violence and bloodshed. The physical closeness of the slaves to their colonial audience entirely changes the context in which commiseration might be deployed. The politics of pity cannot develop in the proximity of suffering masses who want to share the same space and privileges as those who do not suffer, as this contiguity transforms the unhappy masses into violent rebels.[36]

Another important aspect of the slaves' demand for compassion appears in the second letter, where the slaves relate their own suffering within the Christian community to the God-given right to freedom:

> God, who sooner or later confounds the arrogant plans of men, this *God* who is so just knows us deeply, he would know had we ever had any other plan besides patiently enduring the *oppression* of our persecutors; no longer being able to *suffer so many persecutions,* this eternal *God* doubtlessly entrusted Louis XVI the Great Monarch with the responsibility of delivering all the *unhappy Christians, oppressed* by their unjust fellow men, and you were elected, virtuous Viomesnil [governor of Martinique], to announce these good news.[37]

The reference to "oppression," "suffer," "persecutions," and the "unhappy oppressed Christians" places compassion in the theological framework of the Christian community, which unites the baptized through communion:[38] all Christians are equal before God. It is noteworthy that the one who has compassion and suffers with the slaves is God himself. The slaves describe freedom as a God-given right, not as a right granted by man: "Did God ever create any man as a slave? The Heavens and the Earth belong to our Lord as well as everything that lives there." [39] The slaves' reference to God underlines their natural right to freedom that the system of slavery has denied them; they are already free and do not need anybody's pity to recognize that: "We know we are free." [40] God's message of freedom from Viomesnil to the slaves creates a link between the slaves "we" and their reader Viomesnil "you," a link that is governed by God's grace. As universal subjects of God, the slaves enter into a larger framework where all beings are free and equal. In this context, no human obstacles to freedom are possible, and liberty cannot be denied.

This perspective conflicts with the *Amis des Noirs'* argument that liberty must be granted by France and that the French will eventually abolish slavery and the slave trade out of the natural goodness of their hearts. The slaves' recognition of their God-given right to freedom casts their demands in a framework of independence that even the abolitionist discourse does not concede them due to their vile and degraded nature: slaves need to acquire the principles of French civilization before they can be safely entrusted with liberty. Even the *Amis des Noirs* believe that granting freedom without a period of preparation extending over several years would be disastrous not only for the colonies but also for the slaves, who would not know how to behave and take care of themselves.

The slaves' extensive references to God not only reinforce their assertion of autonomy but also reappropriate the religious discourse of the church to a different end. One of the original justifications of the Africans' enslavement during the seventeenth century, which supposedly convinced Louis XIII of the necessity of this practice, was the argument that the heathen Africans would be baptized upon their arrival in the colonies and would thus be saved.[41] In this context, the religious argument justified the institution of slavery. The slave letters reverse this original claim by describing freedom as inherent, God given, and only taken away by the unjust Christian brothers. This reappropriation of religious discourse by the slaves again underlines their autonomy. They establish a direct link with God by interpreting the teachings they received from the church in a way that places them on an equal footing with their oppressors, before God's judgment.

Finally, the slaves empower themselves as they state their cohesion as a group. They begin and end their second letter by underlining their own nationhood: "*The entire Nation of the Black Slaves* humbly beseeches your August person . . . to take a look of humility at the remarks we are taking the liberty to make," "We end our reflections by declaring to you that *the entire Nation of the*

Black Slaves gathered together forms one single wish, one single desire for independence." [42] The slaves' reference to themselves as a united nation creates a space that is separate and independent from that of the colonial system. Abolitionist writings never consider slaves as a group that gains power from its internal cohesion. In these two letters, the slaves autonomously state their united demand for freedom, thus emphasizing their force as a group and making their demands much more foreboding. Even though the threat presented by masses of slaves in revolt was always present in the colonies, the slaves were generally considered to be a blind mass, driven by the inherent violence of their inferior African origin. Here the slaves present themselves as a reasonable nation making demands that are justified, not only by God, but also by European abolitionist discourse. The threat of violence grows out of the refusal to continue living in the state of enslavement, not out of a mere desire for vengeance and blood.

The most original contribution made by the two slave letters from Martinique is the evidence of slave autonomy that was systematically denied by French and colonial authorities, by planters, and by abolitionists. Even if, at best, the rights of slaves were defended by their philanthropic friends, their status as independent and entirely human subjects, equal before God and intelligent enough to interpret the political events of the times, was generally denied them. One of the most striking aspects of the demands formulated by the slaves themselves is the lucid recognition of their rights. The slaves do not implore the pity and commiseration of their white audience in order to receive the "gift" of freedom. On the contrary, they demand the recognition of a right that should already be theirs. Considering the slaves only in terms of their oppression and exploitation is denying the Caribbean nations today the pride of self-liberation and independence. Though the slaves were cruelly exploited, they did not cease to be human beings who were conscious of their situation and who fought for the improvement of their lot. Their struggles were inscribed within the fabric of western colonization and exploitation, influencing and modifying the course of events in profound ways that generally remain unrecognized today.

FROM THE PERSPECTIVE OF COLONIAL PLANTERS

In spite of the various points of contention between the texts of the *Amis des Noirs* and the slave letters, there is a continuity between these discourses that surprisingly is revealed by the writings of colonial planters in their attacks on the *Amis des Noirs'* philanthropic discourse. Writing to the *Assemblée Nationale* and to the *Amis des Noirs*, the colonial planters of the French West Indies underline the connection they see between the abolitionist goals of the *Société des Amis des Noirs* and the violent rebellion of the Martinican slaves in August 1789.

On September 11, 1789, a Martinican planter lays out the series of events leading to the insurrection in Martinique. He refers to the two slave letters discussed above and even mentions a third letter that to my knowledge has not yet been found: "On August 31, *firmly persuaded that they would be supported by the philanthropic Society of Paris, the Negroes dared write three letters to our superiors,* one to the General, the other to the intendant and the third one to the commander of St. Pierre. . . . *These incendiary letters* were immediately followed by the revolt of 300 Negroes from the plantations closest to St. Pierre, who claiming to all be free, refused to work." [43] The letters and actions of the slaves are directly traced to the writings of the *Amis des Noirs* as the slaves execute the ideals of their philanthropic friends. The apparently moderate discourse of the *Amis des Noirs* is thus made to play a fundamental role in colonial events. The importance of ideas coming from France via newspapers and journals is further underlined in the following passage: "Interrogated, they [the slaves] responded that they had been urged to revolt upon the counsel of several learned Negroes from the city of St. Pierre, that they had assured them that for a while the *newspapers coming from France had all been saying that they had distinguished friends in Paris,* who had obtained their freedom; that they should have already received it, but that their masters were opposed to it." [44] According to the planters, the ideals of the Enlightenment were transformed into action not only in France but in the colonies as well; in the hands of the slaves they had given rise to demands for action and change. The planters trace the discursive genealogy of slave violence successively back to the incendiary letters of the slaves, the written news coming from France, the texts of the *Amis des Noirs,* and finally the decision of the king. Emancipation rumors for the first time took on considerable importance during the St. Pierre uprisings. They consisted in the slaves' belief that a distant government, generally the king, had liberated them but that their masters refused to implement this new law. [45]

The planters' accusation of the *Amis des Noirs* is not only a reaction to the slave rebellions in the colonies but also a sign of underlying tensions between France and the colonies caused by the Declaration of the Rights of Man. The planters were extremely concerned about the revolutionary events going on in Paris. This is expressed in a letter from planters in Paris to their compatriots in Saint-Domingue dated January 11, 1790: "[Our wariness] turned into a kind of terror when we saw *the Declaration of the Rights of Man* establish as the basis of the Constitution absolute equality, the identity of rights and liberty for all individuals." [46] The planters from Guadeloupe similarly address their concerns about the Rights of Man to the *Assemblée Nationale:* "As Frenchmen we accept with transport the new constitution the nation gave itself and we place ourselves under its powerful guard. As planters, compelled by the laws of imperious necessity, *we are obliged to make exceptions to some of its principles.*" [47] Deeply contradictory, the colonial discourse agrees with the revolutionary principles of freedom to which all French people are entitled, while maintaining the necessity of legislating exceptions particular to the French colonies. The opposition between the universality of the Rights of Man and the singularity of African slavery on French sugar plantations is the basis upon which the complex interweaving of eighteenth-century discourses on slavery and abolition takes place. The stakes of this contradiction are the most unequivocally expressed in the planters' texts. While the *Amis des Noirs'* discourse often develops inconsistent statements advocating completely opposed positions, and the slaves mainly focus on their inclusion in the circle of free and equal men, the planters clearly elaborate the problematic practical application of the Declaration of the Rights of Man to black slaves in France's overseas possessions. Philanthropic ideals are inconsistent with the entire foundation of the slave economy, based on inequality, the overriding right to possession, and the strict application of economic principles to the mass labor of millions of African and creole slaves. Giving slaves the rights proclaimed by revolutionary France entailed the total destruction of a system that had proven to be profitable for plantation owners, for slave traders, and most importantly for France itself.

Even though the vehement opposition of the planters to the *Amis des Noirs* is partially due to their refusal of France's larger revolutionary ideals, they were also specifically reacting to the *Amis des Noirs'* philanthropic discourse, which brought these ideals uncomfortably close to the planters' social reality. In *Considérations présentées aux vrais amis du repos et du bonheur de la France,* the well-known deputy and spokesperson of the planter class Moreau de Saint-Méry clearly underscores that the *Amis des Noirs'* discourse was not a simple continuation of the philosophical debate regarding slavery, but that it presented abolitionist ideas in a way that for the first time threatened colonial societies:

> Until then, slavery and the slave trade were only the subject of philosophical mediations, of regrets more or less sincerely felt . . . these speculations did not present any danger to public order. . . . At the beginning

of 1788 it was no longer the same thing. Since there were *Amis des Noirs* amongst the members of parliament in England, suddenly increasing numbers of petitions which had the abolition of the slave trade as their objective arrived at this legislative body. . . . These periodical writings [of the *Amis des Noirs*] were passed on to our colonies; and I remember perfectly well that several issues of the *Mercure*, which arrived at the Cap François during the months of April and May 1788 with details and reflections on [the question of abolition,] caused much sensation there.[48]

Moreau de Saint-Méry's brief summary of abolitionist thought highlights the pressure the *Amis des Noirs'* publications exerted on colonial order. The danger of these incendiary writings, as the planter Laborie points out, is that they cross the ocean and communicate themselves like a fire.[49]

Even though the changes proposed by the *Amis des Noirs* appear abstract and unsuited to the urgency of the slaves' misery, the publication and distribution of their pamphlets left its mark on colonial events. An organized pressure group, the *Amis des Noirs* were seen as having helped instigate slave insurrections and thus as having realized the abolitionist ideals of freedom and fraternity. Though the politics of pity developed by the *Amis des Noirs* remained at the stage of plans and calculations without ever leading to abolitionary actions, their texts were considered to have communicated their "fire" to the slaves themselves. The discourses of the *Amis des Noirs*, in the words of Bhabha, had been "appropriated, translated, rehistoricized and read anew" by the slaves: moderate proposals turned into adamant demands for liberty. The hegemonic power structure of the planter society was destabilized by the overlapping discourses and actions of the *Amis des Noirs* and of the slaves. Although the slaves had already extensively developed varied forms of resistance, it is feasible that the *Amis des Noirs'* writings contributed to the crystallization of rebellion. The *Amis des Noirs'* proposals made change conceivable, as is evidenced by the planters' vehement protest. They provided the possibility for a breach in the colonial system of oppression.

Perhaps one of the principal reasons why the *Amis des Noirs* are remembered more for their extreme moderation than for the "incendiary" quality of their writings is that following the attacks from the planters and the successive slave revolts in the colonies, they completely abandoned their original aims, even going so far in 1790 as to deny any previous abolitionary goals: "*We* do not ask that you [the *Assemblée Nationale*] restitute the political rights, which alone attest to and maintain the dignity of man, to black Frenchmen; *we do not even ask for their freedom.* . . . Immediate emancipation of the blacks would not only be fatal for the colonies; it would even be a harmful present to the blacks, who through cupidity have been reduced to a state of abjection and incompetence." [50] This moderation did not escape the watchful eye of the planters, who carefully observed the propagation of the revolutionary principles: "In the first place, we are certain that we mustn't have any fears regarding emancipation; we have just as little to worry about the suppression of the slave trade. . . . The *Amis des Noirs* themselves have changed their mind regarding the former. M. de Condorcet declared this in public in the journal of Paris." [51] Ironically, the planters took the revolutionary ideal of "liberté, égalité, fraternité" more to heart than the *Amis des Noirs*, as they believed this ideal to entail the immediate abolition of slavery in the colonies. The *Amis des Noirs* were taken more seriously by the planters and the slaves than perhaps they imagined. As Bénot states, the disproportionate and even absurd fears of the *Amis des Noirs*, in the face of political adversity, stopped them from following through with a project that had already begun to cause considerable upheaval in the colonies. Nonetheless, the changes they had outlined continued all the same, leading to the mounting resistance of the slaves and a series of slave revolts in the Caribbean. By 1791 the Saint-Domingue rebellions had gained such momentum that the colonial system began vacillating and was forced to take the only action that could save the colonies from total destruction—the abolition of slavery in 1793 and 1794. The slaves led the plans of actions elaborated on a philosophical level to their logical conclusion. The breach that the French Revolution had caused in the plantation system aided the slaves in materializing their own desire for freedom. Ready to die for this cause, they could no longer be stopped.

France's revolutionary strivings for liberty contributed to some of the most controversial discourses and actions on the part of the *Société des Amis des Noirs*, the black slaves, and the colonial planters. The main point of contention was focused on the status of black slaves in the French West Indian colonies at a time when France was building an entirely new constitution based on liberty, equality, and fraternity. Even though France's overseas possessions were to apply the revolutionary principles to all the inhabitants of the colonies, economic and political interests made it inconceivable for white planters, colonial administrators, and slave traders to give up their control over the slave economy. The principles of the Enlightenment, heralded by the *Société des Amis des Noirs* in connection with the immeasurable human suffering caused by slavery and the slave trade, were in direct opposition to the disregard for humanity and justice prevailing in the colonies. The inconsistencies would have hardly seemed to matter, had the slaves themselves not begun playing an active role in the scene of the revolution. Demanding liberty in writing and through rebellion, the slaves set the West Indian revolutionary process in movement. While the planters interpreted the slaves' revolt as an immediate effect of the *Société des Amis des Noirs'* philanthropic writings, it must not be forgotten that the slaves already had their own tradition of revolt, which needed no more than a spark to ignite.

The initiative of the Martinican slaves, which inspired rebellion on other islands of the Caribbean, showed that change does not lie solely in the hands of the oppressor but is produced through contentious exchanges between master and slave. By rising to the awareness of their own nationhood as negro brothers, demanding the return of a God-given right to liberty, the slaves began making their own history. Although, as Glissant so poignantly conveys in his theoretical and literary texts, the history of the French Caribbean is lost, "obliterated in the collective consciousness (memory) through the concerted act of the colonizer,"[52] a return to the primary sources of this combined European and Caribbean history shows that pieces of history made by the oppressed do remain. Patched into the larger context of relations between France and the Caribbean, between the colonial master and the plantation slave, between enlightened ideologies and principles of exploitation, the pieces of independent history born from the slaves' often ignored cry for liberty challenge France's hegemony over the past of French Caribbean nations.

NOTES

1. "Correspondance secrète des colons députés à l'Assemblée Constituante, servant à faire connaître l'esprit des colons en général sur la Révolution," in *La Révolution française et l'abolition de l'esclavage* (Paris: EDHIS, 1968) 8:9. All translations from French are the author's, and unless otherwise indicated, all emphasis is added.

2. Those of mixed African and European descent were often referred to as "people of color." In general, they were emancipated and quite wealthy property and slave owners, but they had absolutely no political rights.

3. In 1781, the marquis de Concordet, one of the *Société's* leading members, had already published *Réflexions sur l'esclavage des nègres*—an essay proposing the gradual abolition of slavery over a period of seventy years—under the pseudonym of Joachim Schwartz.

4. For diverging historical studies of the phenomenon of runaway slaves and maroon bands, see Arlette Gautier, *Les Soeurs de Solitude* (Paris: Editions Caribéennes,

1985); Jean Fouchard, *Les Marrons de la liberté* (Paris: Editions de l'Ecole, 1972); and Yves Debbash, "Le Marronage: Essai sur la désertion de l'esclavage antillais," *Année sociologique* 3 (1961): 1–112, (1962): 117–95. For the influence of the famous poisoner Mackandal, an African slave who fomented an unsuccessful uprising and was burned at the stake in 1758, see Moreau de Saint-Méry, *Description topographique, physique, civile, politique et historique de la partie française de l'île de Saint-Domingue* (Paris: Société française d'histoire d'outre-mer, 1984), 631; Ronald Segal, *The Black Diaspora* (London: Faber and Faber, 1995); 106–7, and Yves Bénot, *La Révolution française et la fin des colonies* (Paris: Edition de la Découverte, 1989), 139–40.

5. Yves Bénot, "La Chaîne des insurrections d'esclaves aux Caraïbes de 1789 à 1791," in *Les Abolitions de l'esclavage de L. F. Sonthonax à V. Schoelcher, 1793–1794–1848*, ed. Marcel Dorigny (Paris: PU de Vincennes, 1995), 181–82; Richard Burton, *La Famille coloniale: La Martinique et la mère-patrie, 1789–1992* (Paris: L'Harmattan, 1994), 25; David P. Geggus, *A Turbulent Time: The French Revolution and the Greater Caribbean* (Bloomington: Indiana UP, 1997), 8; David P. Geggus, "The Slaves and Free Coloreds of Martinique during the Age of the French and Haitian Revolutions," in *The Lesser Antilles in the Age of European Expansion*, ed. Robert L. Paquette and Stanley L. Engermann (Gainesville: UP of Florida, 1996), 282–85.

6. Edouard Glissant, *Le Discours antillais* (Paris: Seuil, 1981), 159.

7. Glissant, *Le Discours antillais*, 159.

8. Glissant, *Le Discours antillais*, 130–31.

9. Glissant, *Le Discours antillais*, 133.

10. Homi K. Bhabha, *The Location of Culture* (New York: Routledge, 1994), 25.

11. Homi K. Bhabha, "DissemiNation: Time, Narrative, and the Margins of the Modern Nation," in *Nation and Narration*, ed. Homi K. Bhabha (New York: Routledge, 1990), 292.

12. Bhabha, *Nation and Narration*, 312.

13. For specific information on the members of the *Société des Amis des Noirs*, see Claude Perroud, "La Société française des Amis des Noirs," *La Révolution française* 69 (1916): 122–47; for general facts on the *Société des Amis des Noirs*, see Daniel P. Resnick, "The *Société des Amis des Noirs* and the Abolition of Slavery," *French Historical Studies* 7 (1972): 558–69.

14. "Discours sur la nécessité d'établir à Paris une société pour concourir, avec celle de Londres, à l'abolition de la traite et de l'esclavage des Nègres" [1788], *La Révolution française et l'abolition de l'esclavage* 6:7.

15. "Règlements de la Société des Amis des Noirs de Paris" [1789], *La Révolution française et l'abolition de l'esclavage* 6:13.

16. For a historical analysis of the *Société des Amis des Noirs* in the context of French abolitionism, see Bénot, *La Révolution française et la fin des colonies;* David Brion Davis, *The Problem of Slavery in the Age of Revolution* (Ithaca: Cornell UP, 1975), 41–148; and William B. Cohen, *The French Encounter with Africans: White Response to Blacks, 1530–1880* (Bloomington: Indiana UP, 1980), 139–40.

17. Hannah Arendt, *Essai sur la révolution* (Paris: Gallimard, 1967), 113–14.

18. Luc Boltanski, *La Souffrance à distance: Moral humanitaire, médias et politique* (Paris: Métalié, 1993), 15–86.

19. *Société des Amis des Noirs*, "Adresse à l'Assemblée Nationale, pour l'abolition de la traite des noirs," *La Révolution française et l'abolition de l'esclavage* 7:4–7.

20. Pétion de Villeneuve, "Discours sur la traite des Noirs," *La Révolution française et l'abolition de l'esclavage* 8:23–38.

21. *Société des Amis des Noirs*, "Description d'un navire négrier," *La Révolution française et l'abolition de l'esclavage* 6:11–12.

22. Jean-Louis de Viefville des Essars, "Discours et projet de loi pour l'affranchissement des nègres, ou l'adoucissement de leur régime, et réponse aux objections des colons," *La Révolution française et l'abolition de l'esclavage* 7:39.

23. Villeneuve, "Discours sur la traite des Noirs," 61.

24. Villeneuve, "Discours sur la traite des Noirs," 70.

25. These two archival documents have been published by Léo Elisabeth, "Saint-Pierre, août 1789," in *Compte rendu des travaux du colloque de Saint-Pierre* 14, 15, 16 (Centre Universitaire Antilles Guyane, December 1973); and by the archivist Monique Pouliquen, *Doléances des peuples coloniaux à l'Assemblée Nationale Constituante, 1789–1790* (Paris: Archives Nationales, 1989). Since I directly consulted the letters in the Archives Nationales de Paris, I am citing them as such in the text.

26. St. Pierre, Martinique, was one of the most important trade and cultural capitals of the French Lesser Antilles until the eruption of the Montagne Pelée in 1902, which completely destroyed the city.

27. Pierre F. R. Dessalles, *Historique des troubles survenus à la Martinique pendant la Révolution, 1794–1800*, ed. Henri de Fremont (Fort-de-France: Société d'histoire de la Martinique, 1982), 20–21. For a description of the negroes of St. Pierre and an analysis of their relationship to the negroes on the plantations during the rebellion, see Elisabeth, "St. Pierre, août 17789," 38–42.

28. Dessalles, *Historique des troubles survenus à la Martinique*, 22–23.

29. Geggus, "Slaves and Free Coloreds of Martinique," 287.

30. Dessalles, *Historique des troubles survenus à la Martinique*, 18.

31. Archives Nationales de France, "Colonies F3 29," folio 84.

32. Archives Nationales de France, "Colonies F3 29," folio 83. The powerful image of torrential streams of blood is reminiscent of the images of revenge conjured in Louis-Sébastien Mercier, where the negro "vengeur du monde" led the oppressed slaves to the revengeful extermination of European nations: "The French, the Spaniards, the English, the Dutch, the Portuguese all fell victim to swords, poison and flames. *The American soil avidly drank the blood it had been awaiting for a long time*," in Mercier, *L'An deux mille quatre cent quarante: Rêve s'il en fut jamais* (London, 1773), 168–69.

33. Bhabha, *Location of Culture*, 37.

34. Archives Nationales de France, "Colonies F3 29," folio 84.

35. Arendt, *Essai sur la révolution*, 123.

36. Arendt, *Essai sur la révolution*, 165.

37. Archives Nationales de France, "Colonies F3 29," folio 84.

38. Boltanski, *La Souffrance à distance*, 20.

39. Archives Nationales de France, "Colonies F3 29," folio 83.

40. Archives Nationales de France, "Colonies F3 29," folio 83.

41. For eighteenth-century references to Louis XIII's acquiescence to African slavery based on religious motivations, see Jean Baptiste Labat, *Nouveau Voyage aux isles de l'Amérique* (Fort-de-France: Editions des Horizons Caraïbes, 1972), 386; Baron de Montesquieu, *De L'Esprit des lois* 2, in *Oeuvres complètes* (Paris: Société les Belles Lettres, 1955), 219; Denis Diderot and Jean Le Rond d'Alembert, "Nègres (*Commerce*)," in *L'Encyclopédie ou Dictionnaire raisonné des sciences, des arts et des métiers* 2, 8 (New York: Pergamon Press, 1969), 81; and P. Henrion de Pensey, *Mémoire pour le nommé Roc, nègre, contre le sieur Poupet, négotiant* (Paris: Imprimerie de J. Th. Hérissant, Imprimeur du Cabinet du Roi, 1770), 6–7.

42. Archives Nationales de France, "Colonies F3 29," folio 84.

43. Archives Nationales de France, "DXXV 117," dossier 914, pièce 3. For similar archival documents of planters' attacks against the *Société des Amis des Noirs*, see Archives Nationales de France, "Colonies F3 29," folio 211 and "DXXV 117," dossier 915, pièce 3 bis.

44. Archives Nationales de France, "DXXV 117," dossier 914, pièce 3.

45. According to Geggus, such rumors would make their appearance again during revolts in Tortola, Venezuela, Dominica, Guadeloupe, and Saint-Domingue during the following years. Geggus, "Slaves and Free Colored of Martinique," 288.

46. "Correspondance secrète," 25.

47. "Cahier adressé à l'Assemblée Nationale par les colons de la Guadeloupe," in Pouliquen, *Doléances des peuples*, 45.

48. Moreau de Saint-Méry, *Considérations présentées aux vrais amis du repos et du bonheur de la France* (Paris: Hachette, 1972), 3–4.

49. P. J. Laborie, *Réflexions sommaires adressées à la France et à la colonie de Saint-Domingue* (Paris: Imprimerie de Chardon, n.d.), 37.

50. *Société des Amis des Noirs*, "Adresse à l'Assemblée Nationale," 2.

51. "Correspondance secrète," 28–29.

52. Glissant, *Le Discours antillais*, 106.

Voices Lost?

Staël and Slavery, 1786–1830

JOHN CLAIBORNE ISBELL

Anne-Louise Germaine de Staël devoted her life to the idea of freedom; unlike many, she also fought against slavery, in life and through her fictions. *Mirza ou lettre d'un voyageur*'s narrator is African; *Histoire de Pauline* opens in Haïti. Staël's later works, from exile, contrast reality and metaphor: spiritual slavery, women's domestic slavery, ancient slavery, serfdom in Eastern Europe. As Napoleon falls, Staël meets William Wilberforce; she publishes a pamphlet calling for a world ban on the slave trade, prefaces her daughter's translation of his *Lettre à Talleyrand*, and campaigns for him in Paris. Her last book ends with talk of the slave trade. After her death, friends and heirs continue her work: perhaps no other Romantics in Europe did as much. Where François-René de Chateaubriand's father, for instance, bought Combourg with profits from slavery, three generations of Staël's family worked in succession to end it.

Today, what does this matter? First, it rebuts a tired myth that Staël and her circle cared only for the rich. Second, it helps to rewrite what ideas like *romantic* and *liberal* meant in postrevolutionary Europe. Third, to the millions taken from Africa and forced into slavery, it returns the near victory of 1814, after that of Wilberforce in England in 1807; more voices in the dark over the next thirty years; and the gift of fiction, which offered models for the freed self.

MIRZA, THE NECKERS, AND THE
SOCIÉTÉ DES AMIS DES NOIRS: 1786–1895

Director of the *Compagnie des Indes,* Staël's father, Jacques Necker, is still an orthodox mercantilist in his 1773 *Eloge de Colbert.* By 1784, the former minister's *De L'Administration des finances de France* notes that, in the colonies, wealth is measured by the number of those who suffer; he adds that unless an international pact were possible, abolition of slavery would benefit economic rivals. State payments to slavers increased in his absence, 1784–88. Necker returns to power in 1788: in May 1789, opening the Estates General as effective prime minister of France, he proposes abolishing the slave trade. He adds that of the state's 3,800,000 *livres* in total grants, 2,400,000 went to slavers, and that Louis XVI has halved these payments. Necker quietly refuses any credit for this idea from his own *Rapport au roi.* Payments are suspended until March 1793, and abolition follows on February 15, 1794. A week after Necker, Wilberforce begins his long campaign in Parliament, citing Necker's example; his ally Thomas Clarkson contacts the Neckers. As Clarkson recalls in 1822, "I received great assistance . . . both from Monsieur, and also from Madame Necker, the latter of whom exerted her influence in various ways in my favour." The new *Société des Amis des Noirs,* led by Brissot de Warville, Etienne Clavière, the marquis de Condorcet, and Etienne Dumont, all friends of Necker's rival the comte de Mirabeau, thanks Necker but regrets his compromise; Necker replies "fairly dryly," and the debate produced various pamphlets, amid the ferment of revolution. Meanwhile, Mme. Necker joins their *Société;* the abbé Raynal and Denis Diderot frequent her salon, where Bernardin de Saint Pierre first read *Paul et Virginie,* and as Clarkson suggests, Mme. Necker may be more committed than her husband.[1]

Staël, too, may have moved Necker toward action. *Mirza* dates from 1786, when Stanislas-Jean Boufflers, governor of Senegal, brought two slaves to France: Staël's Ximéo and Ourika, whom her friend Claire de Duras made famous. Doris Y. Kadish and Françoise Massardier-Kenney have stressed Staël's new voice: Staël avoids clichés of violence or sexuality, focusing "on Mirza, a black woman and a poetess." Identifying the author with a black character "is the opposite of what happens in a work like *Bug Jargal"*—or in Prosper Mérimée, or other male Romantics, except perhaps Charles de Rémusat. Like Duras, Staël's gender "allowed her to be inclusive racially"; although our narrator is male, "both author and addressee are women," as is Mirza, who enters singing of "the horror of slavery." Mirza thus stands alone outside the slave system: after her eloquence saves Ximéo and herself from brutal enslavement, she chooses to die "while Ximéo heads a European-style plantation, answering the naïve and patronizing questions of the European narrator." As Jean Starobinski argues, eloquence since Longinus has been a litmus test for free societies. Ximéo redeems himself by telling Mirza's story, addressing the narrator with "an astonishing 'tu'"—*thou,* the new *tu* of fraternity, as the tale concludes.[2]

Three forces shape Staël's text. First, it answers Jacques Antoine Guibert's *Zulmé* (1786), which presents Staël as a Greek priestess and ends in a declaration of love. Staël thus launches her Romantic career by seeing herself as African. She also draws on her talks with Boufflers, which she records for the king of Sweden as wife of the Swedish ambassador, and on literary tradition. Edward D. Seeber fills a page with parallels between *Mirza,* Louis Claude de Saint-Martin's *Ziméo,* which had seven editions in six years, and Aphra Behn's *Oroonoko,* among the nine best-selling English novels in France during the period. Staël's novelty is best judged in this context: comparing her hero to the Belvedere Apollo is worthy, but it repeats Saint-Martin, whereas her stress on black independence and eloquence, and even her total condemnation of slavery, mark a radical break with the past.[3] Finally, Mirza is in fact a Persian man's name, in reality today as in Joseph Addison or in Charles de Secondat de Montesquieu's *Lettres persanes;* Staël and her successors, from Joseph Patrat in 1797 to George Sand, with *Le Poème de Myrza* in 1835, uniquely make Mirza female and tied to the slave trade.[4] This may seem proof that Staël knew Olympe de Gouges's *Zamore et Mirza,* read at the Comédie française in 1785 and retitled *L'Esclavage des noirs* when performed there in 1789. Gouges's Mirza is indeed female, but only in the rewritten version is she African. Mirza's sex change aptly signposts a female abolitionist tradition here, running from Behn through Staël and Gouges to Sand and Duras; author and public alike know that the name was male, making this change no innocent act.[5]

Two other short *récits* continue Staël's involvement: *Zulma, fragment d'un ouvrage* and the *Histoire de Pauline,* set in Saint-Domingue, whose famous opening, "In those burning climates, where men, occupied only by a barbaric commerce and gain," echoes the first sentence of Saint-Martin's *Ziméo.* Staël claims she wrote *Pauline* in 1786, but there are signs that it records her breakup with the comte Louis de Narbonne in 1794. Narbonne's wife owned sugar plantations in Saint-Domingue that Staël here attacks, rights she had defended in 1792: "they must . . . reestablish your fortune in America." Her salon then welcomed both the *négrophile* Girondists and the planters' Club Massiac, with Theodore and Alexandre de Lameth and Victor Pierre Malouet, whom she later saved, like Narbonne, from the guillotine. Publishing *Mirza* and *Histoire de Pauline* in 1795, a year after the Convention abolishes slavery, thus helps to establish Staël's uncertain revolutionary credentials. Pauline is first married off at twelve to a slaver; Mme. de Lebensei in Staël's novel *Delphine* is first married to an abusive slave owner. The bitter confessional feel continues in *Zulma*, whose native American heroine finds her lover Fernand with a rival named, curiously, Mirza, kills him, and tells the story to her judges. Narbonne's intendant Ferdinand was in Saint-Domingue; *Zulma* is set on the relatively nearby Orinoco. As the comtesse de Pange observes, Staël puts cypresses on the Orinoco and branches on palm trees while her African and American heroines share weapons and names, showing that local color is not her priority.[6]

HISTORY, METAPHOR, AND LOCAL ACTS OF KINDNESS: 1796–1813

After abolition in 1794, the French slavery debate lost focus for the next twenty years: Bonaparte's restoration of slavery, with the ocean controlled by the British, touched France itself little until his fall, though it did make the task of British abolitionism easier. Staël's work parallels these events, with slavery largely a metaphor from history until 1814. Above all, Staël equates slaves and women, as Flora Tristan will. In *De L'Influence des passions sur le bonheur des individus et des nations* she remarks: "Nature and society have disinherited half the human species"; Staël ghostwrote as much for Charles Maurice de Talleyrand in 1791, and her 1788 *Lettres sur Rousseau* talk of "domestic slavery." *Corinne* says, "chain me like a slave to your destiny"; Sapho asks Cléone, "can you not take me for your slave?" *De La Littérature considerée dans ses rapports avec les institutions sociales* elaborates: "Everything bore the trace, among the ancients . . . of the odious institution of slavery." Only with Christianity did women begin to be "half-partners in the human association." Since the manuscript *Des Circonstances actuelles pour terminer la Révolution et fonder la République en France*, Staël's remarks have softened on ancient Athens, where slaves outnumbered citizens four to one; in *De La Littérature*, she notes only its small population, where "women were nothing in life." "Each time," she concludes, "that a lower class has risen from slavery or degradation, the human species has perfected itself further." A telling moment in *Corinne ou l'Italie* shows that Staël's sympathy depends not only on her gender but also on her own wounding from prejudice. Corinne is meeting Oswald: "starting her toilette, her black hair, her complexion a little browned by the sun of Italy, her pronounced features . . . inspired her with discouragement about her charms." Staël's dark-haired heroines are all daughters of Mirza and will face blonde rivals throughout the Romantic age. In 1890, the black author Mrs. A. E. Johnson returns to Staël for her moral novel, *Clarence and Corinne; or, God's Way;* and the moment bears thought, as suffering leads her black Corinne to autonomy.[7]

In 1802, after Britain's return of slave-holding Martinique, Bonaparte re-institutes slavery, thanks in part to Joséphine's *creole party*. The French slave trade briefly resumes during the months of the Paix d'Amiens; slave entry to France is banned; freed soldiers remain free in theory. Staël and Chateaubriand both evoke Toussaint Louverture: Staël writes to Joseph Bonaparte, "Can you deny the perfectibility of the human species when blacks begin to talk consti-tution?"; "Who would yet dare," states Chateaubriand, "plead the cause of the blacks after the crimes they committed?" In September 1803, Staël writes of Toussaint in Haiti, captured in June 1802, and Pélage in reenslaved Guade-loupe, where eight thousand died. The crass refusal to treat with Toussaint has lost the island, with resistors drowned, Staël remarks, as in the Vendée: "they threw eighteen hundred into the sea with no form of trial. There are now in the galleys of Toulon negro generals in general's uniform, and every cruelty which violence and contempt for humanity can invent has been lavished on these un-fortunates." To give an idea of the legislation against this color, she describes Pélage, who had run Guadeloupe but who was seized like Toussaint and taken to France. Bonaparte, she writes, wanted Pélage condemned, but the judges were insisting on actually judging him: "I spoke at length in favor of this Pélage, without whom we would not have kept Guadeloupe." Her informant, a general, "finds it very wicked of the negroes to hang themselves without con-sidering their owner." Mme. de Pange suggests that Pélage's release in No-vember was "doubtless thanks to the intervention of Mme de Staël"; this may indeed be true. Staël was exiled for ten years two weeks later.[8]

DIRECT ACTION AND WILBERFORCE: 1814–1817

Fleeing to London via Moscow in 1812–13, Staël has a thousand plans to end Napoleon's tyranny: putting Jean-Baptiste Bernadotte on the French throne, linking the duke of Wellington and Tsar Alexander, publishing *De L'Alle-magne*. Staël's book talks of spiritual slavery, saying of Hobbes: "He was an atheist and a slave, and nothing is more consequent." Her focus changes when she meets Wilberforce: the man who got the British slave trade abolished now wants a world ban, but with the war's end nearing, the trade is poised to resume in France. In February 1814, Wilberforce hears that Staël wanted to meet him more than "any other person"; the words are from his diary, full of Staël in spring 1814, with an odd soul-searching tone that may suggest that he felt at-tracted by her—common enough. Staël arranges dinner on February 19 at the duke of Gloucester's, with Thomas Erskine and Samuel Rogers. "I must read her *L'Allemagne*," notes Wilberforce; Staël is "quite like her book, though less hopeful," he writes that evening. She invites him again to join her Whig friends, the earl of Harrowby, Sir James Mackintosh, and Rogers: "I will not however, please God, enter and be drawn into that magic circle." On February 22, Wilberforce sends Staël "my books, for which she had almost asked" (a work on Christianity, his famous Yorkshire letter, a pamphlet on India promoting religious instruction). He then writes Staël, coyly refusing dinner. Reversing roles, Staël pursues him: "Do you not believe that it is also being a missionary to speak with people worthy of hearing you?" By March, London society is placing bets: Staël "said she was sure I would come, because I had said I would." Prodded by Thomas Bowdler, Wilberforce dines again with Staël and the Whigs and writes, "She talking of the final cause of creation—not utility but beauty." His diary notes the next day that the fever "is not yet gone off." Thanking the duke of York at Freemason Hall, Wilberforce notes Staël's presence; she describes the scene in her *Considérations sur la Révolution française*. As Wilberforce remarks, Staël also told Mackintosh that he "is the best converser I have met with in this country." [9]

In May of 1814, Staël is back in conquered Paris, with the allied armies. Bernadotte is focused on Norway, to be joined to Sweden in November, but the abolitionist campaign is in full swing: pamphlets, translations, plans. [10] The Treaty of Paris gives France five years to abolish the trade; days earlier, Staël sends word to Wilberforce "that the Emperor of Russia told me that the abolition of the negro trade would take place at the Congress." She writes again in June, asking him to ask the tsar for an interview: "He is truly a generous soul . . . and I have seen him blush at the idea of the negro trade." In Paris, abolition is seen as code to stop France from regaining her colonies. As Spain returns to Santo Domingo, Lord Castlereagh collects proof for Talleyrand that French Saint-Domingue is not to be recaptured; slave trade north of the Niger has ceased, and Wellington backs instant abolition there. [11] Staël's *Oeuvres complètes* date her *Appel aux souverains* from 1814, but the world's catalogs do not mention the pamphlet. I have a copy, and the *Appel* is datable by its text: it mentions Louis XVIII, impossible before April 11, and the forthcoming Treaty of Paris. Staël opens with England's abolition of the slave trade; despite outcries, abolition freed millions without damaging "true" commerce—a pragmatic abolitionist topos of the time. Staël compares this cause to a crusade, writing of war in Africa and ships so crowded that slaves would take up more room dead. Alfred Berchtold mentions that Staël's talk of "long coffins," curiously, is quoting Maximilien Robespierre: she tactfully calls him "a French writer." [12]

In August, Staël writes to Bernadotte: "The human race is far indeed from freedom in this moment." When Wilhelm von Humboldt laments French indifference, Wilberforce replies by asking Staël to "overlook and correct the French of a piece which I am writing . . . I would not impose on you the laborious drudgery of translating the whole." A week later, he replies to Humboldt, proposing a "society of literary men" in Paris and mentioning his new pamphlet for Talleyrand. Humboldt, Prussian envoy at the Congress of Vienna, is doubtful: "this establishment will badly damage the good cause. Everyone will make a fuss about this Society. The memory of that of the *Amis des noirs* will awaken. Some very zealous men . . . are hated for political reasons." Kadish notes in France "a profound mistrust of anti-slavery writing and abolitionism. . . . Little was said about the plight of slaves until the 1820s." She adds that abolitionism was perceived as "a women's issue"; this is true from Aphra Behn to Harriet Beecher Stowe. France has no Wilberforce to rescue the cause from Jacobinism; and power leaves Paris for Vienna after the Congress opens there on August 29. September also sees publication of *De L'Intérêt de la France à l'égard de la traite des nègres* by Staël's friend J.-C.-L. Simonde de Sismondi, with two new editions the same year. Like Benjamin Constant in 1813 in *De L'Esprit de conquête*, Sismondi argues that the slavers are archaic, missing an economic revolution. The immense Spanish American market is the future: "Humanity has become a good calculation." "They reproach the Africans with the barbarism they created," he concludes. Staël shares his themes, writing to Sismondi in October that people like his brochure, which she is distributing: "I gave it first to the Minister of Finance, who arrives at humanity via economy. I hope that they will give up on the Haiti expedition." [13]

With the French press closed to abolitionist articles, Staël's daughter Albertine translated Wilberforce's Talleyrand pamphlet, which Staël prefaced. He wrote back: "I should be void of all feeling, if I were not deeply sensible how much I owe you for all the zeal you manifest for our *good cause*." "This indeed may be justly termed a Holy war," he adds, "Believe me, we cannot fail." He asks Staël to give Sismondi his 1807 volume and a letter of thanks: "Sismondi's pamphlet is excellent." Meanwhile, Humboldt has convinced him that a society must wait. By mid-October, printers have Albertine's translation, but Humboldt now reports that no printer in Paris will print it unpaid. Victor de Pange suggests that Staël write her *Appel* because the French press is closed; the *Appel* is written and published in London, but France's closed press does solicit the Talleyrand pamphlet. John Charles Villiers reviews events: Wellington distributed the pamphlet, along with the 1807 volume, which Staël had got translated at Wellington's suggestion, and its diffusion "secured the notoriety of his pamphlet on the continent." Sismondi writes: "I am persuaded it has been much read at Paris." Villiers later proposes a new translation; Sismondi thinks this pointless and reviews Albertine's work: "as a whole it is written in a manner which makes a profound impression." What matters here is to see Wellington, Wilberforce, Staël, and Sismondi in concerted action, focused on the future of France and of liberty in 1814.[14]

On October 20, Wilberforce writes directly to thank Sismondi. Five days later, he notes: "I have received from Chateaubriand a letter which is far from satisfactory. Such I really grieve to say I should have expected if I had credited what had been reported by his enemies of his trimming politics." Chateaubriand calls the abbé Grégoire a regicide.[15] Meanwhile, Albertine writes to Sismondi that she has translated "a little brochure on the negro trade which Mr. Wilberforce sent to my mother and which Lord Wellington is to see published." The text is more than that, since it contains the first French publication of the infamous slave ship diagrams, a decade before Clarkson's 1821 *Cri des Africains* (a rare lapse in Léon-François Hoffmann's fine survey, which is also missing Joseph Patrat's *Mirza* and Rémusat's *L'Habitation de Saint-Domingue*).[16] However, the two known editions of her daughter's work have no preface by Staël. Did she write one for a projected new edition? I would sooner suspect a political decision on her part. Her text contrasts Wilberforce's struggle with France's anti-British propaganda, talking of methodism and altruism: she mentions "those who split the human species into two halves, of which one, in their opinion, must be sacrificed to the other," and concludes in praise of Wellington. The *Appel* in May had praised the tsar instead; perhaps Staël already sensed his shift toward reaction. She writes to Wilberforce on November 4, as the unprefaced translation appears, thanking him for the "gold pen" that Thomas Babington Macaulay had presented to Albertine. By late autumn, France has abandoned the Saint-Domingue reconquest project, and Wellington announces that French slavers are banned north of the Niger's mouth. These are two small victories for humanity, and Staël's work is part of their story; it may be that she felt her work was done. As Hoffmann remarks, "That Mme de Staël resolutely engaged herself in the abolitionist troops is indisputable." Edith Lucas and Gaston-Martin also plausibly tie Staël's return in 1814 to the resurgence of French negrophile literature.[17]

Sismondi writes to Wilberforce in January and March 1815, as Napoleon leaves Elba, saying that French resistance is not a question of money, as it was in England, but is "tied purely to national passions." On March 29, a week after Constant drafts the famous *Acte additionnel* for the Hundred Days, Napoleon abolishes not slavery but the slave trade; rhetorical gesture or sop to England, it seems worth noting when Staël attacks Sismondi, like Constant, for rallying to the emperor: "have you then forgotten what you wrote last year about England and the negro trade?" After Napoleon's second fall at Waterloo, Louis XVIII maintains this abolition in theory, a long step forward from 1814 and a victory to which Staël, Constant, and Sismondi all contributed. Yet in practice, and illegally, the French slave trade resumes once more.[18]

Staël's last works bear traces of her watershed 1814 campaign. She writes to Thomas Jefferson at Monticello in 1816: "If you succeed in destroying slavery in the South, the world will have at least one government as perfect as human reason can conceive." "Freedom and religion," she writes in 1815, "are bound together in my thought," and her *Dix Années d'exil*, which Staël's son Auguste sent Wilberforce ("full of deep and yet witty remarks"), links slavery and atheism: "the enlightened men in France wanted to console themselves for slavery in this world by seeking to destroy the hope of another." It also has two pages on Bonaparte's violated treaty with Toussaint Louverture, called "doubtless a great criminal" in a remark that shocked Wilberforce, and a defense of Russian serfdom, reflecting Staël's fading hopes for a liberal tsar, the last trace of 1814's Holy Alliance: "this Russian slavery does not resemble in its effects the type we imagine in the West . . . the great and the people sooner resemble what was called the slave family among the ancients, than the state of serfs among the moderns." Staël was less tender in London in spring 1813, when told that Russian serfs were happy and free: "Happy, that's splendid, but free! Among all the definitions of freedom, I have never encountered slavery."[19]

The *Considérations sur la Révolution française*, which Wilberforce thought superb, is sharper: "I must say I am extremely struck with it; I had no idea she possessed so much sound political judgement, combined with considerable shrewdness in discernment of the characteristic traits of human nature in different classes and individuals. How clever are her remarks on the courtier minister, and how skillfully she slides over the weaker parts of her father's character. How much better and more true are her principles than those of our modern factious reformers." Hannah More writes to him, "she appears to me to be a splendid error." Staël's whole sixth part is a hymn to liberty, opening with the chapter "Are the French made to be free?" Alongside placid scenes— the ray of sunlight entering Parliament when the British slave trade is abolished—stands Staël's answer to a nationalist cliché that the *Dictionnaire Napoléon* still repeats in 1989: on the Continent, people said that the slave trade had been abolished "in order to ruin the other countries' colonies. . . . If you'd believed the colonists, you had to be a Jacobin to desire that men were no longer bought and sold." When Britain pronounced abolition, Staël writes, "almost all the colonies of Europe were in her hands." More curious still is Staël's linking of the French and Haitian Revolutions: "No people had been so unhappy for a hundred years as the French people. If the negroes in Saint-Domingue committed still more atrocities, it is because they had been more oppressed. . . . The furies of revolts give the measure of the institutions' vices. . . . They say today that the French have been perverted by the Revolution. And from where, pray, came the disordered urges which so violently developed during the first years of the Revolution, if not from a hundred years of superstition and arbitrary rule?" To Staël, the slavery question is not tangential, it conditions her vision of France and the future, which makes more remarkable her refusal, throughout her career, of the slave-despot metaphor that contemporaries from Robespierre onward were using with abandon. For Staël, slave means slave, not someone in a monarchy. It is fitting that the *Considérations sur la Révolution française*, Staël's last major work, should end with a hymn to human freedom: "Be it a question of the abolition of the negro trade, of the freedom of the press, of religious tolerance, Jefferson thinks like La Fayette, La Fayette like Wilberforce"; it is also fitting that Staël's heirs continued her struggle.[20]

CONCLUSION: 1817–1830

Hoffmann remarks that "the *Société de la Morale chrétienne*, founded in 1821, takes the torch from the *Amis des Noirs*." Before his early death, Staël's son Auguste is the society's president: "This question preoccupies me entirely," he writes. Walter Scott owns Auguste's works; Wilberforce gives him an introduction to Edinburgh society: "You are descended from persons whom Africa must reckon among her benefactors." Broglie and Coppet hold seven Wilberforce letters to Auguste, and a short biography of Auguste by a Mr. Sims, with a few lines Wilberforce wrote for Albertine, saying how much he appreciated Auguste's friendship; Albertine probably gave this to Auguste's widow. Like the work of his sister and her husband, Victor de Broglie, Auguste's work for abolition deserves more study. The two men's first visit to England in May 1822 is indicative. When Chateaubriand proposes breakfast at the embassy, a critic suggests that he wanted to introduce Broglie to Wilberforce; it seems more likely that Chateaubriand, neglected ambassador and supremely gifted self-publicist, hoped to use Broglie to meet Wilberforce himself and failed. Wilberforce preferred to meet Staël's two heirs unencumbered by hangers-on. In March 1823, with Wilberforce's *Appeal* published, Auguste writes "to express the unqualified admiration" he feels. Under the Bourbons, Staël's heirs can only protest, like her friends Sismondi or Constant, laughed at in the *Assemblée* in 1821, who replied that whenever one speaks of whips and torture, it is natural to hear laughter on the right. That year, Albertine writes to Wilberforce about her husband's efforts amid "the indifference of the public," a public more concerned by English self-interest and by Greek Christians under the Turks. Broglie and Constant again speak out against the slave trade in 1822; at Constant's death in 1830, Martinicans are among the forty people who pull his hearse. After the 1830 Revolution, Broglie directly shaped French progress toward abolition: Wilberforce writes that seeing him prime minister gives hope to "the friends of justice and humanity." After 1834, he presides over the *Société pour l'abolition de l'esclavage* and an official commission after 1840. "Many shelves of the library in the chateau of Broglie," notes Victor de Pange, "and four files in the Archives are devoted to the numerous publications and pamphlets for and against the abolition of slavery. . . . Broglie combined with Tocqueville in further efforts and he obtained the King's consent to the ordinances of 1840 and 1845 which at last after so many years completely abolished slavery in the French colonies." But that is another story.[21]

What links these names are Staël and the vision of her work at Coppet. Staël's sex, her religion, and her life of revolution and exile all fed the flame that drove her struggle forward. Anchored thus in the particular, Staël's thought however, trained in the Enlightenment, strives constantly toward universal and timeless truths. This brings a special excitement and power to her discussion of freedom and its dark side, slavery, in the age of the *Déclaration des droits de l'homme*. In the history of abolitionism, many aspects of Staël's thought are curious: her refusal of the slave-despot metaphor; her geographical and historical sweep; her refusal of cheap clichés like the Christian slaves in Greece and Algiers; her talk of domestic and spiritual slavery; her using the Haitian Revolution to understand 1789 in France, or at least 1793. Thirty years of thought about freedom will produce some words on slavery, but Staël and her circle joined deeds to words. Much of Staël's work requires this pragmatic reading, such as the focus on the slave trade over slavery so common to her age, which may suggest people less upset over "property" than over a demonic variant of world commerce. Politics is a messy business: as Joan Baum argues, "Napoleon's orders to restore slavery in the West Indies would free the English abolition movement from the 'taint of Jacobism' and give it new life."[22] Twenty years later, after Wellington's troops fired on the poor at "Peterloo" in 1819, Wilberforce's abolitionism increasingly looked like a distraction for the rich, and he was attacked for valuing distant slaves over English workers.[23] Frankly, it remains true that abolition began in Europe as a Whig enterprise. But that hardly makes it less sincere or its achievement less good.

NOTES

1. Alfred Berchtold, "Sismondi et le Groupe de Coppet face à l'esclavage et au colonialisme," in *Sismondi européen* (Geneva: Slatkine, 1976), 171–72; Jean Vidalenc, "La Traite des nègres en France au début de la Révolution française," *Annales historiques de la Révolution française* (1957): 57; Sue Peabody, *"There Are No Slaves in France": The Political Culture of Race and Slavery in the Ancien Régime* (Oxford: Oxford UP, 1996); Victor de Pange, "Madame de Staël and Her English Correspondents" (Ph.D. diss., Oxford University, 1955), 177; Thomas Clarkson to Auguste de Staël, July 28, 1822, Broglie Papers in Broglie, Normandy; *The Life of William Wilberforce*, by his sons (London: John Murray, 1838), 1:229–30; Henri Grange, *Les Idées de Necker* (Paris: Klincksieck, 1974), 146; Comte d'Haussonville, *Le Salon de Madame Necker* (Paris: Calmann Lévy, 1900), 1:195.

2. John Isbell, "Les Oeuvres complètes de Mme de Staël," *Cahiers staëliens* 46 (1995): 88; Doris Y. Kadish, "The Black Terror: Women's Responses to Slave Revolts in Haiti," *French Review* 68, 4 (1995): 672; Françoise Massardier-Kenney, *Translating Slavery: Gender and Race in French Women's Writing, 1783–1823*, ed. Doris Y. Kadish and Françoise Massardier-Kenney (Kent, Ohio: Kent State UP, 1994), 136, 141–42; Jean Starobinski, "Eloquence et liberté," *Revue suisse d'histoire* 26 (1976): 549–66; Charles de Rémusat, *L'Habitation de Saint-Domingue ou l'insurrection, 1825* (Paris: Editions du C.N.R.S., 1977).

3. Jacques Antoine Guibert, *Zulmé*, ed. John Isbell, *Cahiers staëliens* 47 (1996): 1–15; Anne-Louise Germaine de Staël, *Correspondance générale*, ed. Béatrice W. Jasinski (Paris: Pauvert, 1960–) 2:141; Béatrice d'Andlau, *La Jeunesse de Mme de Staël* (Geneva: Droz, 1970), 108–9; Edward D. Seeber, "*Oroonoko* in France in the Eighteenth Century," *PMLA* 51, 1 (1936): 957–58; Edward D. Seeber, *Anti-Slavery Opinion in France during the Second Half of the Eighteenth Century* (Baltimore: Johns Hopkins UP, 1937); Saint Lambert, *Ziméo*, ed. Mercer Cook and Guichard Paris (Atlanta: Atlanta University, 1936), 7.

4. George Sand, "Le Poème de Myrza," *Revue des deux mondes*, March 1, 1835. Isabelle Naginski showed me Mirza's etymology ("prince" in Persian) and also that combining this title with Sand's simultaneous *Lettres d'un voyageur* produces Staël's full title, a delicate homage typical of Sand.

5. Olympe de Gouges, *Théâtre politique*, ed. Gisela Thiele-Knobloch (Paris: Côté-Femmes, 1970); Léon-François Hoffmann, *Le Nègre romantique, personnage littéraire et obsession collective* (Paris: Payot, 1973), 108.

6. Staël, *Correspondance générale*, 2, i: 31; Berchtold, "Sismondi et l'esclavage," 173; Comtesse Jean de Pange, "Madame de Staël et les nègres," *Revue de France* 5 (1934): 432–34; Simone Balayé, "De la Liberté selon Madame de Staël," *Revue des sciences morales et politiques* 44, 3 (1989): 337–50.

7. Staël, *De L'Influence des passions sur le bonheur des individus et des nations*, in *Oeuvres complètes* (Geneva: Slatkine Reprints, 1967), 137; Staël, *Lettres sur Rousseau* in *Oeuvres de jeunesse*, ed. John Isbell (Paris: Desjonquères, 1997), 38, 46; Staël, *Corinne ou l'Italie*, ed. Simone Balayé (Paris: Gallimard, 1985), 413, 488; Staël, *Oeuvres complètes*, 3 : 503; Staël, *De La Littérature considerée dans ses rapports avec les institutions sociales*, ed. Gérard Gengembre and Jean Goldzink (Paris: Garnier-Flammarion, 1991), 170–71, 123, 62; Dominique Desanti, "Flora Tristan," in Sara Melzer and Leslie Rabine, *Rebel Daughters: Women and the French Revolution* (Oxford: Oxford UP, 1992), 277–78; Charles Maurice de Talleyrand, *Rapport sur l'instruction publique*, in *Cahiers staëliens* 46 (1995): 12–17; A. E. Johnson, *Clarence and Corinne; or, God's Way* (Oxford: Oxford UP, 1988).

8. Jean Martin, "Esclavage," in *Dictionnaire Napoléon*, ed. Jean Tulard (Paris: Fayard, 1989); Staël, *Correspondance générale*, 4, pt. 2: 365–66; François-René de Chateaubriand, *Le Génie du christianisme* (Paris: Flammarion, 1948), 2 : 149–50; Staël, *Correspondance générale*, 5, pt. 1: 23–27; at Chaumont in 1810, Schlegel, Montmorency, and Mme. Récamier participate in a freed slave's baptism, and Staël, finishing *De L'Allemagne*, seems uninvolved: Pange, "Staël et les nègres," 438.

9. Staël, *De L'Allemagne*, ed. Jean de Pange and Simone Balayé (Paris: Hachette, 1958–60) 4 : 37; Wilberforce, 4 : 158–59, 161–67; Staël, *Considérations sur la Révolution française*, ed. Jacques Godechot (Paris: Tallandier, 1983), 529; Pange, *Staël*, 177, 441–49; Jean-Daniel Candaux, *Cahiers staëliens* 20 (1970): 68.

10. Staël to Mary Berry, May 25, 1814, *Extracts from the Journals and Correspondence of Miss Berry* (London: Longmans, Green, 1866), 3 : 24.

11. *Articles additionnels*, in Martin, "Esclavage"; Candaux, *Cahiers staëliens* 20 (1970): 68; Wilberforce, 4 : 210–11.

12. My own *Appel aux souverains*, 7 pp., from the Library Company of Philadelphia and printed by Ellerton and Henderson in London, has some minor variants from the *Oeuvres complètes* text. A second, private copy appears in Simone Balayé, *Madame de Staël et l'Europe* [exhibition catalogue] (Paris: Bibliothèque Nationale, 1966), no. 467. Staël bibliography remains faulty; this article revises my claims in *Cahiers staëliens* 46 (1995): 107–8, redating the *Appel*'s writing and publication to April 11 to May 29 1814, dates of Napoleon's abdication and the Treaty of Paris; Berchtold, "Sismondi et l'esclavage," 175.

13. T. Höjer, "Madame de Staëls Brev till kronprins Carl Johann, 1812–1816,"

Historiske Tidskrift 2 (1960): 172; Kadish, "Black Terror," 669–70; Pange, *Staël*, 446; Berchtold, "Sismondi et l'esclavage," 181–82; Carlo Pellegrini, *Madame de Staël e il gruppo cosmopolito di Coppet* (Bologna: Patròn, 1974), 171.

   14. *Wilberforce*, 4: 212, 215; Pange, *Staël*, 447–49, 187.

   15. *Wilberforce*, 4: 217–18, 213.

   16. Pellegrini, *Gruppo*, 211; Hoffmann, *Nègre romantique*, 188.

   17. Edith Lucas, *La Littérature antiesclavagiste au XIXe siècle* (Paris: Boccard, 1930), 15; Gaston-Martin, *Histoire de l'esclavage dans les colonies françaises* (Paris: 1948), 261, cited in Berchtold, "Sismondi et l'esclavage," 192.

   18. *Wilberforce*, 4:238, 212; 5:17; Pellegrini, *Gruppo*, 173.

   19. "La Correspondance de Madame de Staël avec Jefferson," in *Revue de littérature comparée* (1922): 636; *Lettres inédites et souvenirs biographiques de Mme Récamier et de Mme de Staël*, ed. Baron de Gérando (Paris: Ve Renouard, 1868), 44; *Wilberforce*, 5:108; Pierre Kohler, *Madame de Staël et la Suisse* (Lausanne, Switzerland: Payot, 1916), 623.

   20. Robin Furneaux, *William Wilberforce* (London: Hamilton, 1974), 354–55.

   21. Hoffmann, *Nègre romantique*, 150; World Microfilms (1978), *Anti-Slavery Collection*, reel 18; *Wilberforce*, 5:130, 168; *Lettres de la duchesse de Broglie, 1814–1838*, edited by her son (Paris: Calmann Lévy, 1896), 91–95; Berchtold, "Sismondi et l'esclavage," 177, 179.

   22. Joan Baum, *Mind-Forg'd Manacles: Slavery and the English Romantic Poets* (North Haven, Conn.: Archon, 1994), 100; Moira Ferguson, *Subject to Others: British Women Writers and Colonial Slavery* (New York: Routledge, 1992); Arlette Gautier, "Le Rôle des femmes dans l'abolition de l'esclavage," in *Les Femmes et la Révolution française*, ed. Marie-France Brive (Toulouse: PU du Mirail, 1990), 2:153–61.

   23. William Cobbett was making the charge against Wilberforce's abolitionism from around 1802: see James Walvin, *Slavery and British Society, 1776–1846* (Baton Rouge: Louisiana State UP, 1982), 141.

Transmitting the Sense of Property
Reporting on a Slave Massacre in 1847

GABRIEL MOYAL

This chapter evolved from research on Honoré de Balzac's last novel, *Le Cousin Pons*. One of the working assumptions of that research pertains to the status of the novel's first publication in serial form in a prominent political daily, *Le Constitutionnel*, between March 18 and May 10, 1847. The dates (some months preceding the revolution of February 1848 and almost a year before the decrees of March 4 and April 27, 1848, granting slaves full citizenship) and the subject matter of the novel's plot (the misappropriation of a painstakingly assembled private art collection via the machinations of a group of characters who themselves are manipulated by a multinational banker) determined at once the choice of the novel and much of the methodology adopted for its reading.

Since the novel deals principally with the acquisition of material property (not limited to art objects but including as well food and other personal effects essential to everyday life), looking at the daily in which it was first published seemed all the more pertinent since there was some reason to expect that the erosion of a certain material culture of the self being traced in the novel might well find a counterpart in the newspaper's own representation of everyday life. Indeed, the development of newspaper advertising, and the concurrent invasion of private life by mass-produced personal effects represented in much of that advertising, substantiate many of the difficulties Balzac's main characters experience. In their attempts to maintain an idiosyncratic lifestyle, to cling to their own ethical and aesthetic values, Balzac's aging heroes endlessly confront the assaults of rampant consumerism. In the same way, each installment of the serialized novel that tells their tale is besieged by ever more intrusive advertising.

Another sort of continuity between the serialized novel and the balance of the newspaper's pages became apparent on further reading. The novel's major theme of collecting as an art form is directly represented in opposition to the prevalent modes of thoughtless accumulation and speculative acquisition that the novel's dominant moral voice deplores. Since several of the news stories and much of its business advertising deliberately or unconsciously emphasized the growing rift between rich and poor, between owners and owned, the likelihood of an intricate series of symbolic connections existing between the novel and the apparently discrete news stories reported in the daily imposed itself all the more forcefully.

More ambitiously, one could understand the very layout of the newspaper, the separation of events into news articles, as artificial, as potentially consistent with an almost deliberate misrepresentation of human experience. From this perspective, the division of the paper into columns, *rubriques, chroniques, feuilletons,* and so on became symptomatic of a deliberate dissolution of common human experience into disconnected fragments, of an insistence on the alienation of individual experience. The sense of unity around which dedicated collectors—like Balzac's Pons—sought to organize their existence seemed precisely the thing bourgeois political dailies such as *Le Constitutionnel* were, by their very form, intent on denying. That Balzac could seize the opportunity of his contract with *Le Constitutionnel* to lash out, within the pages of his serialized novel, at the fomenters of the July Monarchy—among whom former editors and managers of the paper figure prominently—only underlines the sense of despondent dissociation at work in the newspaper's mode of operation. Clearly, for *Le Constitutionnel*'s editors and owners, Balzac's serialized novel was simply another disparate segment. In terms of practical management, serials were usually a way of hooking new readers, a piece of popular literature included to beef up the subscriber list and of no possible consequence for the paper's political program.

Given the particular theme of this novel, the time setting of the novel's plot being nearly contemporary with the period of its appearance in the daily, this *feuilleton,* this serialized novel, could not simply be dismissed as another attempt at maintaining (or increasing) the readership of the paper. Reading the novel in the context of its serial publication became a means to project back onto the disjointed fragments of daily history the kind of unity classical novelists sought to maintain in the structures of their works.

Projecting the theme of unity from Balzac's serialized novel onto the daily newspaper in which it appeared underlined the arbitrary quality of the paper's divisions and parcelization of current history and accentuated its possible effects on the understanding of human experience. In the end, such divisions came to be understood as consistent with the elaboration of a sense of artificially rationalized identity, with a proprietary sense of self and of one's place: "we" comes to be seen as "logically" or "naturally" distinct from "them," and "here" appears justifiably distinct from "there," much as what belongs in one column, under one heading of the newspaper rather than another, tends to appear less and less liable to question.

Still, *Le Constitutionnel,* like many newspapers of that time, does not present a harmonious voice. Maintaining a homogeneous ideology in all the sections of the paper was complicated by the material conditions of news gathering and reporting of the time. The specific ideology of the paper is most clearly legible only in its front-page editorials and in the occasional—and in no way consistent—framing of stories gleaned from relatively primitive news-distribution agencies. Often, newspapers of diametrically opposed political stripes published the same stories without comment or modification, without a distinctive mediating frame and with no apparent regard to the effect such stories might have on the advancement of their respective political agendas. In the end, identifying the novel's ostensible social and political values ironically ends up being a simpler task than synthesizing the newspaper's ideology. Bringing together scattered editorial expressions with the often incoherent or divergent political intentions of the different editors and contributors often yields little more than ostensibly contingent or provisional values around most ordinary issues. The liberal tendencies of *Le Constitutionnel* in the period studied—that of the serialized publication of *Le Cousin Pons*—become more clearly specified mostly around particular issues relating, for the most part, to domestic policies of the Guizot government. It is mostly in reaction to instances of electoral fraud, around the presentation of new laws and policies perceived or presented as reactionary or as scandalously ineffective by the newspaper's editors, that an ideology begins to find coherent expression amidst the newspaper's columns.[1] Among the issues addressed in this manner, several articles and editorials on the controversial question of the gradual abolition of slavery in the French colonies can be constituted into a relatively unified cluster with other pertinent fragments of political and economic interest. Though this grouping of newspaper articles remains somewhat ideologically ambiguous, some constants begin to appear that, in turn, can be compared with other contemporaneous writings on slavery in other newspapers, in works of fiction, or in other sources.

In the period under study, *Le Constitutionnel* has become an opposition paper.[2] The vast majority of its editorials are critical of the cabinet and conservative government of François Guizot. In this period surrounding the publication of *Le Cousin Pons,* one of the long-term strategies adopted to discredit the government party focuses on a law presented to the Chamber of Deputies by a member of the opposition to reform the electoral practices and extend the right to vote to a larger portion of the population by lowering the property requirement for voters. This conjuncture brings *Le Constitutionnel* to summon every day its liberal egalitarian rhetoric in a campaign aimed ostensibly at questioning the government's democratic principles. It is in this context that the question of emancipating the slaves in the colonies is again raised in the Chamber of Deputies. In all likelihood, *Le Constitutionnel*'s atypically progressive stance on the question of emancipation during this period is conditioned by this political context. Its expressed commitment to democratic principles in internal electoral policy constrained its editorialists to adopt in turn a position on slavery more in continuity with those principles.

Ever since Napoleon's pragmatic abrogation of the emancipation granted to slaves in all French territories in the initial stages of the Revolution, some French parliamentarians had been active in seeking a restoration of freedom. Various laws and decrees had successfully been passed aimed at improving the lot of the slaves in the colonies. Much as the initial emancipation granted in the heat of revolutionary fervor had been turned into a dead letter by subsequent legislation, these measures mostly remained theoretical—tokens of good intentions with few practical means of application—as long, that is, as the responsibility for the implementation of colonial laws passed in the National Assembly in Paris remained in the hands of colonial councils controlled principally by plantation owners.

Among the interim measures ostensibly intended to prepare the slaves for freedom and the labor market and to ease the colonies into a new economic mode were laws passed to force slave owners to free slaves who could buy their own freedom with savings accumulated from the sale of surplus produce. For example, the law passed on July 18, 1845, stipulated, among other things, that slaves were to be granted parcels of land by their owners, and it instituted the principle of the *rachat forcé,* that is, the obligation to free slaves who could buy their own freedom. As *Le Constitutionnel* points out, however, the law did not set any standards or measurements for the parcels of land to be granted, nor did it establish any equations for working out the amounts to be paid by the slaves for their freedom. It left such vital details to local colonial administrations. More significantly, no effective, practical means were set up to ensure the enforcement of the articles of this law. In its editorial of April 25, 1847, *Le Constitutionnel*, along with some other opposition papers, seized on this omission to further confound and denounce the government party's lack of resolve and negligence. As the paper presents it, the occasion for this editorial is the presentation to the National Assembly of a royal commission report on the actual results achieved since the implementation of the July 18, 1845, law in the colonies:

> What is most striking, at first, is the contrast between the report itself and the supporting documents. Whereas the former offers infinite hope of progress and reform, the latter seem to indicate that, in effect, very little has been accomplished and that there is precious little to be expected in the future. Since the passage into law of the July 18 legislation and its implementation it would seem as though nothing but anarchy has been created. France cannot any longer tolerate that its laws remain as dead letters.
>
> Rather than read the royal report itself, read the supporting documents and you will see that despite exorbitant expense, religious and elementary education is practically inexistent in the colonies, that everyone there seems opposed to official marriages between slaves, that, despite the edict, male and female slaves still cohabit in the same hovels. Hence there is no progress in the dissemination of religious, moral or family values.
>
> The colonial decrees supposedly passed as implementation of the law, those decrees which alone can make the law applicable, are framed in such a way as to be contrary to its intent. Indeed they practically render null and void the law's most important clauses: the conceding [to the slaves] of a weekly day of rest, their right to accumulate savings [toward buying their freedom], the slave's right to own those savings, and finally the obligation to free those slaves who are able to buy their freedom.
>
> It is true however that the edict has actually limited the punishment a master can inflict on a slave. Henceforth the masters, to their regret, can administer no more than thirty lashes and no more than fifteen days in jail; iron chains are to be replaced by wooden shackles. Yet even this relatively humane legislation—an excess of philanthropy according to some—will be of no effect if prosecutors do not indict those who contravene it, if the courts do not punish them—as is now happening.[3]

In reading so systematic a critique of the government's inaction in so admirable a cause, one might be tempted to overlook *Le Constitutionnel*'s own political motivations: one might forget to ask what parts of this editorial simply serve to fulfill the role of an opposition newspaper. The editorial repeatedly admonishes its readers to scrutinize the statistical documents rather than focus on the formal report. It cannily distinguishes for them between fact and what it deems the report's empty rhetoric. Nonetheless, though the colonial slaves are shown as the direct victims, the paper's concern appears, on closer reading, to be primarily for the safeguarding of political principle.

What in the end seems most in question here is the government's ability to maintain the rule of law in its territories. That the colonial councils are able to enact ordinances effectively nullifying any possible effects that progressive legislation might have is, in the end, a constitutional matter. This is further demonstrated in the editorial. First cited is M. J. de Lasteyrie, a pro-abolitionist deputy who demonstrates to the Chamber of Deputies how the colonial councils turn the July 1845 law into a dead letter. The editorial, however, goes on to quote M. Jollivet, an anti-abolitionist member of the Chamber, who "unwittingly ended up defending *the same cause* when he too demonstrated that those parts of the law which, in effect, favor the current interests of the colonials have also not been implemented. Among these are the regulations to be passed in order to control vagrancy, and to create free labor in the colonies."[4] The "same cause" in question here, despite the confusion, cannot logically be emancipation but, rather, effective responsible government. At issue, then, is the government's strength of will and determination—not the humanitarian principles first invoked in reference to M. de Lasteyrie's speech to the Chamber. In the end, the government is denounced, not for failing to safeguard, as it was bound to, principles of humanity, equality, or freedom, but for irresponsible accounting. The government's inability to implement its quasi-humanitarian decisions is, in this editorial, somewhat less damnable than its squandering of the public purse on legislation that, for all its good intent, leaves the slaves in no better a situation.

When it comes to discuss those measures directly affecting the slaves (measures that the colonial councils have had to endorse), the editorial seems to change its tone. Rather than raise questions of principle—as it did in relation to the government's inability to impose the rule of law—it points to the possibly overzealous humanitarianism of the reforms. That a slave owner may administer only thirty lashes or may use only wooden restraints rather than chains and manacles does not prompt the editorialist to raise the question of right, of what principle could possibly entitle a person to treat another in this way. Instead, the editorialist chooses to cite a reaction imputed to unnamed others,

presumably to more reactionary, anti-abolitionist factions—hence the opinion
that relatively humane legislation might turn out to be "philanthropic excess."
Indeed, the syntax of the sentence places the two qualifications in apposition
and grants the second equivalent status via the plural verb (*seront*). Both—
deciding which characterization is the more accurate does not seem pertinent—will be made futile because the government does not take adequate
steps to enforce them. In the context of nineteenth-century society, *Le Constitutionnel* would be the equivalent of a "mainstream," "middle of the road"
paper. Behind its citing of a more extreme opposition to emancipation lurks
the implication that its own position represents an attitude of reasonable
compromise.

To say that *Le Constitutionnel* does not question the right of a slave owner to
whip his slaves does not imply that its editorialists have no principles. Nor
would it be completely accurate to claim that its *only* aim is to discredit the government in order to propel its own faction into positions of power. In effect,
throughout the period studied, *Le Constitutionnel* quite consistently defends
certain principles and remains loyal to the aspirations of what it deems its readership. Ambiguities in its expression, in its political rhetoric, seem to arise
mostly when actual situations raise conflicts or contradictions between the
principles themselves or between principles and the prevailing opinions of the
readers.

Such a conflict seems to have occurred with the royal report on slavery in the
colonies. The outlines of this conflict become clearer as the editorial continues
and expands on the situation of the slaves only to show how it affects the interests of the readers:

> We do not know what the lower house will do now but it seems to us that
> it cannot declare on its order paper that it is indifferent to the suffering of
> humanity and indifferent to the execution of its own laws. In all things
> one must know what it is one wants and do what one does. The govern-
> ment and both its houses have indicated that they intend to prepare the
> slaves for freedom through the implementation of various transitional
> measures. Let these transitional measures be genuinely and loyally ap-
> plied. To do otherwise would give the abolitionists solid grounds to say:
> "As you can see, there is no room for improvement within a slave society,
> all these transitional measures are so many deceptions. This so-called
> provisional situation only doubles your expenses and makes you pay at
> once for the government costs of a slave society as well as for those of

an emancipated society." They would then be justified in demanding the complete and absolute abolition of slavery.[5]

Consistent with the paper's political agenda, the unacceptable indifference to the "suffering of humanity" is here presented as equivalent to indifference to the implementation of the government's own legislation. But in this, the last paragraph of the editorial, the contradicting voice has changed attribution. It is no longer the reactionaries but the abolitionists who are cited as the threat to good judgment and reasoned procedure. It is now this voice that the editorial does not want to see vindicated. For all its deploring of the slaves' conditions, *Le Constitutionnel* does not align itself with the abolitionist position. It is the particular kind of discourse imputed to the abolitionists that is most revealing about where the paper's ideology actually lies. What seems to do most harm, in the editorialist's opinion, is not the intermediary measures in themselves but their cost to the public purse. The taxpayer is forced to support the costs of two regimes: both a slave and a free labor one simultaneously. What is most deplored about government inefficiency is its cost to the property owners who pay taxes, not—as seems sporadically claimed—the fate of the slaves.

This is also what explains the earlier reluctance to invoke humanitarian principle in regard to the new rules governing the treatment of the slaves: the absence of question with regard to the right to own or to punish other humans. Dominating *Le Constitutionnel*'s order of values are the rights to, and of, property. Questioning the slave owners' rights to punish slaves would be at once to question the right of citizens to use and dispose freely of their property.

Yet, despite its questioning the exorbitant costs, *Le Constitutionnel* does not oppose the provisional measures adopted to prepare for full emancipation in the colonies. In continuing to report the discussion of the Chamber of Deputies, the editorial focuses momentarily on what are given by de Lasteyrie as the two most significant clauses of the law: "Thus, the two main provisions of the law which were passed with the intention of allowing the slaves to save some of their earnings in order to later buy their own freedom have been made totally ineffective by these colonial councils. It is solely through the sale of produce from the plot of land granted to him by the law that the slave can hope to accumulate some savings. But how will he manage to do so if the area of land he is granted is not even sufficient for his own sustenance?"[6]

This insistence on granting the slaves a parcel of land, on making their freedom dependent on their ability to purchase it from the colonial plantation owners, in the end fits very well within *Le Constitutionnel*'s ideology. The way things stand, the opposition parties have a grand opportunity to blame the colonial slave owners for perpetuating a situation unsavory to the majority of the population in mainland France and, at the same time, to berate the government party for inefficiency.

But the transitional law of July 18, 1847, has yet other advantages for *Le Constitutionnel*. By instituting the concept of *rachat forcé* as a reform, this law allows everyone to conveniently elude the question of justifying buying back what should never have been sold in the first place. More importantly, for *Le Constitutionnel*, the law provides for a kind of training, a *formation*. If emancipation must—reluctantly—be accepted as inevitable, at least these interim laws should ensure that the newly emancipated population will be initiated to citizenship via the acquisition of property. The first property the slaves must acquire is themselves—a contradiction to all democratic principles, which *Le Constitutionnel* is not interested in drawing out. Instead, it is politically more profitable to play out its righteous indignation at the government or the slave owners.

Nonetheless, *Le Constitutionnel* and its readership must have found some reassurance in the slaves' necessary passage through property. Since the interim measures of July 1845 were passed by the very same government the paper still opposes politically in 1847, its insistence on these particular measures would indicate at least some partial agreement on its part, some willingness to compromise on common grounds. Here again, insistence is underlined by what *Le Constitutionnel* does not discuss and chooses to simply paraphrase: "The members of the lower house, being deeply impressed by the facts presented to it by M. De Lasteyrie, and visibly shocked by the numerous instances of cruel mistreatment at the hands of their masters and of denial of justice also exposed by M. De Lasteyrie, adjourned its discussion to Monday."[7] In its editorial of April 27, 1847, two days later, *Le Constitutionnel* draws heavily on M. de Lasteyrie's second speech to the Chamber of Deputies. This speech also includes narration and descriptions of several instances of mistreatment of the slaves by their owners. Despite announcing, "We will not here repeat the monstrous deeds inflicted on the slaves by their colonial masters," the editorial goes on to cite a number of the more horrid instances presented in the speech. What would seem to have taken place at that very time period is that the paper's management sensed a change in its readership's attitude, one that it likely sees reflected in the reactions of the deputies, the elected representatives in the lower house, to the speech. The deputies now see the colonists', the plantation owners', aggravated mistreatment of the slaves as a form of resistance to the laws they have passed: "if this resistance of the colonies [to the laws passed in the Chamber] takes the form of cruelty, if the colonials take vengeance on the slaves for the compassion their fate has evoked in metropolitan France, if the colonial slave owners, not content with simply ignoring the law, decide to use the law as a pretext to aggravate the evils of slavery, then the mood of the members of the Chamber turns to a kind of anger."

If the newspaper cannot logically reconcile slavery with the grand liberal principles it consistently invokes in favor of freedom of trade, industry, and the disposal of property, then, ideally, the freed slaves should at least, as citizens, have a vested interest in defending and furthering these same principles: they should have property.

The effect of property on the owner is what *Le Constitutionnel*'s editorialists seem to be counting on to ensure a seamless transition from slavery to free labor. What these well-intentioned liberal journalists overlook in their efforts to present slavery as morally neutral is the nature and extent of dispossession that slavery implies. If, for them, *to be* means primarily *to have,* for the slaves they want so eagerly to lead into the promised land of property, *to be* has for too long meant *to be had, to be property.* Yet this very confidence, the absence of irony in this conviction that property will smooth over all differences, is in itself revealing. In their apparent intention to assist the former slaves in their adaptation, the (not-as-yet former) masters are effectively dispossessing them yet again. By making them into owners, they are attempting to restrain, in advance, the choices the newly freed slaves can make. More than simply reimbursing them with grants of land, the masters want to ensure that the imaginations of the newly freed slaves will be guided by the same type of responsibilities that liberal civilization has always represented for their former masters. In this, at least, some measure of appeasement is meant to be derived for the colonists: property will somewhat attenuate the differences, it will make the former slaves less radically different than they had so far been thought to be.

Le Constitutionnel has some immediate reasons to take the position it does. Its committment to defending democratic freedoms is mitigated, in 1847, by the presence in Paris of representatives sent to the capital by the colonists. A very visible and audible delegation of representatives from the colonies is lobbying the houses of government in an attempt to protect and continue to control the slavery-based economies of the colonies. Most of the Parisian newspapers, including *Le Constitutionnel,* take note of their presence at this time.

The efforts of this delegation have, to some extent, been successful. Their concrete presence reminds the editorialists of the bourgeois dailies of the very real interests that liberal rhetoric is in the end engaged to protect. Clearly, the plight of the black slaves described in the Chamber of Deputies, as touching as it may have been, as passionately as it may have been denounced, remains relatively abstract. The fears demonstrated by white French colonists for the future of their way of life, for their incomes, have a more direct impact. As appalling as the scandalous incidents of mistreatment narrated in Parliament may have been, the victims are others, and they are far away.

Le Constitutionnel's editorialists are less concerned with providing their readers with a thorough understanding or knowledge of actual conditions existing in the colonial plantations—and are even less concerned with describing the practices of the slave trade. Whatever information they might transmit regarding plantation conditions and the slave trade has gone through a process of selection. Information that might be damaging to the political platform of the newspaper or to its readership is published only because competing papers publish it. Such information has to be framed, reoriented, or explained in order to present the position of the paper as prevailing despite apparent contradictions. Background historical information is resorted to selectively and only with the purpose of confirming the ideology of the paper or of weakening competing ideologies. In the wide array of conflicting political tendencies available in Parisian journalism in the 1840s, such competition accounts for the circulation of a great deal of contradictory information. In the ensuing confusion lucid exposition becomes more essential than contingent, and simplification and distillation of elaborate data are regularly resorted to.

In this context, the editors of *Le Constitutionnel* will delve into the history of the slave trade or into the actual conditions of plantation slaves in the French colonies only when they have to or when it is useful to them. They will not needlessly tax the consciences of their readers with the true conditions of the production of the sugar on their tables. The history of slavery, with all its ramifications and complicating circumstances, lends itself particularly well to this kind of obfuscation, to games of revelation and dissimulation regarding the credibility and the originality of the information provided daily in the French political press of the period.[8] Access to original sources of information involves an arduous process and requires great dedication—not something the vast majority of journalists can afford. All the more so, information from direct experience would imply sacrificing years of one's life and risking great dangers. Mediated but trustworthy knowledge is, under those conditions, about as much as can reasonably be demanded.

No less a figure than Hegel, whose description of the operations of the mind still dominated the philosophical landscape, had resorted to secondhand reports to inform his history of Africa:

> Negroes are enslaved by Europeans and sold to America. Bad as this may be, their lot in their own land is even worse, since there a slavery quite as absolute exists; for it is the essential principle of slavery, that man has not yet attained a consciousness of his freedom, and consequently sinks down to a mere Thing—an object of no value. Among the Negroes moral sentiments are quite weak, or more strictly speaking non-existent. Parents sell their children, and conversely children their parents, as either has the opportunity. Through the pervading influence of slavery all those bonds of moral regard which we cherish towards each other disappear, and it does not occur to the Negro mind to expect from others what we are enabled to claim.[9]

What Hegel has to say of Africa and Africans cannot be taken in quite the same way as one might want to understand what he has to say of the phenomenology of mind or of the evolution of knowledge. Although he does make his globalizing statements on Africa dependent on a certain form of knowledge, on a certain kind of understanding, it is evident that any knowledge he himself had on this topic was at best secondhand, from missionaries' reports and similar sources available at the time. Hegel indicates this himself, in the same chapter of his *Philosophy of History* where he cites his sources: "the copious and circumstantial accounts of missionaries confirm this."[10] Yet, as this instance might indicate, the fact that firsthand knowledge, or at least better-founded knowledge, appears not to have been considered a requisite to expressing such wide-ranging ideas about an entire continent and its peoples has a meaning of its own. For one thing, Hegel's reliance on secondary information contrasts sharply with the meticulous care he otherwise takes in the preparation and arrangement of his arguments. This vast generalization reflects on the nature of the consciousness at work in knowing and understanding the world. For another, superior knowledge—most often in the form of disproportionately advanced military technology—has long served as a substitute justification for the colonization and enslavement of people by European nations with claims to more evolved forms of civilization.[11] In European discourse on slavery or colonization, superior knowledge operates as a more palatable rationalization than the bare-faced affirmation of superior material power, or of superior military might.

But justification by superior knowledge is only one of the strategies in the arsenal of disculpation, of naturalization of slavery in the learned discourse of the period. The vast array of rationalizations continually invoked should serve as proof that the fundamental unacceptability of slavery survived all attempts at intellectual normalization and kept returning to challenge the ethical foundations of any society that practiced it. Just the same, as long as property and profits could still be shown to be on the side of maintaining slavery, knowledge and reason could always be summoned into service and called upon to generate a rhetoric capable of forestalling abolitionist arguments—or, at least, of delaying any practical effects they might have.

A report of an incident occurring in the middle of the period studied and reported by *Le Constitutionnel* allows us an insight into some of the articulations of knowledge and interest. The incident is an alleged massacre of two thousand slaves on the west coast of Africa. The report is first published by an Irish paper, the *Cork Constitution*, and republished, with some framing, by the *Times* of London. The interest in this instance rests in the fact that *Le Constitutionnel* does not simply reproduce or translate the report but seems to feel compelled to comment on it and to supply—without evidence of any other reliable knowledge of the events—an alternate version of the events.

Here are the two versions as they appeared in the two dailies:

Article appearing in the Times *of London (March 31, 1847):*

Slave Trade—the following has just been received from a very intelligent naval officer at Ascension. The detail is one of the most appalling proofs of the calamities which the slave trade leads to, and we trust the efficiency of the naval blockade may put an end to its being continued in that part of Africa at least for some time to come.—"Ascension, January 1, 1847—we have just received news of a most horrible massacre on the coast. A slave depot called Gallinas, known to have 2000 slaves ready for shipping, was so closely blockaded by our cruisers that the slave owners finding it impossible to embark the slaves, and not wishing to incur the expense of feeding them, actually in cold blood beheaded the whole number, placing their heads on poles stuck in the beach, saying, if you will not allow us to make profit of prisoners we take in war, we will kill all."—*Cork Constitution*

Article appearing in Le Constitutionnel *(April 3, 1847):*

Under the heading, "Atrocious Results of the Cruises on the African Coast," *Le Courrier du Havre* reports that two thousand slaves have been massacred by a slave merchant. These are the circumstances of the alleged crime.

Among the measures decided on in the conferences which took place in London against the slave trade, at the time when the right of inspection was replaced by even more deplorable arrangements, the decision to blockade those points on the coast where the slave traders gather the slaves in order to embark them at the first signal stands as one of the worst.

Thus the officer commanding the English squadron had apparently been charged with blocking an old slave trade center at the mouth of a river called Gallinas. According to the report of one of the British officers, this task had been so thoroughly carried out, the blockade was so complete, that the slave trader, finding himself unable to load his slaves onto his ships, apparently decided to kill them in order to save himself the cost of feeding them.

The British officer was very likely misinformed. It is difficult to believe that a European, even a slave-trader, could have massacred, in cold blood, so many victims, especially as such heartless parsimony would have been self-defeating. The feeding of Negro slaves costs so little on the African coast. And though two thousand of these hapless creatures cost little enough, they still represent a considerable sum when sold.

The slave traders know that the slaves can be loaded onto the ships in a very short time. The cruisers' blockade has hardly diminished the traders' activity, nor has it ceased to bring in large profits.

It is therefore unlikely that a European slave trader was responsible for the massacre of two thousand slaves at Gallinas. Rather, it is more than likely that these unfortunates were beheaded on the orders of native leaders who found themselves unable to sell them. These massacres are regular occurrences on the African coast; it seems certain that they have become more common since the selling of slaves has become more difficult.

This is what happens: the African chiefs bring slaves from the interior to sell to the dealers who are set up on the coast. The dealers, for their part, are reluctant to buy this live merchandise when they feel they are being too closely watched, when they are not expecting, very shortly, a slave-trading ship. The African chiefs kill their prisoners out of sheer barbarity and because they are unable to feed them. Then, when they have an opportunity to quickly load some slaves, the African chiefs raid the surrounding area; the strong seize the weak, the husband sells his wife, the son grabs his father by stealth, friends drag their friends to the coast and the miserable creatures are piled into the holds of the slave-trading ships. In short, the slave trade has not at all diminished—it has only become more horrid. Such seems to be the clearest end-result of the repressive measures our government has so proudly adopted.

The conclusion of *Le Constitutionnel*'s version more than likely alludes to the latest treaty signed by France and Great Britain concerning the mutual rights of inspection of ships suspected of carrying on the slave trade. The "new repressive measures" are most likely a reference to the May 1845 treaty between France and England arranged by Guizot. On one level, this is simply another instance of *Le Constitutionnel*'s turning a news item into an opportunity to embarrass the Guizot government. Guizot's reputed admiration for English political culture ran in complete opposition to post-Napoleonic French nationalism. Anti-British nationalism was particularly exacerbated when conflicts arose between the two nations over colonies and maritime commerce. Colonies, which had been the pawns of endless conflicts between England and France throughout the eighteenth century, and the slave trade, which at this time was of interest almost exclusively to the economies of the colonies, were two particularly thorny issues of Anglo-French relations. The following passage from an article by Serge Daget succinctly sets the political and diplomatic frame in which the question of slavery is debated in the French parliament:

> After the allied victory of 1815, the abolitionist ideology had fewer popular adherents than ever in France, and its activists saw themselves relegated to the role of followers of official decisions. Revolutionary in origin (of heightened significance at a time of monarchical restoration), associated with the defeat and with the English, abolition was written into an additional article in the second treaty of Paris, a move which was first viewed as a machiavellian maneuver executed by the principal victors, the English. The envied rival was using ostensibly humanitarian means to further its ambitions for political, commercial, and indeed military hegemony. Such an attitude was clearly in evidence and did not bode well for the implementation of abolition.[12]

This being said, the aim of the translated article in *Le Constitutionnel* is primarily to clear Europeans, and France in particular, of any part in the reported atrocity while at the same time attributing whatever fault there may be to the pro-English policies of Guizot's government. That the reporting and framing of this news item was primarily important to *Le Constitutionnel* in terms of its potential effect on domestic politics is confirmed by the fact that not all the Parisian papers report this massacre though most seem aware of the translated article that had appeared in *Le Courier du Havre* and in *Le Constitutionnel*. Most tellingly, *Le Journal des Débats,* generally identified by the opposition press as the unofficial voice of the Guizot government, does not report the incident but instead prints only a denial, a few days later, that the event ever took place: "The Cygnet, a British warship recently docked in Portsmouth for some urgent repairs, has brought home reports from the naval squadron stationed on the west coast of Africa. These reports completely deny the contents of a letter published in an Irish paper announcing the massacre of some 2,000 slaves by some slave traders who found themselves unable to embark them. Despite the vigilance of the patrolling cruisers, the slave trade is still relatively active. During its patrol, the Cygnet boarded nineteen vessels having on board a total of some 1,760 slaves. Of the nineteen vessels, fifteen were convicted as slavers." [13] Though *Le Journal des Débats* implicitly concedes that the trade is still very active, its emphasis—like that of the London *Times*—is on the efficiency of the Anglo-French blockade. *Le Constitutionnel* draws from the reported massacre an interpretation completely at variance with that of the *Times* and *Le Journal des Débats*. In order to make the most political mileage out of the incident, the blockade and all treaties related to it must be blamed as reactionary, shortsighted measures. Instead of curtailing the slave trade, they are represented as making things worse for the Africans by cornering the traders and supposedly leading them to all the more desperate acts.

Yet, for all the political intricacy that the question of slavery implies for the liberals who ran *Le Constitutionnel,* some guiding principles seem always at hand to lead them—even out of the muddle of guilt that the massacre of two thousand people represents. The priority now is no longer the very existence of slavery as ultimately the cause of the massacre but whether it was carried out by Africans or Europeans. It is, strangely, a question of self-knowledge, of knowing Europeans to be incapable of barbarity.

Ironically, the whole question is founded on a misunderstanding, a mistranslation of the *Cork Constitution* (or *Times*) article. The last line of the *Times* article has the authors of the massacre refer to slaves as prisoners taken in war, implying tribal wars—which would presumably take place with or without European participation in the slave trade. It also speaks of "slave owners" rather than "traders." *Le Constitutionnel*'s insistence on the innocence of Europeans that is the focus of the French version's long addition to the article reads almost as the effect of guilt-ridden anxiety. In their anxiety the editorialists misread the English article and overlook the exoneration of Europeans already implied in it. Assigning responsibility to others, by claiming barbarity and slavery preceded European participation in the slave trade, serves to divert attention from questions that all too evidently would be raised.

Here again, nothing in the article indicates any firsthand knowledge of Africa, or even of the practices of the slave trade. Rather, readers are driven to accept the words of the authors as true by way of a kind of recognizable inherent logic. The credibility of *Le Constitutionnel*'s interpretation of the events rests on the logic of property, of profit and interest: a logic that the habitual readership of *Le Constitutionnel* understands well. The authors can confidently assert that Europeans did not take part in the massacre and can be sure to be believed without supplying any alternative firsthand evidence simply by demonstrating that such a massacre would not be profitable. Implicitly, readers are meant to understand that only Africans, whose conception of commerce and trade is so widely different from the European one, could so wantonly waste so many profitable assets.

For something purportedly hard to believe ("It is difficult to believe that a European, *even a slave-trader*, could have massacred, in cold blood, so many victims"—emphasis added), something almost "natural" is substituted: the normalcy of "business as usual" no matter what laws may be passed ("The cruisers' blockade has hardly diminished the traders' activity, nor has the trade ceased to bring in large profits"). Once this context of profitability has been established, the logic of property and profit can simply take over the story and supply the more credible version: "Especially as such heartless parsimony would have been self-defeating. The feeding of Negro slaves costs so little on the African coast. And though two thousand of these hapless creatures cost little enough, they still represent a considerable sum when sold."

Proof by profitability is, given the proper context (in this case, a ready, willing, and complicit readership), almost irrefutable. As *Le Constitutionnel* has chosen to use the incident for political purposes rather than attempting to deny its veracity, all that is needed is a suitable culprit. This culprit will be consistent with those same principles that served to cleanse Europeans of responsibility. Exculpation of Europeans from this massacre (one among a likely several: "these massacres . . . have become more common since the selling of slaves has become more difficult") becomes an occasion for exculpation from the guilt of the slave system as a whole. To that end, *Le Constitutionnel* trots out the arsenal of hearsay knowledge of rehearsed clichés on the *moeurs*, or customs, of the Africans that has always, as in Hegel, served to make slavery appear as the lesser of two evil destinies.

But if this hearsay passes for certain knowledge with no evidence, not even a pretense at experience, it is not only because its appeal lies in a need for exoneration, or a desire to be purged of guilt, or even for a political advantage in a crucial economic debate. Rather, the credibility of the hearsay lies in its self-mirroring evidence, in its logic of redundancy. Being alien, being distant, being different, being utterly other turns the Africans into objects and denies them—as Hegel does—the status of self-conscious beings. By exacerbating the representation of this otherness, by pushing its aberrance to the utter limits of recognizable humanness ("the husband sells his wife, the son grabs his father by stealth"), this discourse confirms the other's status as object. It simply repeats, in the manner of an endlessly repeated narration, as well-known, infinitely rehearsed practice, the full extent of the other's otherness. In this purportedly corrected narration, the sense of identity that has all along been denied between Africans and Europeans is also denied between Africans and Africans: their nonhumanity is demonstrated, in the terms of this cliché, by the fact that they do not even recognize their own as their own.

One might want to argue here that at least part of the problem lies with the readiness to suspend disbelief, with the willing accreditation of unsubstantiated, unverified reports, with the fascination for the other's capacity to transcend inhibitions taken for natural. Yet, in a way, some part of this willful ignorance must be attributable to this European inability to know oneself, to understand one's own knowledge sufficiently to recognize oneself in the other. Here, in the liberal perspective that *Le Constitutionnel* represents, property visibly determines this inability even beyond all philosophical proclamations of self-knowledge as a condition of humanness.

NOTES

1. Several Parisian papers were studied and compared with *Le Constitutionnel* for the period of the serialized publication of the novel. The coherence of these clusters is predicated on their confrontation with the serialized novel and as such is necessarily liable to revision when situated in a wider or different time frame.

2. For the evolution of *Le Constitutionnel,* see Eugène Hatin, *Bibliographie historique de la presse périodique française* (Paris: Editions Anthrops, 1965).

3. *Le Constitutionnel,* April 25, 1847, 1. All translations are the author's.

4. *Le Constitutionnel,* April 25, 1847, 1.

5. *Le Constitutionnel,* April 25, 1847, 1. These are the last lines of the editorial on the discussion of the royal report in the Chamber of Deputies that day.

6. *Le Constitutionnel,* April 25, 1847, 1.

7. *Le Constitutionnel,* April 27, 1847, 1.

8. For the difficulties of accounting for or even simply defining slavery, see, for example, David Brion Davis, *The Problem of Slavery in Western Culture* (Ithaca, N.Y.: Cornell UP, 1966), as well as David Brion Davis, *Slavery and Human Progress* (New York: Oxford UP, 1984).

9. Georg Wilhelm Friedrich Hegel, *The Philosophy of History*, trans. J. Sibree (New York: Dover, 1956), 96.

10. Hegel, *Philosophy of History*, 93.

11. In relation to colonization in particular, see, for example, Bernard S. Cohn, *Colonialism and Its Forms of Knowledge: The British in India* (Princeton: Princeton UP, 1996), 4.

12. Serge Daget, "France, Suppression of the Illegal Trade, and England, 1817–1850," in *The Abolition of the Atlantic Slave Trade: Origins and Effects in Europe, Africa and the Americas*, ed. David Eltis and James Walvin (Madison: U of Wisconsin P, 1981), 194. An analogous description of differences between French and English attitudes in regard to slavery can be found in the first pages of chapter 4 of Léon-François Hoffmann, *Le Nègre romantique: Personnage littéraire et obsession collective* (Paris: Payot, 1973).

13. *Le Journal des Débats*, April 5–6, 1847.

TWO

*American
Perspectives*

Haitian Contributions to American History
A Journalistic Record

LEARA RHODES

Two groups of free black Haitians were a part of the history of Savannah, Georgia. I use the name *Haiti* instead of *Saint-Domingue* throughout this argument since the intent of the information is to highlight the contributions that a certain immigrant population made to American history. After the Haitian Revolution in 1804, the name of the Saint-Domingue part of the island was returned to the original Indian name: *Hayti*. By using *Haiti*, I hope to link the history with the present. More Haitians know about their ancestors' contributions to the history of the United States than do Americans, even those Americans living in Savannah, Georgia.

The first group of free blacks from Haiti consisted of over five hundred volunteers who fought on the side of the Americans against the British in the Revolutionary War in 1779. The second group, thirty-three free blacks, moved to Savannah in the 1790s from Haiti. There is little information on either group—but there is little information on any Haitian accomplishment in the United States. Indeed, Roy S. Bryce-Laporte notes that there is a dearth of significant research on the contributions, lives, and roles of Caribbean immigrants in general in the United States.[1] While white historians have all but ignored the fact that Haitians fought on the side of the Americans against the British in the Siege of Savannah in 1779, black historians have magnified the Haitian contribution.[2] The uneven reporting process tends either to silence the event or to evangelize it in the name of ethnic pride. Therefore the purpose of this chapter is to look carefully at the contributions these groups may have made to American history. What emerges as a consistent pattern is that the press did not see blacks and slaves as an issue in the Revolution, and even though these groups of free blacks made significant contributions, they fail to receive the coverage and consideration they deserve.[3] I come to this project as a journalist, a Haitian scholar, and a southerner, born and raised in Georgia, committed to reviewing the material about Haitian contributions sympathetically through a newspaper reader's eyes tinted with a deep southern heritage.

METHODOLOGY

The journalistic record of the time, the newspaper, is used here to document the events through an analysis of press roles in the period. Journalism is a special kind of literary product. Some events were not recorded due to politics during the period of the Revolutionary War; therefore, historical events recorded in the newspapers during that period must also be examined in light of how the press was controlled during the colonial, revolutionary, and party press periods. The newspapers are used to create a more reliable picture of how Haitian military assistance was viewed in the United States. Newspapers, a chief source for the history of ideas, are touted as the genetic memory, as a place to assimilate the collective knowledge of a culture.[4] The problem in using newspapers as historical evidence, however, is that during the American revolutionary period most American newspapers were edited and published by printers who were tradespeople and who were often appointed by the king of England. The printer editors often depended upon each other for their intercolonial news, treating the idea of timeliness carelessly. Local news was neglected in favor of what was happening in England and Europe, with even the most important events sometimes passed over for political motives. It is not surprising, therefore, that newspapers suppressed all but the barest public mention of the Haitians who fought in Savannah. It is difficult to prove from the newspapers if the printer favored either the Patriots (American colonists) or the Loyalists (those loyal to Britain) due to the fact that the newspapers often contained what readers wanted to read. Printers bent to the power of whatever group was in control, and papers printed little news outside of political and commercial affairs.[5]

The *Georgia Gazette*, the only newspaper in Georgia before the Revolutionary War, changed its name three times between 1781 and 1787. Operated by three different printers, the newspaper returned to its original name and its original printer, James Johnston, in 1788. Copies of the newspaper are located in the Savannah Historical Society and in the University of Georgia library. Other newspapers of the period also published articles about Haitians in the United States. These articles appeared in the *Gazette of the State of South Carolina, Boston Gazette, London Gazette, Paris Gazette, New York Royal Gazette, New Jersey Journal, Georgia Journal and Independent Federal Register, Maryland Journal, Baltimore Daily Advertiser, Frederick-Town Weekly Advertiser, City Gazette and Daily Advertiser, Washington Spy, Columbian Museum and Savannah Advertiser* (Chatham County, Georgia), and *Columbian Centinal*. A complete reading of the newspapers from 1763 to 1799 resulted in the identification of 117 articles about Haitians.

NEWSPAPER BACKGROUND

Printers believed they were recording current history.[6] Information was reprinted from other newspapers, and innumerable documents—local, national, and foreign—were published as part of the printer's conception of a newspaper's function. Letters to family members with news of a region were printed in the papers. Printers helped shape history through the content of their papers.

Journalism historians have identified various periods of newspaper history. The periods surrounding the time of the Revolutionary War are the colonial press, the revolutionary press, and the party press.[7] The colonial press, which began in 1765, was not neutral; it simply obeyed the authorities and voiced no opinion of its own. During the Siege of Savannah (1779), the newspapers in New York and in Georgia, regions held by the British, followed the colonial press format. The newspapers published only what the authorities wanted published. These papers were considered Tory papers and were loyal to Great Britain. This loyalty eventually led to some of the newspapers not publishing during the Revolutionary War due to politics and to a shortage of paper. Another facet of the colonial press was that their agenda did not include discussion of blacks except as slaves or criminals. "While a Negro murderer or a drunken sailor might be mentioned by name, [the name of] a reader of the *Gazette* could never be published outside the advertising columns or in official proclamations."[8] The agreement among the newspaper publishers was that first the Revolution would be won, and then other issues would be discussed. Kenneth Stewart and John Tebbel have affirmed that the colonial press was a controlled propaganda medium, not particularly devoted to the truth. The papers printed little news outside of political and commercial affairs. They were directed

toward men and excluded women. In the time frame 1765 to 1782, there were
thirty-nine Patriot papers and eighteen Tory papers. The agenda of the colonial and revolutionary press did not include blacks.[9]

The year 1775 marks the beginning of the revolutionary press, which aimed
at action and subordinated everything to the one glorious idea of independence. Though the Siege of Savannah takes place in 1779, few of the newspapers that published reports of the siege were revolutionary papers. Of the
newspapers that were considered revolutionary papers, only the *Boston Gazette,* which published one article, and the *Charleston Gazette,* which published
three articles, reported the battle. Both of these were Patriot papers.

During the party-press days beginning in 1783, the nation had to be organized; the newspapers were used as political organs by the various parties to
further their dogma. Theories of popular government were held to be the most
important argument of that day.[10] The newspapers in Savannah were no different than those in the rest of the country. However, more importantly in the
South, references to blacks, especially free blacks, created a panic in the slave
owner population. There was great fear that the Haitian Revolution of 1791
would feed the slaves in the South information and demonstrate how they, too,
could rebel. One such case was the Gabriel Conspiracy in 1800, where many of
the conspirators maintained that the plot was "inspired by the examples of
Santo Domingo, and the emancipation of the ancient Israelites from Egypt."[11]
Another case was the Denmark Vesey Conspiracy in Charleston in 1822. The
testimony and other evidence presented in the report on that case indicate that
the leaders of the conspiracy as well as many who agreed to take part were profoundly affected by the black revolution in Haiti. Following the Vesey conspirators' trial, a pamphlet was published in Charleston entitled, "Reflections, Oc-
casioned by the Late Disturbances." That pamphlet listed a number of the
causes for the late conspiracy. The first cause was the example of Haiti.[12]

THE SIEGE OF SAVANNAH

The Haitian role in the Revolutionary War begins with Charles Henri Comte
d'Estaing's military records and reports in newspapers, both in the United
States and in France.[13] D'Estaing sailed from France to Haiti to aid the French
army in their attempt to fight the British. Alfred Nemours draws on documents
in the French naval archives to describe Admiral d'Estaing's arrival at Cap
François in July 1779, his departure in August, his arrival off Savannah in September, and his committing of French and Haitian troops to battle the follow-

ing month.[14] In December 1778, Savannah had fallen to the British, who were threatening Charleston and the Carolinas. Savannah was the first major operation of American troops in combination with those of their new and powerful ally, Louis XVI of France.[15]

The summer of 1779 was a happy one as reported in the *Royal Georgia Gazette*. Scarce news appeared in the *Georgia Gazette* about the war because it had been taken over by the Tories. Johnston, the printer, had been run out of Savannah and accused of treason. John Daniel Hammerer published the paper by authority as a Tory paper from 1779 to 1782. It was the *Gazette of the State of South Carolina* that announced d'Estaing's arrival off the coast of Georgia on September 8, 1779. D'Estaing was not pleased with the American press because of the details published regarding the number of his ships and their arrival off the coast. "It is a terrible thing, the American newspapers, as little truthful as the English gazettes, are even more imprudent and nearly always tell their lies at the most inappropriate time."[16] The *Gazette of the State of South Carolina* announced that militia were turning out in all parts of the state. A Charleston paper (probably the *Charleston Gazette*) wrote that the British in Savannah thought they would be defeated. This article was reprinted in the *Boston Gazette* on November 15, 1779, with a dateline of Charleston, September 22, 1779.

What was common knowledge and not printed in the newspapers was that d'Estaing was a general and vice admiral of France as well as the former governor of Haiti and the recent conqueror of St. Vincent and Grenada. His stopping at Le Cap François was a consequence of the Franco-American Alliance of 1778, according to which France, in return for certain commitments from the Congress, would employ its resources to enable the colonies to win their independence from Britain.[17]

Many troops were enlisted in the West Indies. Whereas the sources verify that troops came from Haiti, reports of the numbers of men who enlisted are inconsistent. The journal of a naval officer in the fleet of the count d'Estaing published in Paris, September 1782, stated that a corps of about 4,000 men was formed, including 800 free mulattoes taken and enlisted in Haiti. These men were on *H. M. S. Ariel*, a British ship captured by the French while on the Georgia coast.[18] Nemours wrote that d'Estaing's expeditionary force was made up of regular French metropolitan troops stationed in Haiti (the regiments of Gatinois, Agenois, and Cambresis), the all-white voluntary grenadiers of Haiti, the free blacks and mulattoes of the voluntary *chasseurs,* or militiamen, and additional free black and mulatto volunteers: the total number of troops was 1,550, of which 800 were native blacks or mulattoes.[19] The *New Jersey Journal*

(June 21, 1780) said the colored troops consisted of 545 volunteer *chasseurs*, mulattoes, and negroes newly raised at Haiti. The *London Gazette* (December 21, 1779) said that the troops included colony troops of Guadeloupe, Martinique, Le Cap François, and Port-au-Prince, besides some hundreds of free blacks and mulattoes, taken on board in the West Indies. The *Royal Gazette* on March 4, 1780, listed the number of troops as 1,000 from the Regiment of the Cape, 700 Martinican volunteers, and 1,000 from the Cape Regiment of Color. Historians have affirmed that the French troops consisted of regiments from Guadeloupe, Martinique, and Port-au-Prince, including a detachment of the Royal Corps of Infantry of the Marine and the Volunteers of Vallelle, the Dragoons, and 156 volunteer Grenadiers, lately raised at Le Cap François.[20] The division of M. Louis-Marie, vicomte de Noailles, included 900 men of the regiments from Champagne, Auxerrois, Foix, Guadeloupe, and Martinique. There were an additional 1,000 men enumerated in the *Paris Gazette* of January 7, 1780, of whom 545 were colored.

Of the troops from Haiti, there were notable men who later became generals, such as André, Beauvais, Rigaud, Villate, Beauregard, Lambert, and Henry Christophe, the future king of Haiti. Claude Adrien cites the generation of Haitian leaders who took part in the Siege of Savannah as Jean-Baptiste Mars Belley, Louis Jacques Beauvais, Martial Besse, and André Rigaud. Lawrence gives a more graphic description of these men:

> But others in d'Estaing's army besides the aristocrats would make names for themselves; for example, a bright-eyed, ebon-skinned boy from the West Indies by the name of Christophe. Henri had come to Georgia either as a volunteer in the colored Chasseurs from Cap François, as some say, or as the serving boy of a French officer, as others contend. Be that as it may, the time would come when this unruly youth was to wear a title greater than any of these beribboned noblemen. For Christophe would one day be King of Haiti and build the fabulous mountain citadel of Sans Souci. A dusky volunteer named Beauvais and André Rigaud, a mulatto, were two of the several other future generals of the black revolt in Haiti who learned their first lessons in war and freedom at Savannah.[21]

Christophe was reported to have been wounded at Savannah. The fact that Henry Christophe was but twelve years old in 1779 lends support to the theory that he came to Georgia as a valet rather than a soldier. Christophe was born October 6, 1767, in Grenada; because his birthplace was a British colony, he preferred his name spelled *Henry* instead of *Henri*.[22]

The free blacks arrived in Savannah under the French command on September 8, 1779. The anonymous journal of a naval officer gives vivid details of the landing of the French troops on that date. D'Estaing ordered six ships under de la Motte-Piquet to proceed a few miles south of Tybee Island to the mouth of the Vernon River and set ashore the corps of about four thousand men. When the ships anchored outside of Savannah, the viscount de Fontanges, the troop commander, was sent to confer with Major General Benjamin Lincoln regarding the combined operation against Savannah. A corps of French West India troops, under the viscount de Noailles, the artillery, and some American militia formed the reserve under General Lincoln.[23]

The men waited for new orders. Benjamin Kennedy in his description of the Siege of Savannah has stated that "it was extraordinary that there were so few sick among the 3,000 men who came from the islands and St. Domingo, who were constantly at arms for nearly a month, most of them without tents, dressed only in linen suffering from heat in the daytime, and freezing to death at night."[24]

D'Estaing formed the first advance guards from the volunteers and Grenadiers. These troops were to advance to the Spring Hill Redoubt, which is on West Broad Street, where the Central Georgia Depot now stands. When the railroad depot was enlarged, thirty skeletons were found and were attributed to be the remains of Haitians who had fought in the Siege of Savannah in 1779 and were buried where they had fallen. The redoubt was a massive frame of green spongy wood, filled in with sand, and mounted with heavy cannon.[25]

On September 24, 1779, M. de Rouvrai (some sources spell his name *Rouvray*) and his Haitian volunteers took part in an action. Their role had been to protect working parties that had been digging trenches three hundred yards from enemy lines. The activity was discovered, and 600 British troops attacked the trenches. These British were repulsed and driven back, but the French and Haitians pursued within range of the British cannon and immediately incurred heavy losses. According to Lt. Col. O'Dune, de Rouvrai's subordinate, de Rouvrai was drunk, and his actions led to the wounding of 150 men and to the death of another 40. Lawrence cites Captain Tarragon's assertion that M. de Rouvrai was no soldier, and that if he had not played into the hands of the British by ordering out the six companies, the French would not have lost a man.[26]

According to de Noailles, the volunteer *chasseurs,* under the orders of de Sabliere, were to make a false attack called for in d'Estaing's orders and to guard the trenches. D'Estaing's printed orders said that the people of color would be treated at all times like the whites. "They aspire to the same honor, they will exhibit the same bravery." However, the official French roster of the forces at Savannah noted that the corps of free negroes was capable only of employment on trenches. Just before the battle, according to Leighton, de Fontanges (some sources spell his name *Fontage*), major general of the army, made changes and mixed the men to form new companies, giving their command to officers unacquainted with their soldiers. This restructuring of the companies, which Clark believed was responsible for the actions of the Haitian troops in the battle, cannot be fully documented.[27] What has been documented is that a corps of French West India troops under the leadership of M. de Noailles, plus the artillery and some American militia, formed the reserve under General Benjamin Lincoln. When the action started, within fifty-five minutes nearly eight hundred men of France, Haiti, and America had been killed or wounded, compared to British losses, according to Lawrence, of only eighteen killed and thirty-nine wounded. The retreat was orderly, capably protected by Noailles, commander of the French reserve.[28]

Nemours wrote, "The black and mixed-blood soldiers and officers of St. Domingo protected the retreat of American and French forces and permitted the embarkment of the French forces." Balch attributed leadership to Fontanges: "He commanded there a legion of mulattos of more than 800 men, and saved the army after the useless assault on the fortifications, by bravely covering the retreat." Adrien asserted that the Black Legion or the Fontanges Legion saved the Patriot army from what might have been annihilation. Madiou, the only Haitian historian located whose writings included the Siege of Savannah, supported the bravery of the Haitian soldiers by suggesting that they covered themselves with glory in the Siege of Savannah. The source of the information cannot be verified but has become canonical among Haitian historians. The Honorable Richard Rush, U.S. minister to Paris in 1849, wrote: "The legion of black and mulatto freedmen, known as Fontanges Legion, saved the army at Savannah by bravely covering its retreat. . . . It was this legion that formed the connecting link between the Siege of Savannah and the wide development of republican liberty on the Western continent." Laurent wrote that "the history of the United States should retain, graven upon its Roll of Honor, the names of these valorous adventurers who bathed with their blood the soil of a nation at birth."[29]

On October 9, 1779, the assault on the Spring Hill Redoubt was where the Fontanges Legion reportedly saved the retreating army of Americans in "the most brilliant feat of the day, and one of the bravest ever performed by foreign troops in the American cause."[30] The *Royal Georgia Gazette* reported that this was a critical moment at hand for Great Britain, and that the troops and militia joined together heartily in the defense of Savannah. The Tory sentiments of the paper were obvious.

The proof of how valiant the Haitian troops were has been hard to come by. What happened October 9, 1779, in Savannah, Georgia, has been difficult to verify. Newspapers, having no organized means of covering the Revolutionary War, relied almost wholly on the chance arrival of private letters and of official and semi-official messages.[31] Existing records are from the reports of French and American officers. There is no firsthand documentation from Haitians, a fact that is confirmed by Heinl and Heinl:

> The entire records of the Haitian government were destroyed when the National Palace exploded in 1869; ten years later, the Foreign Ministry had to ask the U.S. State Department for copies of previous treaties and agreements and related diplomatic correspondence because the ministry's files had been wiped out by fire; within four more years, in 1883, the events of the Semaine Sanglante consumed not only the national archives but virtually every government bureau and its files in Port-au-Prince. In 1888 the reconstituted archives perished when the building burned to the ground. And in 1912, when the National Palace again blew up, the explosion took with it the government's records.[32]

Finding records to verify the Haitian contributions is not the only problem in documenting the role played by Haitians in the Revolutionary War. Fear among the whites in the South as to what blacks would do if armed escalated in 1778 when the *Georgia Gazette* published that two hundred slaves were armed by General Augustin Prevost, a British officer. This was thought by many as unjustified under any circumstances. The paper defended Prevost by calling attention to the fact that the French had initiated the practice by bringing along colored troops from the West Indies.[33]

When the Siege of Savannah was over, many men were dead or wounded. The attempt by the Americans and French to take Savannah had failed, but even though the British still held Savannah, the French soldiers were welcomed home as heroes in France. D'Estaing was greeted in Versailles by great crowds of people who celebrated his win at Grenada and ignored the loss of Savannah.[34] Many of the French officers fought in the French Revolution, and some returned to the American colonies. Many books have been written about the French who fought in the Revolutionary War in Savannah. Their journals have been reproduced and published. Polish officer Casimir Pulaski has been made a hero in Savannah with a monument celebrating his bravery in the battle that mortally wounded him, and the national General Pulaski Memorial Day honors him each year.

The Haitians who died in the Siege of Savannah were buried where they fell. Their bones were found when the railroad depot over their grave was expanded. Some of the Haitians who returned to Haiti became officers and generals who fought many other battles. Beauvais went to Europe and served in the French army. He returned to fight for liberty in Haiti and was captain-general in 1791. Rigaud, Lambert, and Christophe fought for Haiti's freedom in 1790 to make Haiti the first free black republic. The lessons the volunteers learned in the Siege of Savannah have been seen by many historians as the background these men needed to fight for the liberty of their country. Moreover, this experience has been viewed by some as the beginning of freedom for countries all over the Western Hemisphere.[35]

RESULTS

A total of 123 newspaper articles were examined from the time period of 1763, when the first newspaper in Georgia was established, through 1803, when Haitian independence was won. Of the nine newspapers publishing articles about Haitians, only seven articles were about the Siege of Savannah and included numbers and origins of Haitians fighting in the battle. Another twenty-six articles concerned topics related to shipping and trade. The remaining eighty-eight articles were about the French who relocated in the United States as refugees from Haiti at the outbreak of the Haitian Revolution in 1791.

The colonial press period of 1765–75 included only eleven articles about Haitians, all trade related. The revolutionary press period of 1775 to 1783 included seven articles about Haitians, all of which contained statistics on how many mulattoes and blacks there were and from where they were recruited. Only two of the articles were printed in southern newspapers: the *Gazette of South Carolina* and the *Royal Gazette of Georgia*. At the time, the *Royal Gazette of Georgia* was under British guidance, and the article printed was very pro-Britain. Other newspapers printing articles on the Siege of Savannah included two foreign journals: the *London Gazette* and the *Paris Gazette*. Both offered statistics on the number of mulattoes and blacks recruited from the West Indies. There were no articles about Haitians located from the years 1770 to 1778.

During the party-press period, beginning in 1783, only seven articles were printed about Haitians during the years 1783 to 1790. However, beginning with the outbreak of the Haitian Revolution in 1791, the *Georgia Gazette* published eight articles in 1791, eight more in 1792, three in 1793, six in 1794, and ten in 1796. By 1799, the *Columbian Museum and Savannah Advertiser* in Chatham County, Georgia (in which Savannah is located), published fifteen articles on the refugees entering Georgia.

HAITIANS IN SAVANNAH

In 1826, Chatham County registered thirty-three free persons of color from Haiti.[36] The rich cultural diversity in Savannah in the 1820s included immigrants from ten foreign countries. Johnson attributes this rich cultural diversity to the Atlantic slave trade (prior to its abolition in 1808) and the Haitian Revolution (1791–1804). In his book *Black Savannah*, he states that the multiple aspects of social life—the black family, social events, civic organizations, education, and the black church—were the major agents of change in Savannah. Most of the free blacks from Haiti attended the Saint John the Baptist Catholic Church.[37] Laurel Grove Cemetery, set aside for blacks, had tombstones marking the burial sites for some of the free blacks from Haiti. Marianne Marcelene, who died July 9, 1815, at age sixty-seven, was from Port-au-Prince. D'Ariel Marcelene, also of Port-au-Prince, died December 6, 1812. Other graves included the following names: Elizabeth Mirault (December 24, 1895), Jane Mirault (June 4, 1854), Simon R. Mirault Sr. (December 3, 1875—sixty-three years old), Lewis Mirault (1826–forty-seven years old), Rose Mirault (1836), Isaac Emanuel Deveaux, Clodia Deveaux, Jane A. Deveaux (1885), Josephine Mirault (1879), and Capt. Joseph L. Mirault (January 18, 1859–October 7, 1898).

Church records from the Saint John the Baptist Catholic Church in Savannah, Chatham County, provide some data about Haitians. Johnson lists the following information on Haitians in Savannah. Francis Jalineau, a merchant from Haiti, lived in Coosawhatchie, South Carolina, but attended Saint John the Baptist Catholic Church. His wife, Rosette, or Rose, was a free negro woman. Their daughter, Elizabeth, was baptized December 18, 1803; their son, Simon Francois, was baptized June 9, 1807. Francis owned property in Savannah and Cuba. When he died on the way to resettling in Cuba, he left his property to Rose, who was a seamstress. Her property at the corner of Congress and Price Streets was auctioned off in 1844 to pay a $15.00 fine. Rose switched careers in 1848 at age seventy-seven and washed clothes until she died in 1864, when she was ninety-three. She was buried in the Cathedral Cemetery instead of Laurel Grove. Other names in the registry confirm the Laurel Grove grave sites: Simon and Elizabeth Mirault, Josephine Mirault and her son, George Bulloch. In the 1840s, Julien Fromantin of Saint John the Baptist Catholic Church operated a school for black children. This school was illegal, so Fromantin listed his occupation as carpenter. Jane Deveaux operated a school for black children for thirty years.

Indications are that most French-speaking free persons of color in Savannah during the 1800s interacted among themselves and may have kept a social distance from English-speaking people, as Johnson affirms: "Clemente Sabatte Sr. settled in Darien where he married Mary Gary, the American-born mother of Clemente Sabatte Jr. and Hetty, both of whom were born in Darien. . . . Aspasia Mirault, a French *émigré* and confectionery store owner, had a son by James Oliver . . . and Andrew Morel, the tailor, had a son by Eve Wallace . . . while he was still married to his wife, Ann, a native of Saint-Domingue." [38]

Johnson links some of the families together through the second generations: Josephine Mirault married a Bulloch. Mary Jane Mirault, the wife of Josephine's younger brother, Simon, died in 1854. Simon remarried two years later, and the ceremony was recorded in the Catholic church. Johnson attributes the decline of French culture in the immigrants from Haiti as a result of deaths, intermarriage, education, and the termination of the immigration from Haiti.

Two problems may have faced the free blacks from Haiti: the freedom of all free blacks in the United States in the 1820s was difficult to preserve, and first-generation Haitian immigrants had the added difficulty of preserving their French Caribbean culture. [39] They attempted to alleviate the burden of being a foreigner by maintaining close contacts with the Haitian community throughout the city.

DISCUSSION

The original question I pursued was, What contributions have Haitians made in the community of Savannah, Georgia? Of the 117 articles on Haiti published in five newspapers, the topics covered include ships arriving from Haiti and stories on white refugees from Haiti fleeing the Haitian Revolution. A few of the articles mentioned the Haitian volunteers when groups of soldiers were listed. None of the articles reported the retreat and the protection the Haitians offered the American and French troops. No monument was built for the Haitian men who fought in the Siege of Savannah. Therefore, the first group of Haitians left little in Savannah that could be traced to success. They left hundreds of dead soldiers who died during the retreat at Spring Hill Redoubt. What the Haitians took with them, though, was significant. The lessons learned during the Siege of Savannah enabled them to take on leadership roles in the Haitian Revolution. The lifting of the battle flag of freedom was transported from American soil to Haitian soil to South American soil to Central American soil. What the Haitians did in Savannah has had a tremendous impact on freedom throughout the Americas.

The second group of Haitians assimilated into the community and combined with others to create a new life for themselves. Their contributions have been in the everyday realities that face immigrants. The fact that there were no references recorded in the newspapers of the Haitians merging into Savannah black culture does not mean there was no news to report. What it means is that the newspapers of the day found the lives of blacks, free or slave, of no great importance and thus not worth writing about. The renewed fear of black uprisings limited news of the black community. So far as local news was concerned, eighteenth-century papers were neglectful. The history concept of news called for a record, but even the most important events were sometimes passed over from political motives.[40]

Did the Haitians contribute to American history? Yes, through their blood in the battles and through their lifestyle in settling southern cities. Why were their contributions not reported? The reports of the Siege of Savannah were carried in Tory newspapers, which would never promote the courage of free blacks. The agenda of the newspapers in the colonial press and the revolutionary press did not include blacks. The participation of free blacks in the Revolutionary War obviously was not a strong enough event to break racial barriers. Any contribution of free blacks in the 1820s was ignored and not seen as newsworthy enough to warrant coverage in the press. And until the notions change, until the press views minority contributions as significant, it will be the same story: the immigrants who contribute to American history will be underreported and undervalued.

NOTES

1. Roy S. Bryce-Laporte, "New York City and the New Caribbean Immigration: A Contextual Statement," *International Migration Review*, 13 (1979): 214–34.

2. John D. Garrigus, "Catalyst or Catastrophe? Saint-Domingue's Free Men of Color and the Battle of Savannah, 1779–1782," *Revista/Review Interamericana* 22, 1–2 (1992): 109–25.

3. See Humphrey Regis and Leroy Lashley, "The Editorial Dimensions of the Connection of Caribbean Immigrants to Their Referents," *Journal of Black Studies* 22, 3 (1992): 380–91; Patricia Bradley, *Slavery, Propaganda and the American Revolution* (Oxford: U of Mississippi P, 1998).

4. Frank Luther Mott, *American Journalism: A History, 1690–1960* (New York: Macmillan, 1962).

5. Bradley, *Slavery, Propaganda and the American Revolution;* Louis Turner Griffith and John Erwin Talmadge, *Georgia Journalism, 1763–1950* (Athens: U of Georgia P, 1951), 6.

6. Griffith and Talmadge, *Georgia Journalism*, 6.

7. Frederic Hudson, *Journalism in the United States, from 1690–1873* (New York: Harper and Brothers, 1873).

8. Griffith and Talmadge, *Georgia Journalism*, 3.

9. Bradley, *Slavery, Propaganda and the American Revolution;* Kenneth Stewart and John Tebbel, *Makers of Modern Journalism* (New York: Prentice-Hall, 1952), 15; Sidney Kobre, *The Development of the Colonial Newspaper* (Gloucester, G.B.: Peter Smith, 1960), 96–100.

10. Griffith and Talmadge, *Georgia Journalism*, 6.

11. Harvey Wish, "American Slave Insurrections before 1861," in *American Slavery: The Question of Resistance*, ed. John H. Bracey Jr., August Meier, and Elliott M. Rudwick (Belmont, Calif.: Wadsworth, 1971), 22.

12. Monroe Fordham, "Nineteenth-Century Black Thought in the United States: Some Influences of the Santo Domingo Revolution," *Journal of Black Studies* 6, 2 (1975): 115–26.

13. Marmaduke Hamilton Floyd and Dolores Boisfeuillet Floyd, *Collection No. 1308–37: 458, and 37:461* (Savannah: Georgia Historical Society, 1970). Dates covered, 1562–1970.

14. General Alfred Nemours, *Haiti et la guerre de l'independance americaine* (Port-au-Prince, Haiti, 1950), 73.

15. Theophilus G. Steward, "How the Black St. Domingo Legion Saved the Patriot Army in the Siege of Savannah, 1779," *Occasional Papers No. 5* (Washington, D.C.: American Negro Academy, 1899), 4.

16. Alexander A. Lawrence, *Storm over Savannah* (Athens: U of Georgia P, 1951), 13.

17. Steward, "Black St. Domingo Legion," 4.

18. Charles C. Jones Jr., ed., *The Siege of Savannah by the Fleet of Count d'Estaing in 1779* (New York: New York Times and Arno Press, 1968), 59, 15.

19. Nemours, *Haiti et la guerre*, 73; George P. Clark, "The Role of the Haitian Volunteers at Savannah in 1779: An Attempt at an Objective View," *Phylon: The Atlanta University Review of Race and Culture* 41 (December 1980): 356–66.

20. Franklin B. Hough, *The Siege of Savannah by the Combined American and French Forces under the Command of General Lincoln and the Count d'Estaing in the Autumn of 1779* (1866; reprint, Spartanburg, S.C.: Reprint Company, 1975), 145.

21. Vergniaud Leconte, *Henri Christophe dans l'histoire d'Haiti* (Paris, 1931), 2; Steward, "Black St. Domingo Legion," 12; John W. Vandercook, *Black Majesty: The Life of Christophe King of Haiti* (New York: Harper and Brothers, 1928), 11; Claude Adrien, "The Forgotten Heroes of Savannah," *Americas* 30 (1978): 55–57; Lawrence, *Storm over Savannah*, 10.

22. Thomas Balch, *The French in America during the War of Independence of the United States, 1777–1783*, trans. E. S. and E. W. Balch (Philadelphia, 1895), 2, 82; Asa Bird Gardiner, *The Order of Cincinnati in France* (Newport, R.I., 1905), 190; Leconte, *Henri Christophe*, 2; Gerard Laurent, *Haiti et l'indépendance américaine* (Port-au-Price, Haiti: 1976), 145; Adrien, *Forgotten Heroes*, 55; Thomas O. Ott, *The Haitian Revolution: 1789–1804* (Knoxville: U of Tennessee P, 1973), 96 n45.

23. Steward, "Black St. Domingo Legion," 7; Jones, *Siege of Savannah*, 20.

24. Benjamin Kennedy, *Muskets, Cannon Balls and Bombs* (Savannah: Beehive Press, 1974), 63.

25. Adelaide Wilson, *Historic and Picturesque Savannah* (Boston: Published for the Subscribers by the Boston Photogravure Company, 1889); Lawrence, *Storm over Savannah*, 133; George W. Shaffer, former treasurer of the Central Rail Road, to General Henry R. Jackson, president of the Georgia Historical Society, May 1893, Georgia Historical Society, Savannah, Georgia; Steward, "Black St. Domingo Legion," 7.

26. Clark, "Role of the Haitian Volunteers"; Charles C. Jones Jr., ed., *The Siege of Savannah in 1779 as Described in Two Contemporaneous Journals of French Officers in the Fleet of Count d'Estaing* (Albany: J. Munsell, 1874), 57–70; Lawrence, *Storm over Savannah*, 45.

27. Vicomte de Noailles, *Marins et soldats françois en Amerique pendant la guerre de l'independance des Etats-Unis* (Paris, 1903); Roberta Leighton, "Meyronnet de Saint-Marc's Journal of the Operations of the French Army under d'Estaing and the Siege of Savannah, September 1779," *New York Historical Society Quarterly*, 36 (1952): 281; Lawrence, *Storm over Savannah*, 43, 65.

28. Hough, *Siege of Savannah*, 52; Lawrence, *Storm over Savannah*, 113; Kennedy, *Muskets*, 67; Jones, *Siege of Savannah in 1779*, 57–70.

29. Nemours, *Haiti et la guerre*, 73; Balch, *French in America*, 82; Adrien, *Forgotten Heroes*, 55–57; Thomas Madiou, *Histoire d'Haiti*, trans. Theophilus Steward (Port-au-Prince, Haiti, 1847), 1:37–38; Steward, "Black St. Domingo Legion," 4; Laurent, *Haiti et l'indépendance américaine*, 145.

30. Steward, "Black St. Domingo Legion," 2.

31. Frank Luther Mott, *American Journalism: A History, 1690–1960* (New York: Macmillan, 1962).

32. Robert Debs Heinl and Nancy Gordon Heinl, *Written in Blood: The Story of the Haitian People, 1492–1971* (Boston: Houghton Mifflin, 1978), 7–8.

33. Lawrence, *Storm over Savannah*, 27.

34. *Royal Gazette*, December 15, 1779, under the dateline Savannah, November 18, 1779.

35. See Eugene Genovese, *From Rebellion to Revolution: Afro-American Slave Revolts in the Making of the Modern World* (Baton Rouge: Louisiana State UP, 1979); Albert James Williams-Myers, "Slavery, Rebellion, and Revolution in the Americas: A Historiographical Scenario on the Theses of Genovese and Others," *Journal of Black Studies* 26, 4 (1996): 381–400.

36. Chatham County Records, Georgia Historical Society, Savannah, 1826.

37. Whittington Bernard Johnson, *Black Savannah, 1788–1864* (Fayetteville: U of Arkansas P, 1996), 17; register book of the Saint John the Baptist Catholic Church, Savannah, 1796–1816.

38. Johnson, *Black Savannah*, 110.

39. Johnson and Roark, *Black Masters*.

40. Mott, *American Journalism*.

The Tricolor in Black and White
The French Revolution in Gabriel's Virginia

DOUGLAS R. EGERTON

The year 1792 ended in revelry. In countless taverns and public houses along the river, celebrants toasted the birth of the new republic. Hailing one another as "Citizen" or "Jacobin," they spoke with confidence about the coming struggle against the "Tyrants of the World." Optimistic young men banded together in Democratic-Republican Societies or, if stouthearted enough, bragged of enlisting in the "army of the Republic." Tankards were raised to "perpetual alliance between the Republic[s] of America and France," and many a good song was sung, too. The river, however, was not the Seine; it was the James. The taverns stood not in Paris, but in Richmond and Petersburg and Norfolk. But what did a few thousand miles of water signify to men of enlightened goodwill? Republicanism was triumphant on both sides of the Atlantic. The "American public spirit appears to be in our favor everywhere," reported a delighted Jean Baptiste Ternant, the French minister to the United States.[1]

Ternant's letter was posted in December 1792; thereafter it was almost as if a line had been crossed, and with every following month, the two sister republics grew more and more estranged. Specialists in diplomatic history have long sought to explain how the two allies, once staunch confederates in the cause of American independence, descended into the Quasi War by decade's end. The undeniably rash behavior of Minister Edmond Genet, they suggest, together with American abhorrence of the Reign of Terror's bloody excesses and the escalating assaults on American shipping, served to silence Francophile voices. (Although the 1794 toast given in Norfolk—"Liberty to the oppressed, and the

guillotine to the oppressors"—suggests that not as many Americans were sick-
ened by Maximilien Robespierre's handiwork as is often supposed.[2]) Such
explanations undoubtedly have merit. Yet there may be other, less obvious answers as well. For many southern politicians, the French Convention's grudg-
ing acceptance of black liberty—a position forced upon Paris by the rebels of
Saint-Domingue—revealed that too close an association with France could be
deadly. It was not until slaves on the American mainland openly embraced the
twin causes of France and liberty that their terrified owners began to reconsider
their earlier infatuation with Gallic notions of fraternity and equality.

From the start, of course, much of the enthusiasm with which white Virginians greeted news of revolutionary advances in Europe had little enough to
do with republican ideology. Tobacco planters had long chafed under the
French monarchy's refusal to fully abide by the trade agreements of 1778. Confronted with a sovereign blinded by antiquated mercantilist theories, Virginia
agriculturalists had little choice but to fall back into established trading patterns
with Britain, only to watch helplessly as London merchants turned a handsome
profit by reselling their product on the continent. Virginians hoped that the rise
of a new regime in Paris would bring about a more advantageous commerce
in both tobacco and cereal crops, a dream that was more than realized in 1792
when French farmers were pressed into service in the war against Prussia and
Austria.[3]

Nor is there evidence that most Virginians feared that closer trading relations with France would lead to dangerous entanglements on the continent.
Thomas Jefferson, who had been named secretary of state upon returning from
four years as minister in Paris, believed that a vibrant, republican France could
prove a valuable benefactor to his young nation by serving as a counterweight
to hostile British pretensions. But should the revolution fall victim to Austrian
cannon, Britain would emerge from the European vacuum in an even stronger
position, and at length the United States would be forced to militarily protect
its trade and sovereign rights. If for no other reason, Jefferson suggested,
Americans greeted the news of French victories on the battlefield with "universal feasts and rejoicing."[4]

To that hope, Jefferson's protégé, Congressman James Madison, added the
thought that such rejoicing might revive the beleaguered political fortunes of
his emerging party at home. Despite his best efforts, Madison had failed in his
quest to thwart the banking plans and financial schemes of Treasury Secretary
Alexander Hamilton. Perhaps a domestic wave of Gallic enthusiasm might
awaken the sleeping republican instincts of his countrymen in a way that his

learned opposition to Hamilton's program had not. As George Lee Turberville observed, the passions excited by revolution abroad might help to turn the American public against the "endless Funding Schemes, & Factious acts to aggrandize the few at the expense of the great mass of the People."[5]

Yet even pragmatic politicians like Madison conceded that such economic and geopolitical concerns did not create sympathy for France in Virginia but rather served to bolster an already existing empathy for the libertarian ideals of the new republic. Whatever sensible reasons Virginians might have had for cheering the birth of the republic, most agreed with George Lee Turberville of Richmond when he congratulated his own country for first "having made the Rent in the great Curtain that withheld the light from human nature." Certainly the aged George Mason, then in the last year of his life, saw the ideological connection between the two revolutions. "The third Estate," the old patriot observed, "have catched the Flame of American Freedom, and in protecting the Rights & Liberties of others, have learned to assert their own."[6]

But just who were these "others" of whom Mason spoke? Mason surely meant white Americans, but the first hint that some French revolutionaries recognized few exceptions when they spoke of liberty—and thus posed a very real threat to the established southern order—arrived in Charleston, South Carolina, on April 8, 1793, in the person of Edmond Charles Genet. Appointed as the first minister to the United States from the infant republic, the talented young Girondist chose to disembark in the South, where support for the French cause was the strongest. Members of the Republican Society of Charleston, wearing hats decorated with laurel branches, marched to the docks to escort Genet to a reception at his hotel. There patriots offered toasts to the closer "union of the two Republics" and cheered the "speedy revolution of Great Britain and Ireland on Sans-Culotte Principles." Among their number was one Joseph Vesey, a former slave trader who had settled in the city ten years before. Perhaps the old captain's manservant, then still a slave named Telemaque, also witnessed the tumult, for in 1822 the former bondman, under his free name of Denmark Vesey, would attempt to revolutionize South Carolina along similar sansculotte principles.[7]

Encouraged by his tumultuous reception in South Carolina, Genet began a slow overland parade toward Philadelphia, speaking to cheering crowds at virtually every hamlet and crossroads. The minister was in Richmond when word arrived that President George Washington had issued a proclamation announcing that the United States would remain neutral in the contest between France and Britain. Genet was visibly shaken by the news but still hoped to change American foreign policy after presenting his nation's case to the administration; when Senator James Monroe passed the Frenchman on the road near Fredericksburg, he observed that Genet, although now traveling north in great haste, continued to make a favorable impression on the Virginia public.[8]

Nor was Genet the only politician struggling to counter the pro-British policies of the administration. In hopes of keeping the flame of revolution burning, Madison and Monroe penned a series of resolutions designed to be distributed across Virginia. Monroe's rhetoric was the bolder of the two. The senator condemned administrative efforts to distance the American republic from France at a time when it yet struggled against counterrevolutionary onslaughts from "the Priests and Nobles." The two Virginians mailed their resolves to the district courts of Caroline and Charlottesville; Monroe carried his by hand to the courthouse in Staunton, where Archibald Stuart saw that it was formally adopted by the court on September 3. So determined was Monroe to support the French cause that he could not bring himself "to abandon" the minister, even after Jefferson quietly warned his allies that the administration would soon request Genet's recall.[9]

But white southerners were already beginning to abandon Genet, and not merely because of his rude defiance of the still-revered Washington. The Frenchman's enemies in Philadelphia let it be known that Genet was a founding member of the *Société des Amis des Noirs,* the powerful Parisian antislavery society with ties to chapters in London and Philadelphia. Despite the fact that the policies pursued by the *Amis des Noirs* were gradualist in nature, this fact more than any other served to discredit the minister in the eyes of the white South. Southern politicians were all for liberty and equality, but only so long as those ideals were qualified and limited along lines of race and gender. No sooner had the American South realized that Genet—unlike their own revolutionary patriots—actually believed in social revolution, than they began to abandon him.[10]

Genet's problem was not merely that he was an abolitionist but rather that the republic he served was slowly embracing the cause of black liberty. Indeed, most of the French ships in New York harbor, which Genet expected to employ as warships in attacks on British Canada and Spanish Florida, were part of the escort that had ferried Thomas François Galbaud to Saint-Domingue. Galbaud, the governor-general chosen by Genet's fellow Girondists, had the unhappy task of restoring order in the once-profitable Caribbean colony following the revolt of the free mulattoes in the spring of 1791 and the rising of the slaves later that year. Increasingly, the only hope of retaining French control of the colony lay in accepting the *fait accompli* of black freedom.[11]

As white Virginians increasingly came to understand, the revolution in Saint-Domingue began not in the port city of Le Cap François in 1791 but in Paris in 1789. With the calling of the Estates General, a delegation of white planters—most of them French, not Domingan by birth—sailed for the continent in hopes of undercutting the often autocratic power of the governor-general. But the delegation arrived only in time to witness the signing of the Declaration of the Rights of Man and Citizen, a document, not unlike its American counterpart, that spoke in the dangerous language of equality. When Jacques Pierre Brissot de Warville and other leading members of the *Amis des Noirs* asserted that the declaration indeed extended to free mulattoes, a colonial power struggle ensued between the *grands blancs* and the *gens de couleur*. With the free minority at each other's throats, the door to African freedom was opened, and on the evening of August 22, 1791—later known as the Night of Fire—hundreds of slaves on the northern plain of Saint-Domingue rose in revolt and began to put the plantations to the torch.[12]

At length, control of the rebel forces fell to Toussaint, a forty-eight-year-old house servant and folk doctor on the Breda plantation. Shortly after Toussaint reached the age of twenty, Bayon de Libertad, the manager of Breda, gave him forty acres and thirteen slaves to manage; although no official document of manumission formally established his liberty, for more than two decades Toussaint, despite his ongoing duties as coachman, functioned as a free man. Even before that, Toussaint had learned to read and write under the tutelage of his godfather, the priest Simon Baptiste. Perhaps it was this unaccustomed access to the news of the Atlantic world that led Toussaint to demand what he regarded as the universal rights of liberty and equality. Whereas most slave rebels previously sought to escape the world of their captors by establishing maroon colonies high in the mountains, Toussaint's soldiers fought to join it on equal terms. From that moment, the rebel leader—increasingly known to his men as Toussaint Louverture, the soldier who always found his opening—inspired enslaved Americans with an ideology of revolutionary violence that posed a far more dangerous threat to the plantation order than isolated *marronage*. By fighting for the principles that Thomas Jefferson had proclaimed, the Domingan slaves reminded their mainland brethren that the struggle to fulfill the egalitarian promise of 1776 was far from over. All of which was to say that absentee landlords in Paris and nervous planters in Virginia found this black Jacobin to be especially unsettling because he was so much like them.[13]

For white Virginians, the French colony was more than just a distant menace. In the month of June 1793, Louverture's armies fought their way into Le Cap François in a campaign that forced ten thousand colonials to flee Saint-

Domingue. When slave insurgents reached the outskirts of the city, hundreds of destitute whites boarded ships bound for the Chesapeake and the Carolinas. On July 6, portions of the shabby armada washed ashore in Norfolk. "This morning arrived a French 74 Gun Ship with a number of distressed people from Cap François," an overwhelmed Mayor Thomas Newton reported to Governor Henry Lee. "I hear that 150 Sail are expected momently with the remains of the Inhabitants of that Town, it being destroyed by the Negroes." [14]

For mainland authorities, finding food and clothing for those "destitute of the Means of Subsistence" was but part of the problem. Too many Domingan refugees from "the French Island" insisted on "bringing with them a number of Slaves" in vain hopes of rebuilding their plantation society in North America. One specialist has estimated that in the four years following the Night of Fire, no less than twelve thousand Domingan slaves were brought into the United States. For white Virginians, that was twelve thousand too many bondpersons infected with the contagion of liberty. White refugees could be accorded pity, but human property that brought word of a place where enlightened theories of liberty and equality were more than mere slogans was a very real threat.[15]

Within weeks of the refugees' arrival, Norfolk residents began to worry about the impact of the Domingan slaves on their own bondmen. Mainland slaves, of course, needed little prodding to resist their chains, and scholars should resist the temptation to theorize that revolutions in Philadelphia or Paris or even Le Cap François taught allegedly passive Virginia bondmen to be rebellious. But there can be little doubt that Louverture's victorious armies inspired black Americans with a symbol of militant success, and black refugees from Saint-Domingue, some of them—according to Willis Wilson of Portsmouth—veterans of "the insurrection in Hispaniola," reminded mainland slaves that freedom, should they be bold enough to seize it, might be within their grasp. Norfolk authorities immediately noticed that "Our negro Slaves have become extremely insolent & troublesome" due to their "associat[ion] with French Negroes from St. Domingo (with whom the place is also overrun)." Whites near Point of Fork, Virginia, observed the same tendency. "The insolence of [the slaves] is almost a common talk," Earl Langham informed Governor Henry Lee, "particularly since the arrival of the French." [16]

Given the encouraging whispers of the black refugees and the public hosannas to Genet and the natural rights of all men, it did not take long for "insolence," to borrow Langham's term, to revolutionize into collective rebellion. Late one night in July, John Randolph of Roanoke heard several slaves talking quietly below the window of his Richmond home. Easing the window open, Randolph overheard one of the men explaining that some time before mid-October "the blacks were to kill the white people" of the seaboard south. The second man, more timid, doubted it could be done. But the "one who seemed to be the chief speaker, said, you see how the blacks has killed the whites in the French Island and took it a little while ago." [17]

This was not just bold talk. Randolph had overheard a recruiter in the so-called Secret Keeper Plot, a slave conspiracy that spanned several southern states. Within a week, observant whites in Yorktown uncovered written proof that the Richmond insurgent was in constant touch with both creole and "West Indies" rebels in Norfolk and Charleston. According to a letter dropped by "the Black Preacher Gawin"—presumably Gowan Pamphlet, a former slave from Middlesex who upon gaining his liberty formed a black Baptist congregation in Williamsburg—"Six thousand Negroes in South Carolina" planned to rise "in concert with others of the different States to massacre the [white] Inhabitants." Virginia authorities had good reason to doubt such inflated figures, but they had little skepticism about the inspiration. The rebels intended "to set fire first to the Houses," Virginia's Peter Oram warned South Carolina's Governor William Moultrie. "[T]hey say the Negroes of Cap François have obtained their Liberties in this method." [18]

Prior to obtaining his freedom, Pamphlet had been the property of David Miller of Middlesex, who evidently traveled to Charleston frequently in the course of business. Pamphlet may have accompanied his former owner during the summer of 1792, when Miller again journeyed to South Carolina; according to one Virginia official, the black preacher had "just returned from Charleston." Presumably his job was to relay messages from the rebel leader in Charleston to his counterparts in Virginia, known as the Secret Keepers of Richmond and Norfolk. Clearly the plot was tightly coordinated. "We will appoint a Nite to begin with fire[,] Clubs and shot," wrote the Richmond leader in a description sharply reminiscent of Saint-Domingue's Night of Fire, and "we will kill all before us." [19]

Virginia and Carolina officials responded with a show of force. The state of alert not only discouraged black rebelliousness; it also diminished white sympathy for Caribbean refugees and even dampened white enthusiasm for a mother country that had allowed its Caribbean province to fall victim to black control. Norfolk Mayor Thomas Newton breathed a sign of relief that the Secret Keeper plot had come to nothing. The Domingan slaves "brought from Cap François by the unfortunate French Peoples" stood ready, he believed, "to operate against us with the others." Newton reluctantly continued to allow white refugees to land in his city, but he began to enforce older statutes that prohibited the importation of slaves into the state. Too many French planters arrived with their slaves only to "plead ignorance of the law." The mayor wished that "all we had among us could be sent off," a complaint that appeared to be aimed at French planter and black bondman alike.[20]

White Virginians enamored with the French cause initially sought to distinguish between French policy on the continent and the chaos in the Caribbean. Secretary of State Jefferson, who had been in Paris at the time of its adoption, archly observed that the Declaration of the Rights of Man was never meant to be an emancipation decree, and he doubtless attributed Genet's antislavery tendencies to the naive enthusiasm of youth. But Toussaint's victories in the summer of 1793 forced a change in policy that stunned the secretary. In hopes of holding onto the once-lucrative Caribbean jewel, the French commissioner in Saint-Domingue, Léger Félicité Sonthonax, declared slavery abolished on August 29, 1793. Thus it happened that in the same month that Gowan Pamphlet plotted for black freedom on the mainland and Philadelphia crowds cheered the abolitionist Genet, slavery died in the French Caribbean. Having no alternative but to ratify Sonthonax's course, the Paris Convention grudgingly affirmed his decree in February 1794.[21]

Word traveled slowly in wooden ships. But when Louverture learned of the French Convention's action in May 1794, he abandoned his Spanish allies and raised the Parisian standard. Having briefly utilized the Spanish—who controlled the eastern half of the island of Hispaniola in their colony of Santo Domingo—as a counterweight to French authority, the former slave abruptly turned on the enemies of France. His armies forced the Spanish to retreat beyond their colonial borders, and he hurried orders to his sometimes ally André Rigaud to rouse the freedmen against the British invaders, who also coveted the sugar island. In doing so, old Toussaint had ceased to be a slave rebel. He had become General Toussaint Louverture, servant of France. French military policy and black liberation were now one and the same.[22]

Historians have long insisted that Americans turned against France when the republic descended into the bloody nightmare of the Reign of Terror. Certainly the execution of King Louis XVI, who was fondly remembered in the United States as the ally of 1778, gave many moderate Americans pause. But the clamorous reception accorded Edmond Genet just months after the death of the monarch casts doubt on the theory that a majority of white Americans, who had secured their own liberty with the sword, turned suddenly queasy when confronted with the guillotine. But the Convention's decree of February 1794 was an altogether different matter. When Paris and Louverture joined forces, the white South with astonishing rapidity renounced its earlier support of France. "The atheistical philosophy of revolutionary France added fuel to the volcano of hellish passion," recalled one southern planter, "and the horrors of the island became a narrative which frightened our childhood." By abolishing slavery in its Caribbean empire, agreed another planter, France "zealously declared Negro equality."[23]

Sharing that grim assessment was James Monroe. Although still dedicated to a pro-French course, Monroe rightly worried about the impact that Caribbean emancipation would have on Virginia bondmen. "The scenes which are acted in St. Domingo," he fretted, "must produce an effect on all the people of colour in this and the States south of us." Other planter politicians even speculated that the small number of French nationals living in the South might follow the lead of their mother country and throw their efforts behind universal emancipation. The "lower order of Frenchmen" who "fraternize with our Democratic Clubs [might] introduce the same horrid tragedies among our negroes, which has been so fatally exhibited in the French islands," observed one South Carolinian. "Our . . . French friends will do no good to our Blacks," agreed another.[24]

It helped not at all that many New England Federalists, long perceived by southern Republicans as being insufficiently supportive of things French, abruptly turned their geopolitical coats and endorsed both French emancipation and black rebels in Saint-Domingue. Abraham Bishop, a young Yale graduate writing in a Boston newspaper, attacked southern hypocrisy by insisting that Louverture was fighting for the same principles that Washington had fought for in 1776. The Anglo-Americans who attained their liberty "by the sword," Bishop insisted, taught the world "that freedom from the tyranny of men is to be had *only* at the price of blood." But planters, who increasingly employed concepts of race to explain why not all Americans were endowed with certain inalienable rights, refused to see these "cannibals," to borrow Jefferson's delicate description of Domingan soldiers, as fellow brothers in republican revolution.[25]

The very fact that Federalists in the nation's capital increasingly defended Saint-Domingue may have played a significant role in Virginia's growing estrangement from France. As relations between Philadelphia and Paris soured in the wake of John Jay's commercial alliance with Britain, the Adams administration increasingly sought to use Louverture, now lieutenant-governor, both to diminish French power in the Atlantic and to strengthen New England's trade with the Caribbean. In stark contrast to Jefferson's offensive characterization of Louverture's soldiers, Secretary of State Timothy Pickering regarded the black general as "a prudent and judicious man possessing the general confidence of the people of all colours." As a politician possessed of both antislavery and autocratic tendencies, Pickering believed Toussaint was precisely the sort of forceful leader needed to restore order in Saint-Domingue—and perhaps even to guide it toward independence. The alternative was to abandon the freedmen to French jurisdiction, which might arm them against the United States. "Nothing is more clear," he suggested to Adams, "than, if left to themselves, that the Blacks of St. Domingo will be incomparably less dangerous than if they remain the subjects of France."[26]

Of such international intrigues, Virginia slaveholders knew little and understood even less. But for reasons beyond their comprehension, their Federalist adversaries were conducting business with Louverture, even while Paris continued to heap honors and titles upon him. The very plausible notion that Adams and Pickering might successfully seduce Saint-Domingue away from the French empire seemed impossible to readers of the *Fredericksburg Virginia Herald*, which as late as the spring of 1800 continued to discuss Louverture's "fealty to the French Republic." Even the shrewd James Madison, who had reason to know better, later insisted that during the Adams administration Saint-Domingue was "a Dependency or colony of the French Republic" and that "local authorities there," such as General Louverture, must be regarded as authorities of the French nation.[27]

Viewed in this context, the southern hostility toward the Quasi War—the undeclared naval conflict of 1798 with France—must be understood not as sympathy for the government in Paris. Instead, Virginia's nearly collective denunciation of the clash as "an unrighteous, impolitic & distracting war" was born of fear as to how France might use Louverture's armies on the mainland. In South Carolina, Robert Goodloe Harper warned his constituents that the count d'Hedouville, on orders of the Paris Directory, "was preparing to invade the Southern states from St. Domingo, with an army of blacks," in hopes of sparking "an insurrection among the negroes." Scholars today doubt that Paris was planning any such thing, but given the sound and fury of the Atlantic world in the 1790s, white Virginians like David Meade may be forgiven for devoutly believing that the Quasi War would "bring evils upon the three or four Southern States, more terrific than Volcano's [or] Earthquakes."[28]

By the end of decade, France had become a symbol. Blacks throughout the western hemisphere regarded the very word *France* as synonymous with liberty and equality, while whites, including those who once had lifted their mugs in honor of Genet, saw only chaos and racial genocide in the term. Signs of its spreading influence were everywhere. In Albany, New York, a slave set a fire that nearly leveled the town in apparent imitation of the burning of Saint-Domingue. In the Brazilian city of Bahia, four mulattoes were hanged and quartered for the crime of promoting "the imaginary advantages of a Democratic Republic, in which all should be equal." In Jamaica, British officials executed Dubuisson, a white Frenchman from Saint-Domingue, for allegedly trying to rally black support for a French invasion. If Virginia's capital city had once been "Sans-culotte Richmond," sneered the *Porcupine's Gazette* in 1798, it was now "the metropolis of *Negro-land*," a slaveholding society deathly afraid of radical French influence.[29]

The final blow to French fortunes in the seaboard South came in the spring and summer of 1800, when Virginia slaves inspired by the revolutionary currents that washed back and forth across the Atlantic planned to seize their liberty by putting Richmond to the torch. So clear was the influence of Saint-Domingue that one modern writer has mistakenly identified Gabriel, the young blacksmith who masterminded the conspiracy, as a Haitian refugee who arrived on the mainland sometime during the 1790s. The fact is wrong, but the logic, given the symbolic importance of Toussaint Louverture in the minds of Virginia bondmen, is impeccable.[30]

In the aftermath of the failed conspiracy, as white authorities tried and executed twenty-seven slaves for the crime of attempted liberty, the figurative power of France became all too clear. It was not merely that slaves hoped to exploit the chaos of the Quasi War, although one eighteen-year-old recruiter, Ben Woolfolk, did inform the court that "they had understood that the French were at war with this country." For oppressed people around the Atlantic basin, France had become the very symbol of freedom. Among the whites not to be slaughtered by the rebel army, Woolfolk explained, were impoverished women, Quakers, Methodists, "and the Frenchmen, and they were to be spared on account of their being friendly to liberty."[31]

Even more embarrassing for Governor James Monroe were the persistent allegations that two French nationals were deeply involved in the plot. According to one condemned slave, for nearly four years "a Frenchman named Charles Quersey" had been urging "him & several other Negroes, to rise and kill the White people." The young slave testified that he had not seen Quersey for several years, but that recently he had heard that the Frenchman had "been very active in encouraging the Negroes in this business." Even Gabriel's chief lieutenant, his brother Solomon, admitted to the court that Quersey, who had arrived in Virginia during the war and had been "at the siege of Yorktown," planned to join them on the night of the uprising and assist them in fortifying Richmond.[32]

Quersey's partner in international revolution, Alexander Beddenhurst, was an even more mysterious figure. Although known to slaves in Petersburg and Norfolk, Beddenhurst had either business or political contacts in Philadelphia. While in the North, he rented a room from John Boulanger, the proprietor of the "French Boarding-House." The establishment sat on the corner of Coats' Alley, a street heavily populated with artisans and French nationals; as a part of the Sixth Ward, it was also in a section of the city that was the traditional home of Philadelphia blacks.[33]

By the time Gabriel swung from the gibbet in October 1800 — only ten days after the Convention of Mortefontaine ended the Quasi War, and the Treaty of Amiens allowed for Bonaparte's attempt to reimpose white authority in Saint-Domingue — Virginia Republicans had all but turned their backs on France. The eccentric John Randolph continued to open his missives with the salutation of "Dear Citizen," but exactly none of his correspondents returned the favor. As gravediggers in far too many Virginia counties put down their shovels, the price of befriending a nation that endorsed black liberty came at too high a price. Gabriel and his black Jacobins wielded swords forged of scythes, not guillotines, but the Virginia planter class had no desire to play the role of Louis Capet, the ill-fated French king.[34]

Modern defenders of the Republican leadership correctly observe that Jefferson and Madison always placed the fortunes of their nation above all others, including France. They observe that Francophile passion was methodically corroded by the death of Louis XVI, the foolish behavior of Edmond Genet, Robespierre's bloody reign, and especially Napoleon Bonaparte's destruction of civilian power. These unhappy events were indeed important. But there are other points to be made as well, and France's all too brief endorsement of black liberty has not been accorded the importance it deserves in explaining why white Virginians fled the French cause. Writing from Paris in 1787, Jefferson pronounced "a little rebellion now and then [to be] a good thing." The "tree of liberty," he lectured a shocked William Smith, "must be refreshed from time to time with the blood of patriots and tyrants." Such sentiments were possible when tyrants bore the names of George III and Louis XVI. But when the patriots became Toussaint Louverture and Gabriel, and the tyrants were Governor James Monroe, Virginia planters quickly perceived the folly of their actions. The liberty poles came down, only to be replaced by the gallows.[35]

NOTES

1. James Sidbury, "Saint-Domingue in Virginia: Ideology, Local Meanings, and Resistance to Slavery, 1790–1800," *Journal of Southern History* 63 (1997): 536; Dumas Malone, *Jefferson and His Time* (Boston: Little, Brown, 1948–81), 3:44.

2. Toast given in Norfolk, February 8, 1794, quoted in Philip S. Foner, ed., *The Democratic-Republican Societies, 1790–1800: A Documentary Sourcebook of Constitutions, Declarations, Addresses, Resolutions, and Toasts* (Westport, Conn.: Greenwood Press, 1976), 347.

3. Robert McColley, *Slavery and Jeffersonian Virginia*, 2d ed. (Urbana: U of Illinois P, 1973), 50–51; Ralph Ketcham, *James Madison: A Biography* (New York: Macmillan, 1971), 340.

4. Noble E. Cunningham Jr., *In Pursuit of Reason: The Life of Thomas Jefferson* (Baton Rouge: Louisiana State UP, 1987), 180; Ketcham, *Madison*, 337.

5. Ketcham, *Madison*, 338; George Lee Turberville to James Madison, January 28, 1793, in Robert A. Rutland, ed., *The Papers of James Madison* (Charlottesville: UP of Virginia, 1962–1991), 14:444–45.

6. George Mason to Samuel Griffin, September 8, 1789, in Robert A. Rutland, ed., *The Papers of George Mason, 1725–1792* (Chapel Hill: U of North Carolina P, 1970), 3:1171–172.

7. John Lofton, *Insurrection in South Carolina: The Turbulent World of Denmark Vesey* (Yellow Springs, Ohio: Antioch Press, 1964). For the early life of Telemaque, see also Douglas R. Egerton, *He Shall Go Out Free: The Lives of Denmark Vesey* (Madison, Wis.: Madison House, 1998), chapters 1–2.

8. James T. Flexner, *Washington: The Indispensable Man* (Boston: Little, Brown, 1969), 287; Harry Ammon, *James Monroe: The Quest for National Identity* (New York: McGraw-Hill, 1971), 99.

9. James Madison to Thomas Jefferson, September 2, 1793, in James Morton Smith, ed., *The Republic of Letters: The Correspondence between Thomas Jefferson and James Madison, 1776–1826* (New York: Norton, 1995), 2:816–17; Ammon, *Monroe*, 104.

10. Conor Cruise O'Brien, *The Long Affair: Thomas Jefferson and the French Revolution* (Chicago: University of Chicago Press, 1996), 285.

11. Harry Ammon, *The Genet Mission* (New York: Norton, 1973), 121.

12. Winthrop D. Jordan, *White over Black: American Attitudes toward the Negro, 1550–1812* (Chapel Hill: U of North Carolina P, 1968), 376; Thomas O. Ott, *The Haitian Revolution, 1789–1804* (Knoxville: U of Tennessee P, 1973), 21, 28–42.

13. Martin Ros, *Night of Fire: The Black Napoleon and the Battle for Haiti* (New York: Sarpedon, 1994), 8–9; Eugene D. Genovese, *From Rebellion to Revolution: Afro-American Slave Revolts in the Making of the Modern World* (Baton Rouge: Louisiana State UP, 1979), xix, 92–93.

14. Sylvia Frey, *Water from the Rock: Black Resistance in a Revolutionary Age* (Princeton: Princeton UP, 1991), 229; Thomas Newton Jr. to Governor Henry Lee,

July 6, 1793, in H. W. Flournoy, ed., *Calendar of Virginia State Papers and Other Manuscripts* (Richmond, 1875–93), 6:437.

15. William Moultrie to General Assembly, November 30, 1793, in Records of the General Assembly, Governor's Messages, South Carolina Department of Archives and History (hereafter RGA, GM, SCDAH); Norfolk Mayor John Cowper to James Monroe, March 11, 1802, Executive Papers, Library of Virginia; David P. Geggus, *Slavery, War, and Revolution: The British Occupation of Saint-Domingue, 1793–1798* (New York: Oxford UP, 1982), 305.

16. William Wilson to Governor Henry Lee, August 21, 1793, in Flournoy, ed., *Calendar*, 6:490; Isaac Weld, *Travels through the States of North America* (1807; reprint, New York, 1968), 1:175–76; David Bedinger to unknown, March 5, 1797, Bedinger Letters, Duke University Library; Earl Langham to Governor Henry Lee, August 3, 1793, in Flournoy, ed., *Calendar*, 6:470.

17. Deposition of John Randolph, July 22, 1793, in Flournoy, ed., *Calendar*, 6: 452–53.

18. William Nelson to Thomas Newton, August 8, 1793, RGA, GM, SCDAH; Peter Oram to William Moultrie, August 16, 1793. On Gowan Pamphlet, see Frey, *Water from the Rock*, 37, 316, and Mechal Sobel, *The World They Made Together: Black and White Values in Eighteenth-Century Virginia* (Princeton: Princeton UP, 1987), 189.

19. Peter Oram to William Moultrie, August 16, 1793, in RGA, GM, SCDAH; Secret Keeper Richmond to Secret Keeper Norfolk (copy); Lt. Governor James Wood to William Moultrie, August, 1793; Sidbury, "Saint-Domingue in Virginia," 542.

20. Julius S. Scott, "The Common Wind: Currents of Afro-American Communication in the Era of the Haitian Revolution" (Ph.D. diss., Duke University, 1986), 277; Thomas Newton to James Woods, no date, RGA, GM, SCDAH; Tommy L. Bogger, *Free Blacks in Norfolk, Virginia, 1790–1860: The Darker Side of Freedom* (Charlottesville: UP of Virginia, 1997), 25–26.

21. O'Brien, *Long Affair*, 283; Ott, *Haitian Revolution*, 82.

22. Lester D. Langley, *The Americas in the Age of Revolution, 1750–1850* (New Haven: Yale UP, 1996), 119; Scott, "Common Wind," 246–47.

23. Alfred N. Hunt, *Haiti's Influence on Antebellum America: Slumbering Volcano in the Caribbean* (Baton Rouge: Louisiana State UP, 1988), 124; Michael Mullin, *Africa in America: Slave Acculturation and Resistance in the American South and the British Caribbean, 1736–1831* (Urbana: U of Illinois P, 1992), 218.

24. James Monroe to John Cowper, March 17, 1802, Executive Letterbook, Library of Virginia; Hunt, *Haiti's Influence*, 110, 116.

25. David Brion Davis, *Revolutions: Reflections on American Equality and Foreign Liberations* (Cambridge: Harvard UP, 1990), 50–51; Donald R. Hickey, "America's Response to the Slave Revolt in Haiti, 1791–1806," *Journal of the Early Republic* 2 (1982): 368.

26. Ralph Adams Brown, *The Presidency of John Adams* (Lawrence: UP of Kansas,

1975), 156; Gerard H. Clarfield, *Timothy Pickering and the American Republic* (Pittsburgh: U of Pittsburgh P, 1980), 198; Hickey, "America's Response," 365.

27. *Fredericksburg Virginia Herald,* 16 May 1800; James Madison to Thomas Jefferson, April 20, 1804, in Smith, ed., *Republic of Letters,* 2:1319.

28. David Meade to Judge Joseph Prentis, September 7, 1798, Prentis Family Papers, Alderman Library, University of Virginia; Robert Goodloe Harper to constituents, March 20, 1799, in Elizabeth Donnan, ed., *Papers of James A. Bayard, 1796–1815* (Washington, D.C.: Carnegie Institute of Washington, 1915), 2:90.

29. Gary B. Nash, *Forging Freedom: The Formation of Philadelphia's Black Community, 1720–1840* (Cambridge: Harvard UP, 1988), 174; Robert R. Palmer, *The Age of Democratic Revolution: The Struggle* (Princeton: Princeton UP, 1964), 338; Scott, "Common Wind," 298; *Porcupine's Gazette,* April 3, 1798.

30. Colin Wilson, *A Criminal History of Mankind* (New York: Putnam, 1984), 477. Wilson also has Gabriel committing "various murders of whites before his army was taken up by the militia," although, in fact, his conspiracy never got off the ground. Gabriel was almost certainly born on the Prosser plantation in Virginia. In 1783, then a seven-year-old boy, his name appears on the list of slaves belonging to Thomas Prosser Sr. See Henrico County Personal Property Tax, 1783, Library of Virginia.

31. Confession of Ben Woolfolk, September 17, 1800, Executive Papers, Negro Insurrection, Library of Virginia.

32. Confession of Young's Gilbert, September 23, 1800; Confession of Prosser's Solomon, September 15, 1800, Executive Communications, Letterbook, Library of Virginia.

33. Unsigned letter to editor, September 13, 1800, in *Fredericksburg Virginia Herald,* September 23, 1800. For the evidence regarding the two Frenchmen, see Douglas R. Egerton, *Gabriel's Rebellion: The Virginia Slave Conspiracies of 1800 and 1802* (Chapel Hill: U of North Carolina P, 1993), appendix 2.

34. John Randolph to Creed Taylor, September 13, 1798, Creed Taylor Papers, Alderman Library, University of Virginia; Robert W. Tucker and David Hendrickson, *Empire of Liberty: The Statecraft of Thomas Jefferson* (New York: Oxford UP, 1990), 80.

35. Walter LeFeber, "Jefferson and an American Foreign Policy," in Peter Onuf, ed., *Jeffersonian Legacies* (Charlottesville: UP of Virginia, 1993), 375; Thomas Jefferson to James Madison, January 39, 1787, in Julian P. Boyd, ed., *The Papers of Thomas Jefferson* (Princeton: Princeton UP, 1950–97), 11:92–93; Thomas Jefferson to William Smith, November 13, 1787, 12:345–57.

Greedy French Masters and Color-Conscious, Legal-Minded Spaniards in Colonial Louisiana

KIMBERLY S. HANGER

The recorded words and actions of free blacks, or *libres*,[1] reveal much about their attitudes toward the dominant white population as the regime changed from French to Spanish rule in colonial Louisiana during the eighteenth century.[2] *Libre* notions of hierarchy and what constituted a just, equitable society were also transformed with the spread of the French and Haitian Revolutions, momentous events that touched every part of the circum-Caribbean and altered the nature of slave and free black resistance to discrimination.[3] Although people of African descent did not constitute one monolithic group and their viewpoints varied, terminology found in several documents indicates that in general they perceived their actual and former French masters as reaping the advantages of their labor without providing them any benefits such as the possibility of freedom and, once free, the respect due them as productive, property-holding citizens. Slaves and *libres* thus looked to the incoming Spanish bureaucracy to confer on them these privileges with the intent of using hostilities between the two groups of whites to their advantage. What they confronted was a Spanish system of law and custom that purposefully delineated differences among its subjects, constructing and maintaining inequalities based on race, color, religion, occupation, gender, wealth, and lineage. From the Spanish perspective, it went against nature for all persons to be equal.[4]

Colonial New Orleans was a community, like so many others in the Americas, in which the upper sectors desired to maintain order and hierarchy, preferably by way of legislation and judicial compromise but through force and authoritarian measures if necessary. In the ideal Spanish world everyone was to be cognizant of his or her proper place. New Orleans, however, rarely fit this ideal. By the late eighteenth century the "city that care forgot" was a vibrant port with people moving in and out, establishing relationships across racial and class boundaries, and generally challenging any kind of stable social order. It had a resident population that grew from about three thousand to about eight thousand between 1770 and 1805, with a large transient group adding to this number. The percentage of *libres* rose from 10 to 20 percent of New Orleanians over the same period; two-thirds were female. The rest of the population was about evenly divided between whites and slaves, with varying numbers of *indios* and *mestizos* residing in and around the city.[5]

In Louisiana, as in many areas of Spanish America, the crown fostered the growth of a free black population in order to fill middle-sector occupations, defend the colony from external and internal foes, and give African and creole slaves an officially approved safety valve to their desires for freedom. Colonial policymakers envisioned a society in which Africans would seek their freedom through legal channels, complete with compensation for their masters, rather than by running away or rising in revolt. In turn, slaves would look to the Spanish government to "*rescatarnos de la esclavitud*" (rescue or ransom us from slavery) and subsequently protect their rights and privileges as freedmen.[6] Spaniards in Louisiana did this, not because they valued the humanity of slaves any more than French masters did, but rather as a result of very practical concerns. Spanish administrators faced French merchants and planters who professed questionable loyalty and at times outright hostility toward Spain's rule in the colony. According to one scholar, "the slaves were the wedge between countervailing French planter power and official Spanish authority, and the governors seem at times to have sought the approval of slaves in order to make them a counterpoise to the planters, whose allegiance to Spain was far from certain."[7] Faced with a potentially restless multitude of African slaves and a small but vocal ensemble of resentful colonials, Spain courted the favor of any and all segments of Louisiana's society and encouraged the immigration of loyal subjects.[8]

Spain has a rich legal tradition, and peninsular and colonial Spaniards were very legal minded. When Spain assumed effective control of Louisiana in 1769, royal officials reorganized its legal system and required that for almost any business transaction to be legitimate or any civil, criminal, or ecclesiastical case to be pursued, it had to be recorded before a notary. Slave manumissions and suits for freedom or change in master constitute part of this notarial register, and the Spanish era witnessed a dramatic increase in the frequency of slave emancipations, at least those noted in the official record.[9]

Much of this boost in the number of manumissions was due to the change in laws governing slavery and ways to escape slavery that the Spanish crown instituted upon taking over the colony. Its aim was to make colonial laws conform to those prevailing throughout the empire. For the governing of slaves and free blacks, Spanish Louisiana codes (commonly referred to as "O'Reilly's Laws" in reference to the early Spanish governor who proclaimed them) primarily drew upon provisions of *Las siete partidas* (Law of Seven Parts, compiled by the court of Alfonso the Wise in the thirteenth century) and the *Recopilación de leyes de los reinos de las Indias* (Compilation of the Laws of the Kingdoms of the Indies, which drew together diverse legislation applying to Spain's New World empire in 1681),[10] and also were influenced by the French *Code Noir* (Black Code) that had been issued for the French West Indies in 1685 and introduced in Louisiana in 1724. The *Code Noir* imposed harsh penalties upon erring slaves and "proved to be one of the more oppressive slave codes in the Americas." It did, however, grant *libres* full legal rights to citizenship, even though this provision was inconsistent with preceding articles of the code that provided for unequal punishments and restricted *libre* behavior.[11] In addition, local regulations frequently impinged upon these rights, denying free blacks legal equality with white citizens.[12] After assuming control of Louisiana in 1769, Spain imposed its laws on the colony, overriding the *Code Noir* in the face of French planter resistance. By and large, Spanish officials enforced their government's laws, at least in the capital of New Orleans where the bureaucratic and judicial structure was strongest. For example, even though the planter-dominated *cabildo* (town council) wrote and passed a much harsher slave code in 1778, the Crown never approved it, and judges continued to follow imperial law.[13]

Included in Spanish law emanating from Cuba and implemented in Louisiana was the codification of a customary practice known as *coartación:* the right of slaves "to purchase their freedom for a stipulated sum of money agreed upon by their masters or arbitrated in the courts."[14] Louisiana's *Code Noir* had permitted masters over the age of twenty-five to manumit their slaves, with prior consent from the superior council (the French colonial governing body). Spanish regulations, however, did not require official permission for masters to free their slaves and even allowed slaves to initiate manumission proceedings on their own behalf. The slaves or their friends or relatives could request a *carta de libertad* (certificate of manumission) in front of a tribunal. Two and sometimes three assessors declared the slaves' monetary value, and upon receipt of that sum, the tribunal issued the slaves their *cartas*. Under Spanish law slaves did not have to depend upon the generosity of their masters to attain freedom; rather, the slaves relied on their own efforts and the aid of a favorable legal system. The institution of self-purchase "expressed the Spanish recognition (1) that slavery was not the natural condition of men; (2) that slaves had a right to aspire to freedom; and (3) that masters had a right to just return for their property." [15] It also acknowledged the slave's property rights or *peculium.*

Louisiana slaves and parties arguing on their behalf recognized support from Spanish officials for "a cause so recommended by the law as that of liberty" and began to realize that their "aspirations for liberty rested on the administration of justice by the Spanish in the colony." [16] Some scholars claim that Spanish administrators continued to apply the French *Code Noir* after occupying the colony. A thorough examination of primary sources definitively shows, however, that "the judicial authorities of Spanish Luisiana routinely applied Spanish rather that French law between 1770 and 1803." [17] My own research in notarial and judicial documents confirms these findings. The slaves and their representatives repeatedly stated their recognition of a change in slave law and those laws that governed freedmen in the transition from French to Spanish rule.

Indeed, the text of several Spanish documents indicates that slaves and free persons acting in the interest of slaves were aware of and acted upon the privileges extended to them by Spain. Both white and free black masters and their slaves noted differences between French and Spanish law and attitudes. Of course, one must remember that they used language designed to win the approval of Spanish justices and thus probably emphasized the positive aspects of Spanish law. The free *morena* Angela Perret was one who observed a change in the status of slaves. The ancient custom of treating slaves as *bienes muebles* (movable property or chattel) no longer prevailed, and now even *libres* could manumit their slaves without seeking special permission from the government. Perret thus sought a formal recording of the fact that she had "rescued from slavery" ("*ella rescate de esclavitud*") her daughter and two grandchildren.[18] And much later in 1803 another slave, the *moreno* Juan Bely, referred to his right to petition the tribunal for liberty against the wishes of a reluctant slaveholder. Bely asserted he had continually requested that the widow and testamentary executor of his late master (don David Ross) issue him a *carta* at the price of his estimated worth. For this reason he exercised rights conceded him by the Spanish Crown according to royal decree in order to name an estimator: "*En cuya virtud usando del derecho que S.M. por Real Cédula me concede, nombro por mi tasador don Fernando Alzar*" (By virtue of which and under the power granted to me by Royal Decree by His Majesty, I name Don Fernando Alzar as my estimator).[19]

In all likelihood, as the Spanish period transpired, New Orleans slaves—like Juan Bely—and interested parties acting on their behalf gained greater experience that allowed them to take advantage of the privileges Spain's judicial system offered. With the exception of the last decade, the number of cases brought before governors' and *alcaldes'* (magistrate and member of the *cabildo*) tribunals rose dramatically during the era under study.[20] Like Africans in other colonial regions, slaves in New Orleans often had to struggle to secure their rights. Nevertheless, in most cases, *coartación* offered advantages to slaveholders, slaves, and the Spanish government alike. All three groups acted according to their best interests. The crown benefited from a growing *libre* population that tended to accept its middle status in a three-tiered society, aspired to attain the privileges of white subjects, and supplied the colony with skilled laborers and defensive forces. *Coartación* provided slave owners with incentives that encouraged slaves to work more productively, reduced their provisioning costs, and compensated them at the slaves' estimated fair values. Legal manumission also acted as an effective form of social control by holding out liberty as a "carrot" to obedient bondpersons. In turn, the system facilitated slaves' efforts to acquire the necessary cash or goods with which to purchase freedom independent of their masters' will.

The case of the *moreno* slave Luis Dor versus the free *parda* widow María Gentilly dramatically reveals the protection from the Spanish legal system that slaves sought in order to secure their freedom. It also discloses the struggles in which free blacks (women in particular) engaged in order to protect their rights from what they perceived as greedy French masters who abused the system but disguised themselves as humane.[21] In 1794 Dor sued the estate of the deceased free *pardo* Esteban Lalande, Gentilly's former husband, for collection of a 230-peso debt. Dor had begun by suing Lalande directly the year before, but he had died before the case was settled. Although Dor claimed that both Lalande and Gentilly had affixed their marks to the promissory note when he loaned Lalande the money, Gentilly asserted that Lalande had forged her mark and that she was not responsible for repaying the loan. Her part of the estate was exempt from seizure because it was mainly made up of her dowry, and "the woman's dowry is always sacred, and protected by royal laws and natural laws," no matter what it was used for, even to purchase one's freedom, which is what Dor intended to do with the repaid loan. Coincidentally, Dor's owner, don Joseph Dusuau, demanded a sum exactly equal to the amount Dor was trying to recover, a fact that did not escape Gentilly's attention. In her initial petition to protect her holdings while her husband was still alive, Gentilly challenged Dor's assertion to first claim on her property simply because he intended to use the money to purchase his freedom:

> My adversary also says that I well know the money he claims is to purchase his liberty, and that as respects my dowry, even if my demands were legitimated, his rights to payment prevail, principally because it would be invested to ransom him from the slavery and captivity in which he finds himself. I ask: From what code did he take this law? Who told him, that a debt contracted by a husband to a slave who wants to free himself with it, that for this reason a wife is obligated to pay the debt from her goods, if the husband himself is insolvent. Perhaps my opponent's lawyer does not know that the dowry a woman and the rest of her goods have the right of precedence in all possible cases, that even the Royal Treasury itself sacrifices that to which it is owed by the husband, to leave intact that belonging to the wife, which it views as a sacred thing.

Once Lalande was dead and no longer culpable, his widow had to intensify her defense by lashing out against not only Dor but also his French master and others like him. After all, as we have seen, Spanish courts favored the cause of manumission, and Gentilly and her legal counsel must have realized that the judge would look sympathetically on Dor's claim. Gentilly first tried to convince the court that Dor had performed services way beyond his initial worth and that, if Dusuau were truly acting humanely, he would free the slave without any monetary compensation. Once again in her words: "It is very certain that the slave Dor is a slave skilled in many valuable procedures, of good conduct, and of much usefulness to his master. Because of all this, which is public and well known, his master is not being generous or appreciative of his slave, notwithstanding the very exorbitant benefits that he has reaped from the slave's personal work during many years, to give him freedom for the so-called modified price of 230 pesos, which can only be had by reclaiming a loan made to my husband." Gentilly continued her attack on Dor's master, while pointing out the travesty he and other French planters made of Spanish attempts to do good:

> Many repeated times I have observed in this province that a large proportion of masters promise to free their slaves and with that they frustrate the slaves [Gentilly had been born a slave herself and freed without conditions by her white father], and they mock the rulings and decrees of the

[Spanish] tribunals. No one better than those of this province can testify to the repugnance and brash resistance with which the *citizens of French origin* [emphasis added] living in these provinces are opposed to freeing their most loyal slaves, even after many years of service and at an advanced age, even those who want to pay for their liberty by compensating their masters with a major part of their value or after a tribunal or knowledgeable appraiser has determined a just price for the slave. One of these is don Joseph Dusuau, a citizen of this city always accustomed to having servants attend to him, and who believes in the same maxims and harbors the same hostilities toward his slaves as do the rest of his compatriots. It cannot be presumed, however, that every rule has its exception and that he has now in his power the will to carry out on his own motivation an act so humane as to manumit his slave Luis Dor for the mere sum of 230 pesos, when he is worth much more. Because even if it is natural and just, it would be sensible for him and others like him to show an excess of generosity in cases like this one [especially if he appropriated funds from a woman's dowry that he had no other way of recouping anyway].

In other words, Dusuau could afford to appear to be humane and generous at the expense of a mere woman, a nonwhite woman in particular. Gentilly challenged the court to decide what was more just: to protect her dowry rights as a woman or to advance the cause of freedom by taking money from her and giving it to Dor so he could purchase his freedom. Unfortunately for Gentilly, Spanish justice weighed in for the latter.[22]

Spanish jurists did not always rule in the slave's favor, however, even when it seems they should have. When the *morena* slave María Luisa Saly appeared before the governor's tribunal in 1781, she accused her master of having stolen the 250 pesos she had given him toward her *coartación* price of 300 pesos, the amount he had paid for her two years prior. Saly earned these sums peddling the pigs and birds she raised. Her master, Matheo Parin, alias Canon, agreed to free her because she had been his concubine for several years, but apparently their relationship turned ugly when she actually asked him to fulfill his promise. According to Saly, Canon began to "treat me with extreme cruelty," placing her in fetters, beating her with a stick and his bare hands so that she was scarred and bruised, and locking her in her room. On one occasion Canon stripped from her a necklace of fine garnets and took from her pocket the keys to her room and four and a half pesos of silver, all of which indicate the rather favored lifestyle to which she had become accustomed. Canon eventually ended the relationship and hired Saly out at the rate of six pesos per month. Having managed to save a bit more than that sum each month, Saly was now ready to pay Canon the remaining fifty pesos of her self-purchase, but he denied that she had paid him the first 250 pesos or that they had any *coartación* agreement. Canon stood by his story and furthermore asked the governor to condemn Saly to perpetual silence about the matter because she was just trying to pester him into selling her to another master. On the legal advice of his counsel, the governor sided with Canon; he warned Saly that she was not to make any future demands on her owner and must respect him "as a slave should her master."[23] Even though slaves had a legal right to purchase their freedom or change masters if they could prove abuse, and even though the law forbade masters from living with their slaves as husband and wife, Saly lost the case. A disobedient, disrespectful slave whose pigs and birds, separate bedroom, fine jewelry, and extra earnings had made her "uppity" posed too great a threat to a social hierarchy based on color, slave status, and gender.[24]

This color-conscious hierarchy of the Spanish was never challenged more than during the era of the French and Haitian Revolutions. The words and actions of the free *pardos* Pedro Bailly and María Cofignie constituted only a few of the many threats to Louisiana's hierarchical system and a plantation society based on racial deference and control, not to mention threats to a tenuous balance of international politics between imperial rivals Spain, France, and Great Britain. In 1794, at the height of the French and Haitian Revolutions, Louisiana's governor tried Bailly before a military tribunal and found him guilty of "having burst into tirades against the Spanish government and of being a manifest follower of the maxims of the French rebels" and of "having professed ideas suggestive of revolution." He was sentenced to prison in Cuba. A court presided over by the previous governor had acquitted Bailly of similar charges in 1791, when fears of interracial conspiracies against Spanish authorities and Louisiana's slaveholding system were not so rampant.[25]

Testimony gathered during the two Bailly trials reveals many of the frustrations free blacks experienced in a racially stratified society and their desire to obtain the equality and brotherhood that revolutionary France appeared to offer.[26] Bailly preached to whomever would listen that the Spanish government valued the *pardos* during the era of revolution only because they were essential to the defense of the colony; under usual circumstances officials degraded them. One such emergency arose in 1793, when the governor ordered troops, including free black militiamen, to Fort Placaminas at the mouth of the Mississippi

River in order to fend off a feared attack by French revolutionaries in the Caribbean. While stationed at Placaminas, Bailly had the audacity — or courage, depending on one's perspective — to explain to one white officer, don Luis Declouet, that his commander, Colonel St. Maxent, referred to the *pardos* as *mon fils* (my son) and other similar terms during this time of crisis, but afterward he would surely treat them as if they were dogs. If they were among the French, however, Bailly believed that *pardos* would be treated as the equals of whites, as they should be.

The testimony of this officer, Declouet, provides valuable insight into Bailly's thoughts, words, and actions, in particular his resentment of being the target of discrimination simply because he had African ancestry. One day when both were at Placaminas, Bailly asked Declouet for information about the French enemy. Certain that French rebels would attack the colony, Declouet responded that Louisiana troops had to prepare to meet and defeat the French, not only because they were enemies of the state and religion, but also because they constituted a foe to all humanity. An aroused Bailly replied: "Humanity! Humanity! I am going to speak frankly to you, sure that you are a man of honor. Sir, I do not see that any acts of inhumanity have been committed. It is true that they have done wrong by murdering their king, but sir, the French are just; they have conceded men their rights."

Declouet asked Bailly to elaborate, to what rights did he refer? Bailly answered:

A universal equality among men, us, people of color. We have on the Island of Saint-Domingue and other French islands the title *ciudadano activo* [active, participatory citizen]; we can speak openly, like any white persons and hold the same rank as they. Under our [Louisiana] rule do we have this? No, sir, and it is unjust. *All of us being men, there should be no difference. Only their method of thinking — not color — should differentiate men* [emphasis added]. Under these circumstances of war the governor treats us with certain semblances, but we are not deceived. Señor Maxent politely received us here at Fort Placaminas, telling us that on this occasion there would be no differences between us and the whites, implying that at other times there are distinctions. Every day Señor Maxent invites officials of the white militia to eat at his table. And why are we not paid this same attention? Are we not officers just as they are?

Declouet tried to calm Bailly and dismiss what he considered ridiculous pretensions by noting that among whites themselves distinctions had existed since the beginning of time. This differentiation constituted one of the most indispensable and sacred characteristics of human society, toward which all should tend rather than reject or scorn, and was indeed how the Spanish corporatist system functioned.

Declouet's words failed to satisfy Bailly, however; he still maintained that "whites derive excess benefits from their rights." Bailly demonstrated his point by providing examples of the inferior status and unjust treatment he experienced as a person of African descent. One day a Mr. Bernoudy approached Bailly on the levee and said "My mulatto, you are a good man, do me a favor." This expression upset Bailly, and he responded: "*Mi mulato! Mi mulato!* When was I ever *your* mulatto?" Bailly resented Bernoudy treating him this "foolish way"—in other words, as a slave. On another day Bailly was at the notary's office when a Mr. Macarty had the audacity to remark that the free *pardos* were ruined by their associations with slaves and that if *pardos* wished to be regarded more highly, they ought to discontinue any fraternization with the tainted slaves. He referred to free *pardos* as "riffraff, thieves whom the governor should expel from the colony." With good reason these words angered Bailly; he told Mr. Macarty that if there were among them such persons, he should name them and not insult everyone. To which Macarty replied that Bailly was the principal thief and threatened him with his walking stick. Bailly further illuminated the legal and social systems' lack of justice. Although he brought charges against Macarty, officials punished him with a mere fine, not for insulting free *pardos* as a group and Bailly in particular, but rather for showing disrespect for the government by criticizing the governor's policies. Bailly then asked Declouet the rhetorical question of what the government would have done to him if he had talked to a white person the way Macarty had spoken to him. "And you call this justice? No sir, and I am as much an officer as you are."

Bailly also discussed this topic of racial equality, or lack of it, with another white officer, don Manuel García. Following his usual complaint about St. Maxent's unwillingness to share his table with *pardo* officers, Bailly proceeded to state that one's skin color was an accident or chance occurrence. Pigmentation should not constitute a reason to differentiate between *pardos* and whites. Bailly then praised the French because they rewarded or punished subjects only on their merit and conduct.

Unlike Bailly, most people of French descent living in Louisiana—black and white—supported the strong sense of hierarchy associated with the Spanish monarchy and France's *ancien regime*. French planters and slave owners desperately wanted to prevent the chaos and disruption spurred by the French and

Haitian Revolutions from spreading into Louisiana; all of a sudden, their Spanish rulers began to look pretty good to them. When the free *parda* María Cofignie was involved in an altercation on a New Orleans street in 1795, white witnesses considered her words and actions "the most vile atrocities that were as outrageous . . . as those that have caused a revolution" in France and its Caribbean colonies. Like free blacks in Saint-Domingue, Cofignie "talked of the whites in general with disdain and great contempt." Such slanderous words were especially effective coming from free blacks because the law demanded that they show respect for all whites, their actual and symbolic former "masters."[27] Frustrated with a patriarchal, racist society that discriminated against them as nonwhites and, for females, as women, free blacks occasionally lashed back at their oppressors with venomous tongues, as Bailly had done to Mr. Bernoudy in the example above.

Cofignie was another free *parda* who resented this preferential treatment for whites and the humiliating behavior expected of free people of color. In May 1795 don Pedro Favrot, a captain of the fixed regiment, brought charges against Cofignie for insulting his daughter Josefina.[28] According to the testimony of white neighbors who witnessed the incident, Cofignie's young *pardo* son was playing with some children on the sidewalk in front of the Favrot home on Conti Street. They told the *mulático* (little mulatto) to leave them alone; he then threw dirt in Josefina's face; and the other children chased him to his mother's house on the same street, whereupon Cofignie furiously confronted the *señorita* and referred to her as a *hija de puta* (daughter of a whore or prostitute)—a definite insult. Berating Josefina for threatening her son, Cofignie decried the actions of Josefina and *other persons of French descent like her* [emphasis added], who, "just because they are white, believe that we [*libres*] are made to be scorned, spurned, and slighted. I am free and I am as worthy as you are; I have not earned my freedom on my back" (i.e., as a prostitute). These egalitarian sentiments upset the white witnesses and the Favrot family, as noted in their above-mentioned remarks.

Bailly and other *libres* reflected the conflicting sentiments that prevailed in Louisiana and other parts of the Americas during the age of revolution. As loyal Spanish subjects and members of the free *pardo* and *moreno* militias, most of them defended Louisiana against a likely invasion by French radicals attacking from both the Gulf and the upper Mississippi, as well as from internal disturbances fomented by pro-French agitators and discontented African and creole slaves.[29] As Bailly discovered, most *libres* were reluctant to go so far as to take up arms against white persons, not only because whites could call on well-trained police forces, but also because many *libres* were linked to whites by kinship and patronage networks and had a direct stake in Louisiana's slaveholding system. Statements made by free blacks disclose the loyalty many sustained for their white patrons and kin and for the Spanish government, no matter how unequal its system of privileges and rewards. According to the free *pardo* Esteban Lalande, who testified against Bailly, the *pardos* had received favorable treatment from whites during French rule of the colony and freedom from slavery under the Spanish regime. The French were their fathers and the Spaniards their liberators. Emphatically stating that they were the sons of whites and had their blood, Lalande and other *pardo* witnesses asserted that they were incapable of murdering their white relatives and benefactors.[30] Although they resented being treated as second-class citizens, most merely wanted to reform the system rather than overthrow it, and most remained loyal to the Crown. They opted for peaceful paternalism rather than revolutionary equality. Nevertheless, they could concur with much of what Bailly said.

Indeed, Bailly did voice many of the concerns of the *pardos*, at least for those who had risen above poverty and could afford the luxury of worrying about such abstract concepts as equality and justice. A few, like Bailly, joined the Jacobins in advocating the overthrow of a discriminatory Spanish government and the institution of liberal French laws that guaranteed free blacks equal rights as citizens. According to standards of the time, his cause was not even that radical and closely paralleled the aims of most *gens de couleur libres* of Saint-Domingue—that is, to gain citizenship rights for free *pardos* equal to those of whites but not to abolish slavery.[31]

It seems that Bailly, Cofignie, Gentilly, and other free blacks longed for a utopian society that revolutionary France appeared to espouse, one founded on liberty, equality, and fraternity. It would be a society absent the color consciousness of the Spanish system and the desire of greedy French masters to exploit their slaves to the fullest and to force deference from their former slaves. Gentilly wanted her rights as a woman protected, no matter what her color or status as a former slave. Whites of French descent who witnessed the altercation between Cofignie and Josefina Favrot decried as an "atrocity" Cofignie's assertion that she was "free and . . . as worthy as you are"; in their minds such notions were as "outrageous" as those that had started the revolution in Haiti. The ideals of radicals in France and the example set by rebellious free blacks in Saint-Domingue and the other French islands, coupled with his own personal experiences of racial discrimination, also motivated Bailly to speak out against local injustice, even advocating the use of force if necessary. Like that of

Cofignie, Bailly's determined effort to secure equal rights for free *pardos* did not succeed: he landed in jail, Louisiana never experienced a revolution like the one in Saint-Domingue during its early phase, and free black rights and privileges deteriorated even further under United States rule. Without the protection of a paternalistic Spanish government, as race conscious as it was, *libres* in New Orleans encountered continuing attacks on their status as a distinct group; as the nineteenth century unfolded, local whites stepped up efforts to define and treat all persons of African descent like slaves.[32]

NOTES

1. Throughout this work I use the inclusive somatic terms *free black*, *free person of color*, and *libre* to encompass anyone of African descent, that is, any free nonwhite person whether he or she be pure African, part white, or part Native American. The exclusive terms *pardo* (light-skinned) and *moreno* (dark-skinned)—preferred by contemporary free blacks over *mulatto* and *negro*—are utilized to distinguish elements within the nonwhite population.

2. Louisiana's colonial period lasted from 1699, when the French established a permanent settlement in the area, to 1803, when the United States purchased it. France ceded Louisiana to Spain in the Treaty of Paris of 1763, and Spanish administrators governed the colony until 1803. During French and Spanish rule, Louisiana's value to Europeans was mainly strategic. Both countries viewed Louisiana as useful within the context of larger geopolitical considerations: they wanted to keep the colony out of the hands of archrival England. Although European rulers put more resources into the colony than they got out, France hoped that by occupying Louisiana it could gain access to silver mines in northern New Spain. Spain, in turn, sought Louisiana as a protective barrier between those same mines and Britain's increasingly expansive North American colonies to the east. For more on Louisiana's early history and its geopolitical role, refer to Bennet H. Wall, ed., *Louisiana: A History* (Arlington Heights, Ill.: Forum Press, 1990), and David J. Weber, *The Spanish Frontier in North America* (New Haven: Yale UP, 1992).

3. On this topic, see David Barry Gaspar and David Patrick Geggus, eds., *A Turbulent Time: The French Revolution and the Greater Caribbean* (Bloomington: Indiana UP, 1997).

4. Lewis Hanke, *The Spanish Struggle for Justice in the Conquest of America* (Boston: Little, Brown, 1949); Lyle N. McAlister, "Social Structure and Social Change in New Spain," *Hispanic American Historical Review* 43, 2 (April 1963): 349–70; and Lyle N. McAlister, *Spain and Portugal in the New World, 1492–1700* (Minneapolis: U of Minnesota P, 1984), 24–40, 398–401.

5. Kimberly S. Hanger, *Bounded Lives, Bounded Places: Free Black Society in Colonial New Orleans, 1769–1803* (Durham, N.C.: Duke UP, 1997), 22.

6. Herbert S. Klein, *African Slavery in Latin America and the Caribbean* (New York: Oxford UP, 1986), 217–41.

7. Quote from Thomas Marc Fiehrer, "The African Presence in Colonial Louisiana: An Essay on the Continuity of Caribbean Culture," in *Louisiana's Black Heritage*, ed. Robert R. Macdonald, John R. Kemp, and Edward F. Haas (New Orleans: Louisiana State Museum, 1979), 18; Carl A. Brasseaux, *Denis-Nicolas Foucault and the New Orleans Rebellion of 1768* (Ruston, La.: McGinty, 1987); Laura Foner, "The Free People of Color in Louisiana and St. Domingue: A Comparative Portrait of Two Three-Caste Slave Societies," *Journal of Social History* 3, 4 (1970): 415–16, 418–19. A "tenuous allegiance of the dominantly French planters to the Spanish regime" posed perennial challenges to Spanish administrators in Louisiana. An analysis of the correspondence of Governor Carondelet, who served during the era of the French Revolution, particularly highlights this dilemma (see Fiehrer, "African Presence," 16, 25).

8. Gilbert C. Din, "Proposals and Plans for Colonization in Spanish Louisiana," *Louisiana History* 11, 3 (1970): 197–213.

9. Hanger, *Bounded Lives, Bounded Places*, 20, 26–33.

10. Hans W. Baade, "The Law of Slavery in Spanish Luisiana, 1769–1803," in *Louisiana's Legal Heritage*, ed. Edward F. Haas (Pensacola, Fla.: Perdido Bay Press for the Louisiana State Museum, 1983), 50–55; Frederick P. Bowser, "Colonial Spanish America," in *Neither Slave nor Free: The Freedmen of African Descent in the Slave Societies of the New World*, ed. David W. Cohen and Jack P. Greene (Baltimore: Johns Hopkins UP, 1972), 21–22; McAlister, *Spain and Portugal in the New World*, 25, 435–36.

11. *Code Noir*, applied to Louisiana March 23, 1724, French Judicial Records, Louisiana State Museum Historical Center; Klein, *African Slavery*, 195. Although Klein and other scholars of comparative slave societies note the harshness of the *Code Noir*, most Louisiana historiography claims that it was mild (see Baade's discussion of Louisiana scholarship in "Law of Slavery," 43–53). The *Code Noir* most certainly was more humane than British or Dutch slave law, but much more restrictive and favorable to the slave owner than were Iberian codes.

12. Baade, "Law of Slavery," 48–53; Gwendolyn Midlo Hall, "Saint Domingue," in Bowser, *Neither Slave nor Free*, 172–92.

13. Baade, "Law of Slavery," 64–67.

14. Derek Noel Kerr, *Petty Felony, Slave Defiance, and Frontier Villainy: Crime and Criminal Justice in Spanish Louisiana, 1770–1803* (New York: Garland, 1993), 152.

15. Baade, "Law of Slavery"; quotations from James Thomas McGowan, "Creation of a Slave Society: Louisiana Plantations in the Eighteenth Century" (Ph.D. diss., University of Rochester, 1976), 194.

16. Orleans Parish Notarial Archives, Court Proceedings of Francisco Broutin, no. 11, folios 74–100, March 17, 1792.

17. Baade, "Law of Slavery," 43.

18. Orleans Parish Notarial Archives, Acts of Andrés Almonester y Roxas, folio 165, May 4, 1772.

19. Orleans Parish Notarial Archives, Court Proceedings of Narciso Broutin, no. 60, folios 1495–1501, September 14, 1803.

20. Hanger, *Bounded Lives, Bounded Places*, 26–27.

21. This case and the one that Dor first pursued against Lalande can be found in "Luis Dor, negro esclavo contra Estevan Lalande, pardo libre," Orleans Parish Notarial Archives, Court Proceedings of F. Broutin, no. 21, folios 1–99, January 31, 1793, and "Luis Dor, negro esclavo de Dn. Joseph Dusuau contra la Sucesión de Estevan Lalande, mulato libre," Orleans Parish Notarial Archives, Court Proceedings of F. Broutin, no. 31-A, folios 1–43, January 10, 1794. The translation provided here is the author's.

22. In all fairness to Dor, it appears that Lalande and Gentilly had entered into joint agreements on numerous occasions (for example, see Orleans Parish Notarial Archives, Acts of Pedro Pedesclaux, no. 15, folio 721, December 10, 1792). Records indicate that Gentilly and Lalande had no children together. Once Lalande died and Dor won the case, Gentilly would have had to use what assets remained to support herself, although given her assertive nature, previous high standing in the community (as indicated by the witnesses who supported her claims), and property base, she probably did well.

23. "María Luisa Saly contra Matheo Parin, alias Canon, su amo," Louisiana State Museum Historical Center, Spanish Judicial Records, January 23, 1781.

24. The case also underlines the importance of recording a *coartación* agreement in writing, or at least having reliable witnesses to the arrangement or a third party to hold the money as it accumulated.

25. The two Bailly trials are "Criminales seguidos de oficio contra el Pardo Libre Pedro Bahy," Spanish Judicial Records, October 7, 1791, and "Testimonio de la Sumaria contra el Mulato libre Pedro Bailly, Theniente de las Milicias de Pardos de esta Ciudad, por haver prorrumpido especies contra el Govierno Español, y haverse manifestado adicto a las máximas de los Franceses rebeldes," Archivo General de Indias, Estado 14, no. 60, February 11, 1794.

26. The following discussion and assessment of Bailly's activities in 1791 and 1793–94 are derived from testimony in the two trials, cited above.

27. See articles 52 and 53 of the French *Code Noir* as applied to Louisiana in 1724, and Bowser, "Colonial Spanish America," 40–42. Another excellent source on laws pertaining to slavery is Alan Watson, *Slave Law in the Americas* (Athens: U of Georgia P, 1989).

28. "Criminales seguidos por don Pedro Fabrot contra María Cofinie, parda libre, sobre palabras injuriosas," Spanish Judicial Records, June 8, 1795.

29. For more on the spread of the French Revolution in Louisiana and activities of various groups, see Gwendolyn Midlo Hall, *Africans in Colonial Louisiana: The Development of Afro-Creole Culture in the Eighteenth Century* (Baton Rouge: Louisiana State UP, 1992), 316–74; Kimberly S. Hanger, "Conflicting Loyalties: The French Revolu-

tion and Free People of Color in Spanish New Orleans," in Gaspar and Geggus, *A Turbulent Time*, 178–203; Kimberly S. Hanger, "A Privilege and Honor to Serve: The Free Black Militia of Spanish New Orleans," *Military History of the Southwest* 21, 1 (1991): 80–82; Paul F. Lachance, "The Politics of Fear: French Louisianians and the Slave Trade, 1786–1809," *Plantation Society in the Americas* 1, 2 (1979): 162–97; Ernest R. Liljegrin, "Jacobinism in Spanish Louisiana, 1792–1797," *Louisiana Historical Quarterly* 22, 1 (1939): 47–97.

30. Testimony given by Esteban Lalande, in "Criminales seguidos de oficio contra el Pardo Libre Pedro Bahy," Spanish Judicial Records, October 7, 1791.

31. Geggus, "Racial Equality, Slavery, and Colonial Secession during the Constituent Assembly," *American Historical Review* 94, 5 (1989): 1290–1308.

32. Among the many works to examine the declining status of free people of color in antebellum New Orleans and Louisiana are Baade, "Law of Slavery"; Ira Berlin, *Slaves without Masters: The Free Negro in the Antebellum South* (New York: Pantheon, 1974); Caryn Cossé Bell, *Revolution, Romanticism, and the Afro-Creole Protest Tradition in Louisiana, 1718–1868* (Baton Rouge: Louisiana State UP, 1997); John W. Blassingame, *Black New Orleans, 1860–1880* (Chicago: U of Chicago P, 1973); McConnell, *Negro Troops;* and Judith Kelleher Schafer, *Slavery, the Civil Law, and the Supreme Court of Louisiana* (Baton Rouge: Louisiana State UP, 1994).

Francophone Residents of Antebellum Baltimore and the Origins of the Oblate Sisters of Providence

DIANE BATTS MORROW

In a modest brick row house on George Street in Baltimore on July 2, 1829, Sulpician priest James Hector Joubert received the professions of the four charter members of a pioneering sisterhood. Caribbean emigrants Elizabeth Clarisse Lange, Marie Balas, Rosine Boegue, and Therese Duchemin dedicated themselves as "a Religious society of Coloured Women . . . [who] renounce the world to consecrate themselves to God, and to the Christian education of young girls of color."[1] This otherwise unremarked occasion inaugurated the Oblate Sisters of Providence, a community of free women of color who were "French in language, in sympathy, and in habit of life," and the first permanent Roman Catholic sisterhood of African descent in the world.[2]

This essay examines the impact of the French cultural heritage of three significant participants in early Oblate history on their respective responses to life in antebellum Baltimore. Oblate cofounders Lange and Joubert formed part of the Francophone diaspora to the United States fleeing revolution early in the nineteenth century. Although born in Baltimore in 1809, Therese Duchemin claimed Saint-Domingan ancestry through her mulatto emigrant mother. Joubert, Lange, and Duchemin all drew on such fundamental components of their French identity as language, worldview, and Roman Catholicism to adapt to Anglophone, slaveholding Baltimore.

Two streams of immigration that converged in Baltimore in the 1790s enabled the organization of the Oblate Sisters almost forty years later. As the see, or official seat, of the first diocese of the Roman Catholic Church formed in the United States in 1789, Baltimore proved a logical haven for Catholics fleeing revolutions in France and the Caribbean.

The extreme anticlericalism espoused by the proponents of the French Revolution prompted a group of French diocesan priests, the Society of St. Sulpice, to establish a mission on more hospitable shores. Between 1791 and 1793, nine Sulpician priests and seven seminarians arrived in Baltimore. The priests fulfilled their society's mission by establishing St. Mary's Seminary to educate priests and St. Mary's College as a preparatory institution for the seminary.

The second stream of immigration began in 1793 and spanned almost twenty years, as several contingents of Saint-Domingan refugees arrived in Baltimore. Located on the western third of the Caribbean island of Hispaniola, the colony of Saint-Domingue had developed into France's most profitable overseas possession in the eighteenth century. The labor of African slaves on Saint-Domingan plantations enriched French planters and the Empire alike. In 1791 Saint-Domingan slaves seized the opportunity and the inspiration provided by the French Revolution to strike for freedom. Beginning in 1793 Saint-Domingans of all racial categories fled from the anticipated retributions of the former slave revolutionaries in Saint-Domingue.

French Caribbean exiles sought refuge in New Orleans, Charleston, Philadelphia, and other port cities in the United States.[3] Yet well-established commercial relations between Maryland planters and merchants and Caribbean planters made Baltimore a particularly logical terminus for the émigrés.[4] Hundreds of negroes and mulattoes, many of whom identified with or belonged to the Caribbean planter class in terms of sympathies, self-interest, education, and wealth, composed a significant portion of these successive waves of French Caribbean immigration.[5] In Baltimore, shared traditions attracted Sulpicians and Saint-Domingans to each other, bound together by their French language and cultural heritage, their profession of the Roman Catholic faith, and their common experience of flight from radical revolutions at home that undermined their privileged positions.

In 1796 the Sulpician priests began conducting Sunday catechismal classes or religious instruction in French for the community of black Saint-Domingan émigrés who congregated in St. Mary's Lower Chapel at the Sulpician Seminary on Paca Street. In 1827 James Joubert inherited responsibility for these classes. Frustrated by the inadequate response of his pupils, Joubert conceived the idea of a school to facilitate religious instruction. When the Englishman James Whitfield became the fourth archbishop of Baltimore in January 1828, Joubert submitted his school proposal to Whitfield, who approved the plan.

To staff his school Joubert approached Caribbean emigrants Elizabeth Lange and Marie Balas, two educated women of color and experienced teachers who already conducted their own school for children of their race in their home. Lange and Balas also informed Joubert "that for more than ten years they wished to consecrate themselves to God for this good work, waiting patiently that in His own infinite goodness He would show them a way of giving themselves to Him." Joubert concluded, after consulting with Archbishop Whitfield, that a community of black women religious would suit his purposes as well.[6]

No reliable statistics documented the actual number of black Saint-Domingan *émigrés* entering Baltimore between 1793 and 1810, but sources estimate between five hundred and a thousand black Francophone refugees. The significance of the influx of black Saint-Domingan refugees lay in their ethnic consciousness and consequent formation of a discrete black Catholic congregation at St. Mary's Lower Chapel, served by the French Sulpician priests. Before the Francophone black emigration, Baltimore black Catholics "were absorbed in the parish churches and were taken for granted."[7]

Much of the life of Oblate cofounder Elizabeth Lange remains undocumented prior to 1828. Born of racially mixed parentage probably in the 1780s in either Saint-Domingue or Cuba, Elizabeth Clarisse Lange apparently enjoyed a relatively privileged life, including a formal education, probably in Saint-Domingue.[8] The Sisters of Notre Dame du Cap-François had established an academy for girls in Le Cap, Saint-Domingue, in 1723. After 1774 this school accepted mulatto and black pupils as well.[9] Elizabeth Lange and other early Oblate members of Caribbean origin may have enrolled in this convent school. Such an educational experience would have exposed these young girls of color to the religious life as an appropriate and viable vocation.

Lange emigrated to the United States, where she may have resided briefly in Charleston, South Carolina, and Norfolk, Virginia.[10] Financial support from her father's estate allowed Lange to maintain her independence in the slave city of Baltimore, where she resided from at least 1813.[11] The Oblate Sisters of Providence did not own slaves. Yet Elizabeth Lange, and later the Oblate community through her inheritance, clearly benefited from the institution of slavery, which generated planter wealth. Late nineteenth-century Oblate accounts state that "Sister Mary [Lange] especially was very often the recipient of large sums of money, sent from her home in Santiago."[12] Oblate *Annals* document that Lange had inherited "$2000 left her by Monsieur Lange her father" and had "received in settlement $1411.59 which was due her" in 1832 and 1833 respectively.[13] Like her cofounder of the Oblate Sisters, James Joubert, Elizabeth Lange probably maintained more direct connections with slave society than acknowledged in previous accounts. Unlike Joubert, Lange became an anomaly in her adopted home of Baltimore. Forced to flee her homeland, Elizabeth Lange was a genuine victim of the slave insurrection so constantly feared yet seldom realized in United States slave society. But as a free woman of color, she elicited little sympathy from southern slaveholders or other white people who noted her "of color" designation more assiduously than either her planter connections or her free status.

Oblate member, superior, and historian Sister Mary Theresa Catherine Willigman provided the most comprehensive and reliable information on the nineteenth-century Oblate experience in general and on individual Oblate members Sisters Mary Elizabeth Lange and Marie Therese Duchemin in particular.[14] Willigman's knowledge of Lange derived from personal experience, as she had lived in the Oblate community from 1840, when she was five years old. Lange served as mother superior of the Oblates from 1828 to 1832 and from 1835 to 1841; she then formed part of the Oblate staff at St. Mary's Seminary until 1850. When she returned to the convent from the seminary, Lange served as novice mistress from 1850 until 1855; she became assistant superior in 1857 and director of an Oblate school at Fells Point in east Baltimore in 1858.[15]

Two significant traits of Lange particularly germane to the focus of this study emerge from Willigman's portrayal. Willigman remembered that "Sister Mary was very good but a very strict observer of the Rule and made no allowance for small omissions." Even in her advanced years, Lange "was exact to the regular daily exercises." She enjoyed reminiscing about her life in the West Indies, "but no matter how interesting the fact was she was telling, if the bell for silence rang, there was an end for that time." Yet Lange's devotion to regulatory observance represented no simplistic obsession with ritual. She fully comprehended the spiritual component embodied in the Oblate Rule. Lange once admonished a sister not to focus on the ritual of rosary recitation in the chapel to the neglect of her spiritual communion with the presence of God in the Blessed Sacrament.[16]

Every religious community requires a strict observance of its rules from every member. Yet because the social order of the Caribbean with which Lange was familiar no longer prevailed in Baltimore, she may have sought in her strict personal observance of the Oblate Rule not only the customary assurance of pursuing the path toward spiritual perfection but also some sense of social stability. In her native country Lange had enjoyed a doubly privileged status as functions of her freedom and her color. The privileged position of free mulattoes in a three-tiered caste system pervaded slave society in the Caribbean and Latin America, whether under French, Spanish, or British rule.[17]

Upon arriving in the American South, Caribbean refugee Lange undoubtedly experienced a cultural assault on two significant determinants of her social
identity. Unlike the free black communities in the Caribbean, or even in New
Orleans, Charleston, or Savannah in the United States, the Baltimore black
community maintained no color hierarchy in which light-skinned mulattoes
dominated darker people.[18] Baltimore's less color-striated black community at-
tenuated Lange's formerly privileged social status based on color. She suffered
a second diminution of social status perpetrated by the white community. Lange
soon discovered that U.S. society discriminated against nonwhite people cate-
gorically—slave or free, mulatto or black. The diminution of freedom and
color as guarantees of her personal social status in Baltimore probably increased the appeal of institutionalized religious life for Lange.

Willigman also noted Lange's resistance or aversion to the English language: "Sister Mary was a very accomplished scholar in French and Spanish;
she never tried to acquire English; she however spoke and understood the language well enough to direct the Community, though in business matters Sisters
[Marie Therese Duchemin and others acted as] her auxiliary." On another occasion Willigman recalled, "A little girl one day hearing [Lange] say that she
was 'French to her soul,' stopped suddenly and said, 'Oh, Sister Mary, is your
soul French too?'"[19]

Lange personally preferred French to the English language, perhaps in response to the unwelcome experience of the pervasive and indiscriminate racism
inherent in American society. To this highly cultured and sensitive individual,
the English language symbolized most palpably the society that rejected her
humanity. If Anglo-American culture promulgated such attitudes, Lange
countered it with her "French soul": the pursuit of spiritual perfection and
egalitarianism and immersion in her Francophone cultural identity.

The spiritual commitment and determination of Elizabeth Lange and the
other charter Oblate members alone could not have accomplished the foundation of the Oblate Sisters of Providence in 1828. Societal and episcopal attitudes
and traditions regarding race and gender necessitated white male advocacy to
validate this black sisterhood in antebellum America. James Joubert proved to
be one of the most exceptional of those individuals who transcended contemporary prejudices and proscriptions to advance the Oblate cause.

Born in France of a noble family in 1777, James Hector Nicholas Joubert de
la Muraille attempted careers as a soldier and as a tax official in France. From
1800 to 1803 Joubert served as a tax official in Saint-Domingue. He fled from
there to Cuba in 1803 as a refugee from the slave revolution and then emigrated

to Baltimore in 1804. Joubert entered St. Mary's Seminary to study for the priesthood in 1805 and joined the Society of St. Sulpice shortly after his ordination in Baltimore in 1810. Not only did Joubert serve as disciplinarian and treasurer of the Sulpician St. Mary's College, but he also instructed the students in French and geography. He eventually realized his life's vocation ministering to the needs of the black French Caribbean refugee community in Baltimore.[20]

Joubert's three-year sojourn in Saint-Domingue exposed him to a slave society that allowed a modicum of social and civil parity between white citizens and free people of color. In Saint-Domingue Joubert experienced the social analogue of the Roman Catholic Church's spiritual approach to the institution of slavery: although a social evil, slavery in principle did not constitute a sin; enslaved status—however socially degrading—did not deprive individuals of their humanity or spiritual equality before God.[21] Informed by both his Saint-Domingan social experience and the church's nuanced distinctions between social and spiritual equality, Joubert advocated forcefully for the spiritual cause of the free Oblate Sisters in antebellum Baltimore, where a racially based slave culture denigrated all black people, slave and free.

Joubert brought to his new vocation finely honed administrative skills of discipline, attention to detail, and organization developed in his previous careers as soldier, tax official, and teacher. His noteworthy skills recommended him to secular and sacred agencies beyond the Sulpician community. He represented the French government in extended negotiations with the Haitian regime for payment of indemnities owed Saint-Domingan refugees. Both in 1832 and again in 1841 the Holy See considered installing Joubert as bishop and vicar apostolic to Haiti.[22] In July 1841 the papacy issued apostolic briefs appointing Joubert vicar apostolic to the Republic of Haiti and elevating him to the rank of bishop. That December Joseph Rosati, the bishop of St. Louis newly assigned as apostolic delegate to Haiti, came to Baltimore specifically to recruit Joubert for Haiti. A debilitating illness ultimately prevented Joubert's departure from Baltimore.[23] However, in his mission to legitimize the first community of black women religious in the eyes of both church and society, Joubert utilized fully those diplomatic skills that had recommended him to both sacred and secular authorities.

Rosati's initial negotiations with Haitian president Jean Pierre Boyer appeared promising. A Baltimore Catholic publication even reported in 1842 that "President Boyer was much pleased to learn [of] the existence of the society of colored sisters in Baltimore, and has directed the secretary of state to write to Rev. H. Joubert, their superior, for the purposes of procuring their services in

Hayti."[24] Evidently this proposed initiative never materialized, as Haiti and the papacy did not effect diplomatic relations until 1860.

As a society of priests, the Sulpicians subscribed to a modified form of Gallicanism, a French clerical movement that promoted the development of particular, autonomous, national churches over a culturally homogeneous, universal structure centralized under papal authority.[25] Within the Sulpician mission in Baltimore, Joubert belonged to the faction that represented a traditionalist view characterized as "introverted, rigorous, and narrow minded" in its monolithic focus on the Sulpician mission in the United States to train seminarians.[26] Yet this traditionalist faction constituted the most devoted advocates for the Oblate Sisters within the Sulpician community.

The opposing group represented an "Americanist" position characterized as cosmopolitan, expansively open to American culture, and intimate with the Baltimore social elite—both Catholic and Protestant. Although the Americanist Sulpicians endorsed undertaking external ministries beyond the Sulpician mission of the seminary, they consistently refrained from overt demonstrations of support for the Oblate community.[27] In its openness to American culture, this faction may have absorbed the pervasive influence of racism as well. Evidently ethnicity played no pivotal role in these coalitions, as each one claimed both French and American members.

The frequency and intensity of the conflicts between these two factions accelerated from June 1827 through 1829—concurrent with the founding of the Oblate community—in escalating cycles of resignations, dismissals, and appointments to various college and seminary positions. Joubert wrote the Sulpician superior in France opposing the Americanist faction's plan to "appoint young Americans to positions of power and thereby become 'absolute master of the Community and its institutions.'" Joubert's fears of a "young American" usurpation of Sulpician directorship proved prescient, for the Americanist faction "constituted the triumvirate that would rule the archdiocese until . . . 1840."[28] Certainly in his lifetime the fifty-year-old Joubert—former soldier, bureaucrat, teacher, and survivor of both the French and Saint-Domingan Revolutions—had witnessed the human cost of promulgating social and political ideologies. Perhaps he surmised the grave ramifications of the opposing coalition's eager embrace of a racist American culture for his ministry to black people in general and the fledgling Oblate community in particular.

The tentativeness implied in Joubert's own words recalling his intention to found "a kind of religious society" indicated his awareness that in proposing this society of black women religious he ventured into uncharted territory.

When the Oblate community began, Joubert, who served as its spiritual director, was not certain church authorities would sanction these black women religious.[29]

Joubert crafted the Oblate Rule in consultation with his mentor, the Sulpician superior Jean Marie Tessier, and the Oblate Sisters themselves. Scholars disagree about the originality of the Oblate Rule formulated in 1829.[30] Had Joubert substantially duplicated a conventional religious rule, he himself would have publicized that fact to expedite ecclesiastical recognition of the Oblate community. Elizabeth Bayley Seton had founded the Sisters of Charity of Saint Joseph in 1809. As an American community dedicated to an active or service ministry—not a contemplative, cloistered existence—and organized in the archdiocese of Baltimore under Sulpician auspices only twenty years earlier, this sisterhood constitutes the closest analogue to the Oblate Sisters of Providence. The American Sisters of Charity adopted as their own the Rules and Constitutions of the French Daughters of Charity of Saint Vincent de Paul, incorporating an elastic clause allowing "such modifications in the Rules as the difference of country, habits, customs, and manners may require."[31]

Both Joubert and Tessier knew about the Rules and Constitutions of the Sisters of Charity because of the long and intimate association of the Sulpician society with that sisterhood. However, the Oblate Rules and Constitutions bore little resemblance to those of the Sisters of Charity—in terms of the former's brevity, their focus on the educational mission of the Oblate Sisters, their acknowledgment of the allowance for close Oblate ties with the Baltimore black laity, and the marked omission of the Sulpician superior from the Oblate chain of command.[32] The racial identity of the Oblate membership may have convinced Joubert of the appropriateness—if not the necessity—of formulating the Oblate Rules and Constitutions to accommodate the particular Oblate situation within the antebellum Catholic Church and southern society. Although characterized as a Sulpician traditionalist, Joubert transposed Gallican encouragement of national peculiarites into the incorporation of racial peculiarities in the evolving American Catholic identity with the formation of the Oblate Sisters of Providence.

Joubert had observed the widespread devotion of black Catholics to St. Benedict of St. Philadelpho, known as the Moor, who shared both their African ancestry and experience of slavery. Joubert requested a plenary indulgence for the Oblate Sisters and all Catholics celebrating St. Benedict's Feast Day in the Oblate chapel. Rome granted Joubert's request in May 1833.[33] In presenting his case for the indulgence celebrating St. Benedict the Moor, Joubert revealed aspects of his own thinking about race and religion. Socially conservative if spiritually egalitarian, Joubert accommodated slavery, as did virtually the entire American Catholic Church establishment. Indeed, recently rediscovered evidence indicates that Joubert himself may have owned a slave in 1808.[34] No abolitionist, Joubert commended St. Benedict as a role model to black people for transcending temporal inequities, pursuing a life of Christian perfection, and earning his spiritual reward in heaven.

Yet Joubert was personally sympathetic to black people both as individuals and as a despised minority. Throughout his ministry Joubert demonstrated a marked respect for the humanity of black people and treated them as active agents in their own salvation rather than as passive recipients of an externally imposed regimen. His response to the black Catholics' expressed devotion to St. Benedict the Moor demonstrated his ability to consider black people collaborators in formulating a more personalized religious environment. His sensitivity to the crucial importance for black Catholics of identifying with a fellow black person revered and canonized by the institutional church revealed Joubert's spiritual egalitarianism. Joubert recognized and addressed black Catholic emotional and psychological needs as well as spiritual and temporal needs. Although a white male in the antebellum South, James Joubert championed the cause of the Oblate Sisters of Providence because of his commitment to spiritual equality for black people, informed by his social experiences in Saint-Domingue and his uniquely personal application of Gallican perspectives to the racial realities of the antebellum southern Church.

The historical record most adequately documents the pre-Oblate life of the fourth and youngest charter Oblate member, Sister Marie Therese Duchemin, in part because of her later departure from the Oblate Sisters to found a community of white women religious, the Sisters, Servants of the Immaculate Heart of Mary.[35] On June 1, 1829, Joubert recorded in the Oblate *Annals* that Lange and Balas presented to him "as a novice a young lady of 19 years whom they had raised, and who had been living with them for some years . . . [who] was very pious and also was very capable of rendering great services to the institution."[36]

Although raised by Elizabeth Lange and Marie Balas, Therese Duchemin was no orphan. Her mother, Betsy Maxis Duchemin, had lost her parents in the Saint-Domingan Revolution in 1793 and emigrated to the environs of Baltimore in the care of a prominent family, the Duchemins, who managed to escape Saint-Domingue with their fortune intact. Late in her life Sister Therese revealed her personal recollections of her early years to Sister Mary James, a

Sister of the Immaculate Heart of Mary, in conversations that occurred between 1885 and 1892, the year of Sister Therese's death.[37] Sister Mary James recalled that "later on when she saw her father (for the only time in her life) she
was taken to the door of a drawing room in the Howard home outside of Baltimore, and told that the visiting English Major was her father. It seems she did
not speak to him, but she went back again and again to look at him. She never
mentioned whether he saw her or not, or even whether he knew of her existence . . . but all her life she instinctively disliked the English and loved the
French passionately."[38]

Sister Mary James further recalled that Therese Duchemin "was placed in
the care of some French ladies who trained her so carefully that later on those
who met her believed her to have come from France. Later some of these ladies
formed a Community known as the Oblates of [Providence], which Mother
Theresa says she joined as one of the first members."[39]

Sister Therese firmly endorsed the quality education she received from Elizabeth Lange and Marie Balas over sixty years after the fact and forty years after her estrangement from the Oblate community. Furthermore, the erroneous
impression that she had attended school in France echoed a frequent assertion
that the original Oblate members "were from Saint Domingo, though they had
some of them, certainly, been educated in France."[40] Significantly, Sister
Therese identified the Oblate Sisters exclusively as French, avoiding any reference to their racial identity in her recollections.

The exact year Elizabeth Lange and Marie Balas assumed custody of
Therese Duchemin remains uncertain. Church records place Duchemin in the
city of Baltimore in 1822 when she was twelve years old, so she may have lived
with them at that time.[41] The constant example of both her teachers' lives undoubtedly inspired Duchemin to profess herself as a religious. But Sister Mary
Lange evinced intelligence, determination, initiative, leadership, and deeply
felt personal reasons for preferring Francophone to Anglo-American culture.
In Lange, Duchemin probably recognized a kindred spirit.

The French language figured prominently in Oblate communal affairs. Non-
Francophone sisters and students acquired at least a rudimentary knowledge
of French to communicate effectively with Sister Mary Lange, Sister Rose
Boegue, and Elizabeth Du Moulin, an elderly widow who boarded at the
Oblate convent and spoke only French. As part of the daily regimen of sister
and student alike, Lange read a chapter of the New Testament in French before
the noon meal. From the foundation of the school the sisters taught the French
language as an integral part of their school's basic curriculum.[42] But the Oblate

community and school did not function in a Francophone cultural vacuum in 1830s Baltimore. In 1796 the Sulpician priests had initiated religious instruction for black Saint-Domingan refugees in St. Mary's Lower Chapel in the French language. By the 1820s African-American Catholics also attended these classes, now conducted in English.

As their first decade progressed, the Oblate Sisters documented an increasingly pronounced preference for sermons in French. An *Annals* entry of 1833 reported the delivery of a sermon in French without comment; but an entry of 1837 reported a sermon "in French to the great satisfaction of the Sisters." In 1838 some Oblate Sisters assisted Mass at St. Mary's Seminary to hear a sermon in French as "it was preached here [St. Frances Chapel] in English." [43] In the 1830s French sermons in the Oblate chapel were exceptional; [44] nevertheless, the Oblate Sisters attempted to accord the French language a significant presence in the evolving cultural life of their community.

Francophone tendencies persisted in liturgical observances in the Oblate chapel through 1843. Duchemin assumed the duties of community annalist in 1838.[45] She shared with Lange strong Francophone predilections. It proved no coincidence that beginning with Duchemin's tenure as annalist in September 1838, Oblate *Annals* noted every instance of French hymns or sermons at Oblate chapel services. This trend continued in the early 1840s. On Easter Sunday in April 1841, "Mass began a quarter of an hour earlier than usual, but what was more remarkable, we had a sermon in French preached by Father Director. Until now in spite of all the representation made on the subject, he had continued to preach in English; and when we had sermons in French, they were always preached by strange priests, but at last he decided to give a French sermon a month." [46] The monthly French sermons in the Oblate chapel occurred almost without exception until Joubert's death in 1843. In October 1842 Duchemin noted, "The usual sermon (French) was preached by the Reverend Father Fredet after the gospel and not at the end of Mass as Father Joubert ordinarily did through an excess of compliance with the Americans." [47]

Joubert was not the instigator of the Francophone innovations in the Oblate chapel. He resisted instituting French sermons and accommodated Anglophone adherents by rearranging the order of the liturgy on Sundays featuring such sermons. Evidently Duchemin concurred with neither concession to "Americans." Although she cited "all the representation" in favor of French sermons, the available evidence does not clarify the extent of the Francophone impulse within the Oblate community beyond Duchemin and, perhaps, Lange in the early 1840s.

The Oblate Sisters elected Duchemin mother superior in June 1841 for the customary three-year term, evidently because the serving assistant superior, Sister Chantal Noel, had died on the eve of the 1841 election "which would have made her Mother Superior." The occasionally harsh assessments of Oblate novices first apparent in the *Annals* in 1838 continued in the early 1840s. On August 29, 1841, an exasperated Duchemin observed in an *Annals* entry, "It is something to have to deal with silly women!" [48]

Duchemin did not restrict her critical scrutiny to the novices; she also recorded perceived transgressions or lapses in the professed Oblate members as well. In the assembly of October 26, 1840, "Father Director read only two articles of the rule which furnished him with ample means for scolding. One of these articles had been violated the day before." According to Duchemin's reports, vigilance against "the faults which exist in all religious communities" formed a recurrent theme in Joubert's instructions to the sisters. On April 3, 1842, Duchemin noted, "It has been some time since we had Assembly, but today Father Director assembled the Sisters to scold them." [49] In the assembly of September 25, 1842, Joubert warned the community against "useless visits"— evidently social or family visits, not the authorized home visits associated with the Oblate teaching mission: "He spoke heatedly of the dangers to which we would expose ourselves by neglecting our own affairs in this regard, so much so that the astonished Sisters felt that there was a snake in the grass somewhere. And they were not mistaken. Undoubtedly Father Joubert knows well what he is talking about and has some ones of us in mind, as this is his style." [50]

Duchemin's own style warrants consideration. A strict adherent to the rules, Duchemin approved when Joubert "observed to the letter that which is said in *Christian Perfection* in regard to the observance of the rules, 'that the reprimand and correction should follow the faults against the rules so that one can say that the observance of the rules is in its vigor.'" She noted that the love felt by the sisters for Joubert and his manner of censure "in a way so polite" effectively ameliorated the sting of the reprimand.[51] Evidently Duchemin failed to cultivate or imitate either characteristic she noted in Joubert. Her critical observations may have indicated her own doubts about the spiritual worthiness of her community, then fifteen years old. Oblate annalist and Mother Superior Duchemin found fault with her community, whereas Joubert and others did not.

As spiritual director of the Oblate Sisters of Providence, Joubert had secured the Oblate Sisters in their service ministry. But his declining health, especially after 1841, had circumscribed his effective functioning as Oblate spiritual director. Joubert's death in 1843 and the subsequent alienation of the Sulpician priests and diocesan authorities from the Oblate community exposed the Oblate Sisters to the spiritual influence of the Redemptorist priests. The

Redemptorists substituted an infusion of a more traditional, Eurocentric spiritual perspective, a perspective unfamiliar with cultural conditions in the United
States, for the Sulpician Gallican influence, which was mediated by lengthy experience in the United States, as the major spiritual guidance for the Oblate
community.

Initial Oblate contact with the Redemptorists occurred in July 1843 when
Louis Gillet, a Belgian Redemptorist and gifted preacher who spoke French exclusively, celebrated two masses in the Oblate chapel. Gillet preached for an
hour to the sisters on the obligations of the religious profession. Oblate Superior and annalist Duchemin noted, "He explained to us very well what a spouse
of Jesus Christ must do in order to remain faithful to her divine Spouse." For
Duchemin, the medium of the French language proved as significant as the
message of spiritual discipline. Years later, her confidant in the community of
the Sisters of the Immaculate Heart of Mary recalled that Duchemin "used to
tell of her joy in hearing a sermon in real French from Father Gillet when he
first came to America." [52]

Duchemin herself later recorded a third-person account of her spiritual
struggle: "Although belonging already to a religious Society, she had for a long
time felt the desire of consecrating herself to God in a religious order of strict
observance . . . she placed herself under the guidance of a [Redemptorist priest
and] . . . discovered to him everything that passed in her soul . . . her Director,
instead of sending her to a convent already established, as she wished, decided
upon sending her to the Reverend Father Gillet, another Redemptorist who
had charge of the parish of Monroe." [53]

On September 9, 1845, Sister Marie Therese Duchemin left the Oblate community for Monroe, Michigan, where she and Gillet cofounded the Sisters, Servants of the Immaculate Heart of Mary. Duchemin discarded her black racial
identity, rejecting a former ally in the Oblate community who wished to come
to Michigan, "as her color was too dark." [54] Duchemin's own physical appearance "displayed none of the physical evidences of her mixed blood. She was
fair, had blond hair and blue eyes." [55]

Sources differ about the impact of Duchemin's rupture with the Oblate community on the integrity of her French cultural identity. Several secondary
sources maintain that Duchemin "from now on became another entity. No
longer was she the French-speaking Mere [sic] Marie Therese but Mary Maxis,
later Sister and then Mother Mary Theresa, who used English exclusively, and
who wished apparently to break completely with the past, especially with the
Oblates." [56] Although resonant with dramatic potential in their implication of a
total identity crisis on Duchemin's part, these undocumented assertions prove

inconsistent with the evidence. The area of Michigan where Duchemin relocated supported a sizeable Francophone population. Duchemin could not have communicated with her cofounder, the exclusively Francophone Louis Gillet, in English. Furthermore, French was the language of the Immaculate Heart of Mary Sisters still in 1851, as well as that of their original Motherhouse Chronicles.[57] Significantly, while Duchemin divested herself of her former racial identity in 1845, she clung steadfastly to her status as a Roman Catholic woman religious and her French cultural heritage for the rest of her life.

French cultural identification informed the perspectives and actions of Sister Mary Elizabeth Lange, Father James Hector Joubert, and Sister Marie Therese Duchemin—three Francophone individuals functioning on the periphery of French national culture. Deprived of the opportunity to replicate in her adopted state of Maryland her accustomed, socially privileged status as a free woman of color, Elizabeth Lange asserted herself through total immersion in the spiritual and cultural dimensions of her identity. She rejected the English language, symbol of the culture that denied her humanity, and fervently embraced institutionalized religious life, which promised spiritual perfection and spiritual, if not social, egalitarianism within that most stable and enduring of social institutions, the Roman Catholic Church.

James Joubert utilized his social experience of slave and free society in Saint-Domingue in his creative application of Gallican national prerogatives to the racial situation in antebellum U.S. society. He deftly negotiated uncharted paths to incorporate the Oblate community into the Roman Catholic Church as a legitimate component of its evolving American branch, in spite of the sisters' anomalous status as free women of color in the slaveholding South.

Sister Marie Therese Duchemin promoted strict religious discipline and French language liturgies as an Oblate Sister of Providence. Although in 1845 she abandoned her black racial identity, her membership in the Oblate community, and the city of Baltimore, Duchemin retained allegiance to her French cultural heritage and her commitment to institutionalized religious life as permanent features of her identity. In significant ways the lives of each of these Francophone residents of antebellum Baltimore reflect the fact that they remained "French in language, in sympathy, and in habit of life."

NOTES

1. The Original Rule of the Oblate Sisters of Providence, quoted in Thaddeus Posey, "An Unwanted Commitment: The Spirituality of the Early Oblate Sisters of Providence, 1829–1890" (Ph.D. diss. Saint Louis University, 1993), appendix 1, 314.

2. Grace Sherwood, *The Oblates' Hundred and One Years* (New York: Macmillan, 1931), 5, 118; John T. Gillard, *Colored Catholics in the United States* (Baltimore: Josephite Press, 1941), 118.

3. Gillard, *Colored Catholics*, 79–80.

4. Glenn O. Phillips, "Maryland and the Caribbean, 1634–1984: Some Highlights," *Maryland Historical Magazine* 83, 3 (1988): 202–5; Posey, "Unwanted Commitment," 39–40.

5. Gillard, *Colored Catholics*, 76–79; Michael F. Rouse, *A Study of the Development of Negro Education under Catholic Auspices in Maryland and Washington, D.C.* (Baltimore: Johns Hopkins UP, 1935), 32; Clarence K. Gregory, "The Education of Blacks in Maryland: An Historical Survey" (Ed.D. diss., Columbia University Teachers College, 1976), 78–79; Barbara Misner, *"Highly Respectable and Accomplished Ladies": Catholic Women Religious in America, 1790–1850* (New York: Garland, 1988), 45.

6. A translation of *The Original Diary of the Oblate Sisters of Providence*, typescript copy (hereafter cited as *Annals*), 1, Archives of the Oblate Sisters of Providence.

7. John T. Gillard, *The Catholic Church and the American Negro* (Baltimore: St. Joseph's Society Press, 1929; reprint, New York: Johnson Reprint, 1968), 14–15; Gillard, *Colored Catholics*, 63, 88, 99, 76–79.

8. Current historical evidence identifying Lange's country of origin proves inconsistent. Information from the United States Census Population Schedules lists her birthplace variably as the West Indies (1850), Saint Domingo (1860), and Cuba (1870 and 1880). See U.S. Census, no. 7–10 (1850–80), Population Schedules, State of Maryland, Baltimore City, Ward 12 (1850), Ward 11 (1860–80).

9. Jean Fouchard, *Les Marrons du syllabaire: Quelques aspects du problème de l'instruction et de l'éducation des esclaves et affranchis de Saint-Domingue* (Port-au-Prince, Haiti: Editions Henri Deschamps, 1988), 67–70. I thank Doris Kadish for providing this reference.

10. Lange obituaries in the *Baltimore Sun*, February 4, 1882, and the *Baltimore Catholic Mirror*, February 11, 1882; Sr. M. Theresa Catherine Willigman, "First Foundress of the Oblates," 1, typescript copy, n.d., Archives of the Oblate Sisters of Providence; Maria M. Lannon, *Response to Love: The Story of Mary Elizabeth Lange* (Washington, D.C.: Josephite Pastoral Center, 1992), 3–4; "Where He Leads I Will Follow," (pamphlet, n.d.), 3, Archives of the Oblate Sisters of Providence.

11. Records of Confraternities: "Registre, Confrerie du Rosaire," May 30, 1813, "Elizabeth Clarisse." RG 1, Box 17, Sulpician Archives, Baltimore.

12. Willigman, "First Foundress," 8, Archives of the Oblate Sisters of Providence.

13. *Annals*, 20, 23.

14. Posey, "Unwanted Commitment," 21; Misner, *Highly Respectable*, 297.

15. Willigman, "First Foundress," 4, 5, 9, 11–12; Posey, "Unwanted Commitment," 338–39.

16. Willigman, "First Foundress," 12, 16, 12–13.

17. See August Meier and Elliott M. Rudwick, *From Plantation to Ghetto*, 3d ed. (New York: Hill and Wang, 1976), 69–71, 74–75; David Brion Davis, *The Problem of Slavery in Western Culture* (Ithaca: Cornell UP, 1966), 273–86.

18. Meier and Rudwick, *Plantation to Ghetto*, 89–90; Willard Gatewood, *Aristocrats of Color: The Black Elite, 1880–1920* (Bloomington: Indiana UP, 1990), 157–58; Christopher Phillips, "'Negroes and Other Slaves': The African-American Community of Baltimore, 1790–1860" (Ph.D. diss., University of Georgia, 1993), 36, 80–82, 126–27.

19. Willigman, "First Foundress," 13, 15.

20. Charles G. Herbermann, *The Sulpicians in the United States* (New York: Encyclopedia Press, 1916), 232–33; Sherwood, *Oblates' Hundred*, 7; Christopher Kauffman, *Tradition and Transformation in Catholic Culture: The Priests of Saint Sulpice in the United States from 1791 to the Present* (New York: Macmillan, 1988), 113–14; Joubert obituary, *Baltimore American*, November 15, 1843.

21. For a thorough discussion of the antebellum Catholic Church's position on slavery, see James Hennesey, *American Catholics: A History of the Roman Catholic Community in the United States* (New York: Oxford UP, 1981), 143–49; Richard R. Duncan, "Catholics and the Church in the Antebellum Upper South," 77–98; Randall M. Miller, "A Church in Cultural Captivity," 11–52; and Randall M. Miller, "The Failed Mission: The Catholic Church and Black Catholics in the Old South," all in *Catholics in the Old South*, ed. Randall M. Miller and Jon L. Wakelyn, 149–70; John C. Murphy, *An Analysis of the Attitudes of American Catholics toward the Immigrant and the Negro, 1825–1925* (Washington, D.C.: Catholic UP of America, 1940), 33–51, 76–79, 136–44; Cyprian Davis, *The History of Black Catholics in the United States* (New York: Crossroad, 1990), 35–57.

22. Hebermann, *Sulpicians*, 232–33; Sherwood, *Oblates' Hundred*, 7; Kauffman, *Tradition and Transformation*, 113–14; Indemnities, RG 41, Box 2, Sulpician Archives, Baltimore; "Excerpts from Louis Deluol's Diary Concerning the Oblate Sisters of Providence," comp. John W. Bowen, August 27, 1832, December 1 and 8, 1841, Sulpician Archives, Baltimore; *United States Documents in the Propaganda Fide Archives: A Calendar*, ed. Finbar Kenneally, O.F.M., et al. (Washington, D.C.: Academy of American Franciscan History, 1966–87), vol. 1, section xi, 1489; section xiii, 2059; vol. 3, 799–800, 809; vol. 4, 586, 597, 665.

23. *Annals*, 87; Kenneally et al., *Calendar*, 3:799–800, 809; 4:582, 585–86, 597, 665; "Deluol's Diary," December 1 and 8, 1841.

24. "History: Newspapers; Undated, 1829—General," in *The Religious Cabinet: A Monthly Periodical* (Baltimore: John Murphy, 1842), Folder in C/OSP, Josephite Archives, Baltimore.

25. Kauffman, *Tradition and Transformation*, xiv, xvi, 31, 55, 58–66, 71–72, 110–11, 157.

26. Kauffman, *Tradition and Transformation*, 120.

27. Kauffman, *Tradition and Transformation,* 119, 120.

28. Thomas Spalding, *The Premier See: A History of the Archdiocese of Baltimore, 1789–1989* (Baltimore: Johns Hopkins UP, 1989), 128.

29. Posey, "Unwanted Commitment," 117.

30. Kauffman, *Tradition and Transformation,* 114; Spalding, *Premier See,* 108; Misner, "Highly Respectable," 62; Posey, "Unwanted Commitment," 117.

31. Ellin M. Kelly, *Numerous Choirs: A Chronicle of Elizabeth Bayley Seton and Her Daughters,* vol. 1, *The Seton Years, 1774–1821* (Evansville, Ind.: Mater Dei Provincialate, 1981), 268.

32. Kelly, *Numerous Choirs,* 243–80; Posey, "Unwanted Commitment," 314–25.

33. Joubert to Kohlmann, March 10, 1833, *Propaganda Fide Archives,* Congressi: America-Antille, 1820–34, vol. 4, folios 490r to 493r, microfilm, University of Notre Dame Archives; Davis, *History of Black Catholics,* 19; *Annals,* 26–27, 32.

34. "Registre, Confrairie du Scapulaire," July 17, 1808, "Marie Magdelaine–N[egress]–Joubert," Sulpician Archives, Baltimore.

35. Sherwood, *Oblates' Hundred,* 30–31, 108; Lannon, *Response to Love,* 28–29; Sr. M. Immaculata Gillespie, *Mother M. Theresa Maxis Duchemin* (Scranton, Pa.: Marywood College, 1945), 13–24; Sr. M. Rosalita Kelly, *No Greater Service: The History of the Congregation of the Sisters, Servants of the Immaculate Heart of Mary, Monroe, Michigan: 1845–1945* (Detroit: Congregation of the Sisters of the Immaculate Heart, 1948), 37–46; Sr. Maria Alma, *Thou, Lord, Art My Hope! The Life of Mother M. Theresa: A Pioneer of the Sisters, Servants of the Immaculate Heart of Mary* (Lancaster, Pa.: Dolphin Press, 1961), 1–33; Joseph B. Code, "Mother Theresa Maxis Duchemin," *America* 74 (December 22, 1945): 317–19; Sr. Diane Edward Shea and Sr. Marita Constance Supan, "Apostolate of the Archives—God's Mystery through History," *Josephite Harvest* 85 (1983): 10–13; Sisters, Servants of the Immaculate Heart of Mary, *Building Sisterhood: A Feminist History of the Sisters, Servants of the Immaculate Heart of Mary* (Syracuse: Syracuse UP, 1997), 5–9, 31–73.

36. *Annals,* 4.

37. The manuscript notes, known as the *West Chester Notes,* dictated by Sister Mary James to Sister Maria Alma, February 22, 1920, recalled these conversations.

38. *West Chester Notes,* typescript copy, 2, Villa Maria House of Studies, West Chester Motherhouse Archives, Sisters, Servants of the Immaculate Heart of Mary.

39. *West Chester Notes,* 3.

40. Moses B. Goodwin, "Schools and Education of the Colored Population," in *Special Report of the United States Commissioner of Education on the Condition and Improvement of Public Schools in the District of Columbia* (Washington, D.C.: Government Printing Office, 1871), 205.

41. "Auxiliatrice," June 9, 1822; "Scapulaire," September 17, 1826, Sulpician Archives, Baltimore.

42. Sherwood, *Oblates' Hundred,* 5; *Annals,* 18; Willigman, "First Foundress", 10; *Annals,* 15; *Metropolitan Catholic Almanac and Laity's Directory* (Baltimore: Fielding Lucas, 1834–57), 1834, vol. 70.

43. *Annals,* 13, 31, 59, 66, 70, 23, 49, 56.

44. *Annals,* 71, 72; Hebermann, *Sulpicians,* 233.

45. Misner, *Highly Respectable,* 48; Sherwood, *Oblates' Hundred,* 108; Spalding, *Premier See,* 501 n 32.

46. *Annals,* 83.

47. *Annals,* 2.

48. "Souvenir of Love," manuscript copy, 57, Archives of the Oblate Sisters of Providence; *Annals,* 85–86.

49. *Annals,* 80, 70, 78, 82, 93.

50. *Annals,* 2.

51. *Annals,* 80.

52. Sherwood, *Oblates' Hundred,* 98; *Annals,* 116–17; *West Chester Notes,* 4.

53. Kelly, *No Greater Service,* 45.

54. "Memories of Sister Marie Therese Duchemin," typescript copy, n.d., 4, Archives of the Oblate Sisters of Providence.

55. Gillespie, *Mother M. Theresa,* 14; Alma, *Thou, Lord,* 7–8; Gillespie, *Mother M. Theresa,* 15.

56. Gillespie, *Mother M. Theresa,* 24; Shea and Supan, "Apostolate of the Archives," 12; Code, "Mother Theresa Maxis," 318.

57. Kelly, *No Greater Service,* 91, 764 n 36.

THREE

Caribbean
Perspectives

Creole, the Language of Slavery

ALBERT VALDMAN

The field of pidgin and creole studies, subsumed under the French-derived term *Creolistics* (*la créolistique*), has become in recent years one of the most active areas of linguistic inquiry. The term *Creole* is derived from a Portuguese word meaning "raised in the home," and it was loaned into Spanish to denote persons or animals of European origin born and raised in the overseas colonies. The notion of mixture has formed the central semantic component of the word ever since it was applied to language. It appears in all dictionary definitions— for example, that provided by the *American Heritage Dictionary:* "A type of mixed language that develops when dominant and subordinate groups that speak different languages have prolonged contact, incorporating the basic features of the dominant language with the grammar and an admixture of words from the subordinate language, and becoming the native tongue of the subordinate group." [1] This definition fails to capture features that are specific to these languages, for it could be applied to most languages of the world. Certainly English, with its largely Latin-derived lexicon and Germanic base, fits the criterion of mixture. The definition also suggests that a language can be identified as a Creole on the basis of showing particular linguistic features. In fact, with regard to all aspects of their structure, Creoles do not differ from other natural languages. There are no typological features of, for example, Haitian Creole (HC) that mark it specifically as a Creole.

Creole languages can be identified as such only on the basis of historical evidence: they are languages whose origin and date of birth can be traced with great precision, within a period of about fifty years. Whereas we cannot pinpoint within a period of one or two centuries when *oïl* dialects, the ancestors of present-day Standard French (SF), emerged from Vulgar Latin, we know that

Saint-Domingue Creole, the ancestor of present-day HC, was formed between about 1650, when French settlers established themselves on Tortuga Island, and the development of large-scale plantations on the western end of Hispaniola toward the end of the seventeenth century. Most of the languages clearly identified as Creoles are linked with the worldwide expansion of Western European powers (Portugal, Spain, France, the Netherlands, and England) from the sixteenth to the eighteenth centuries, and in particular with the establishment of plantocratic societies. In their most perfected form—the most prosperous was the French colony of Saint-Domingue, the Pearl of the Antilles that generated more than half of France's foreign trade—these societies were based on the agro-industrial production of cash crops (indigo, coffee, cotton, and sugar) with the aid of slave labor imported from Africa. There is then an intimate link between Creoles and the type of slavery practiced by Western European powers in the mercantilistic age: Creoles are literally languages of slavery.

From the emergence of creole studies in the late nineteenth century through the writings of the eminent German Romanist Hugo Schuchardt, theories about the genesis of creole languages rather than descriptive and comparative work have dominated the field. Until recent years, Creolists have paid insufficient attention to the reconstruction of the sociocultural matrix in which creole languages originated. An example of the type of reductionist matrix posited by early Creolists is offered by Suzanne Comhaire-Sylvain, a Haitian linguist whose Sorbonne dissertation was directed by the French Africanist Lilias Homburger. It should be added that to Comhaire-Sylvain's credit, hers was one of the first solid pieces of descriptive research on Haitian Creole. In the introduction to her book, she guardedly places the birth of the language off the northwest coast of Hispaniola on Tortuga Island, a den of Dutch, English, and French pirates who preyed upon the Spanish galleons loaded with the gold and silver of the Incas and Aztecs that sailed through the Windward Passage between Cuba and Hispaniola: "In my opinion, Haitian Creole was probably born on Tortuga Island during the seventeenth century, beginning on the day when a Negro slave decided that he would try to speak the language of his master, the French freebooter, in order to make himself understood. There was a mutual attempt toward accommodation."[2]

This somewhat romantic view of the genesis of Creoles is reductionist in several ways. First, language contact is not a one-on-one affair but involves the interaction of whole social groups. If pirates owned slaves, it was not primarily as cheap labor but as captured chattel to be sold. Second, the agro-industrial sugar plantations required an extensive infrastructure that could not be improvised in the pirate stronghold of Tortuga Island, nor in the buccaneer establishments across the Windward Passage on the coast of Hispaniola where pairs of Europeans (*matelots*), sometimes aided by a white bondsmen (*engagé*) or an African slave, cured meat (*boucaner*) for eventual sale to pirates. Third, Saint-Domingue was a relatively late colony. Its establishment was preceded by the colonization of St. Kitts (Saint-Christophe) around the early 1620s and of Martinique and Guadeloupe a dozen years later. The first colonists on Tortuga were French settlers who had been evicted from St. Kitts by the English with whom they had shared the island. In all probability it was on St. Kitts that the first French-based Creole of the Caribbean originated. From that focal point—at least in the form of a model if not as a fully constituted language—it was transported to later French colonies in the Caribbean.

Robert Chaudenson divides the development of plantocratic societies into two phases: *société d'habitation* and *société de plantation*.[3] In the former social context, because of the small size of productive units (agricultural or other), the slaves interacted with Europeans and had ready access to their speech, whatever that might have been. As the comparative demographic figures in Table 1 (part a) show, it was not until the formal cession of the western part of Hispaniola to France according to the terms of the Treaty of Ryswick (1697), more than thirty years after the main influx of French settlements in that area, that the servile population of Saint-Domingue outnumbered the Europeans. Thus, an indigenous Saint-Domingue Creole could not have been formed until the beginning of the eighteenth century. Table 1 (part b) also shows the gradual increase in imported labor after the *société d'habitation* was established.

The figures in Table 1 (part c) also indicate that the proportion of the free white and servile black populations remained in balance in Louisiana during the French and Spanish colonial periods, and that Louisiana did not become a *société de plantation*, a plantation colony proper, until its sale to the United States in 1803.

Figure 1 presents a model for the diffusion of French-based Creoles in the New World. The first creolized variety of French probably originated in the first French Antillean settlement on St. Kitts. That pre-Creole developed from the attempt of slaves to acquire vernacular and regional varieties of French, with some possible influence from a rudimentary trade jargon used to communicate with the Carib inhabitants of the Lesser Antilles. That form of speech was exported to Guadeloupe, Martinique, and possibly French Guiana, where it stabilized into first-generation Creoles. This is indicated by the heavy solid lines in the figure. From Guadeloupe and Martinique, the Creole was exported

TABLE 1

Demographics of French Plantocratic Societies

a) *Saint-Domingue*				
Year	Whites	Slaves	Free Blacks Mulattoes	Total
1665		1,500		1,500
1681	4,336	2,312		6,648
1697	8,000	5,000	500	13,500
1700	4,000	9,000		13,000
1715	6,600	30,651	1,404	38,655
1739	11,540	117,411	3,588	132,539
1754	14,253	172,188	4,911	191,352
1775	32,650	249,098	7,055	288,803
1784	20,229	298,079	13,257	331,565
1789	30,831	434,429	24,848	490,108

b) *Estimated Number of Slaves Imported into Saint-Domingue*					
1651–1675	1676–1700	1701–1720	1741–1760	1761–1780	1781–1791
3,000	71,600	70,600	79,400	158,800	286,000

c) *Louisiana*								
	1710	1721	1727	1732	1741	1746	1763	1788
Servile	10	533	1,561	3,600	4,000	4,730	4,598	20,673
Free		1,082	1,450	1,720	1,200	3,650	3,650	18,737

Sources: Robert Cornevin, *Haïti, que sais-je?* (Paris: PU de France, 1982); Philip Curtin, *The Atlantic Slave Trade* (Madison: U of Wisconsin P, 1969); Orlando Patterson, *Slavery and Social Death* (Cambridge: Harvard UP, 1982); John V. Singler, "African Influence upon Afro-American Language Varieties," in *Africanisms in Afro-American Language Varieties*, ed. Salikoko Mufwene (Athens: U of Georgia P, 1992); Gwendolyn Midlo Hall, *Africans in Colonial Louisiana: The Development of Afro-Creole Culture in the Eighteenth Century* (Baton Rouge: Louisiana State UP, 1992).

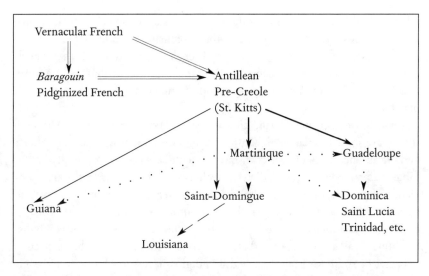

Figure 1. Diffusion of French-Based Creoles in the New World

to the neighboring islands of Dominica and Saint-Lucia, as well as to Saint-Domingue and more distant islands of the eastern Caribbean, such as Trinidad and Grenada. These, then, are second-generation French-based Creoles; this is indicated by the dotted lines. As the broken line indicates, Saint-Domingue Creole influenced the development of Louisiana Creole, a third-generation Creole. Because Louisiana was settled late, it reflects features of the early forms of French-based Creoles of the Caribbean basin. The light solid lines between St. Kitts and Saint-Domingue and French Guiana suggest that the Creoles of these territories also reflect earlier features that developed in that original French settlement. The specific features of the various French-based Creoles result from complex restructuring determined by such factors as the African languages spoken by the slaves, the varieties of French used by the Europeans, and the slaves' access to these French varieties as determined by social and political conditions, and, centrally, by the relative proportion of the servile and European components of the population.[4]

To summarize, any explanation of the genesis of the languages that are a direct result of the particular form of slavery associated with the mercantilistic European agro-industrial colonial establishments must take into account the cultural, social, and political conditions that existed in these establishments.

Therefore, the reconstruction of the sociohistorical context of French plantocratic societies is the most urgent task that Creolists must undertake.

This essay focuses on two aspects of French-based Creoles as they developed in French plantocratic societies: the nature of the contribution of African
languages to the emergent languages and the function of Creole once it had
become established.

First, however, some clarification is needed about terminology. Although
they share some fundamental features, such as the structure of the verb phrase
and the absence of gender, French-based Creoles are no more mutually intelli-
gible than so-called Occitan dialects such as Gascon, Auvergnat, Languedo-
cian, and modern Provençal. The reason the latter speech varieties are viewed
as dialects of the same language rather than autonomous languages rests on historical and ideological grounds, as is always the case in the troublesome distinction between language and dialects. At one point in history, the vernacular
varieties of southern France existed in a diglossic relationship with the same
culturally dominant language, literary Provençal, the language of the Trouba-
dours. In addition, on the basis of shared linguistic and cultural traits and historical links, particularly subjugation by Northern French warlords during the
Albigensian Crusade, such Occitanists as Robert Lafont have constructed a
mythical entity, Occitania. No such strong cultural and ideological link exists
among the territories stretching from the Indian Ocean to Louisiana, the
Caribbean, and the coast of South America where French-based Creoles are
spoken. Nonetheless, despite great differences in their present demographic
makeup and culture, all these territories are united by their common origin in
French plantocratic societies. The same general sociocultural matrix served as
the melting pot in which a language shared by all members of these societies
developed, and it is natural that the same term was used to refer to that language: *le créole*.

Except for Dominica and Saint-Lucia, whose inhabitants refer to the ancestral vernacular as *patois*, the term *kreyòl* is used by native speakers to refer to
the language. Some well-intentioned linguists, most of whom are not members
of creole-speaking communities but who are seeking to cleanse the term of its
deprecatory association with slavery and with admixture, prefer labels that refer only to the territory: Saint-Lucian, Mauritian, Louisianan, Haitian, and so
forth.[5] Not wishing to be *plus royaliste que le roi*, I prefer to adhere to local usage. In this essay the term *creole* refers to French-based Creoles in general and
the more descriptive labels associating the term with the territory to refer to
specific languages, for example, Haitian Creole (HC).

CREOLE: AFRICAN GRAMMAR CLOTHED IN FRENCH VOCABULARY

Because most present-day speakers of Creole are descendants of African slaves, the conventional wisdom affirms that it is a mixed language deriving its lexicon from French, the language imposed by the colonial masters, and its grammar from the slaves' native African tongues. This view appears all the more plausible in light of the survival of African traits in other private cultural spheres: witness the preservation of animist religions in the form of vodun in Haiti and Santeria in Cuba. Gwendolyn Midlo Hall offers solid evidence for an unusually cohesive and heavily Africanized culture in lower Louisiana reflected by the Brer Rabbit and Brer Bouki folktales and a cuisine making heavy use of *gumbo*, the term of African origin for okra.[6]

The African origin of creole grammar is not a novel point of view. More than a hundred years ago Lucien Adam launched the notion of hybridization in his book *Les Idiomes négro-aryen et malayo-aryen*. The distinct racist overtones of the time reflected by the title also colored the author's definition of creole languages on the whole. For Adam, these languages represented an "adaptation of French, English, and Spanish to the phonetic and grammatical mind-set of a linguistically inferior race."[7]

Almost seventy-five years later, in one of the earliest descriptions of her native language, the Martinican *béké* (white) Elodie Jourdain characterized it in terms that are today even more offensively racist. She announced that her book purported to show what became of a great language of civilization as it passed through "black brains and throats."[8] An ideologically more neutral form of the Africanist hypothesis was proposed by Suzanne Comhaire-Sylvain, who in her description of the language systematically compared its features to that of Ewe, a Kwa language spoken in present-day Benin (formerly Dahomey). She concluded that although the influence of French syntax is evident, that of African languages was preponderant, and she characterized HC as French vocabulary shaped by the mold of African syntax.[9] More recently, the Québécois linguist Claire Lefebvre has attempted to demonstrate that HC derives from a relexification of Fongbe, another Kwa language.[10]

Arguably the vocabulary of French-based creole languages is derived mainly from French. Even in HC, which contains many African-based words from vodun, more than 90 percent of the vocabulary can be traced to present-day SF or regional northern French dialects.[11] There is, however, considerable debate about the source of the grammar. So far, no scholar has demonstrated, with support from carefully documented comparative studies, an irrefutable link between the grammar of a specific African language or groups of African languages and that of a particular French-based creole language or this entire group of Creoles. In judicial terms, one would say that the evidence for the African origin of creole grammar is largely circumstantial: the languages were created mainly by African slaves, and it stands to reason that they should show the influence of their various native languages.

The offensively couched assertions by Adam and Jourdain, as well as the views of modern-day substratists (sometimes also termed "substratomaniacs"), rest on the reductionist comparison of Creole with SF. Indeed, when compared with SF, Creole appears extremely deviant. But the linguistic distance between the two languages shrinks if instead one chooses as the starting point vernacular varieties of French. In the two sample sentences below, Louisiana Creole (LC) and HC sentences are compared with SF and vernacular spoken French forms and structures; vernacular variants are shown in parentheses. These examples demonstrate that LC is closer to French and that, with regard to both lexicon and grammar, vernacular forms constitute more plausible models for the Creole forms.

LC	Fo tu le piti vj⁓e isit astèr la.	"Il faut que tous les enfants viennent ici maintenant. (Faut que tous les petits vientici à c't heure-là/à ce coup-là.)"
HC	Se pu tu piti jo vini isit kunje a.	
LC	Mo va kupe zo lalãg.	"Je couperai votre langue (moi je vas couper à vous-autres la langue)."
HC	M a kupe lãg nou.	

It is also unlikely that in the seventeenth- and eighteenth-century French plantation colonies the Europeans with whom slaves were in contact spoke anything that resembled the *Bon Usage* that Vaugelas offered as a model for cultivated French people.[12] In the report that drew conclusions from the linguistic survey he had undertaken between 1791 and 1794, the abbé Grégoire underscored the obstacles faced in spreading the ideology of the Revolution when fewer than one-sixth of the population of France mastered SF.[13] Although many of the colonists were not native speakers of northern French regional dialects (*patois*), their everyday speech reflected these dialects and the plebeian vernacular speech, thus differing markedly from that of the *Bon Usage*. It is the former variety of French rather than the latter that formed the speech input the slaves transformed into Creole.

It is undeniable that there are features of Creole that appear to be modeled on African forms. But in many instances these features seem to have developed by the convergence of features of vernacular or regional French and African ones. One such example is the postposition of determiners that appears to be modeled on Ewe and various Western African languages, such as Igbo and Yoruba. The following examples show the postposed demonstrative determiner of HC and LC with the corresponding feature of Ewe and Yoruba of which it appears to be a calque. For the sake of convenience, I provide the English and French equivalents for the Creoles and a translation that gives the meaning of each constituent element for the African languages:

HC	kay-sa-a 'that house'; Fr. 'cette maison *(là)*'
LC	kab~an *sa la* (mez~ø *sa a la*)
Ewe	afe *a*
Yoruba	ile *yen*
	house *that*
HC	moun *sila yo* 'these people'; Fr. 'ces gens *(là)*'
LC	mun *sa je*
Ewe	ame *sia wo*
	people *that Plural*

The colonial vernacular provided the servile learners two cues for the demonstrative semantic notion, as shown in the following Cajun French example:

Est-ce que *ce* chemin-*là* est mauvais?   *Is this(-here) road bad?*[14]

Faced with the task of acquiring the colonial vernacular without input enriched by focus on form, the learners did not extract the phonologically weak and semantically depleted preposed *ce*. In their approximative system they generalized instead the postposed deictic particle, *là*.

If we view the languages the slaves carried over from Africa as a sort of filter that screened the input to which they were exposed in the plantation colonies, it is not surprising that the presence of the postposed deictic—*là*—would lead them to interpret it as equivalent to the matched features with which they were familiar. The restructuring of the French input by convergence is much more complex than the mere transfer of native language patterns or, as Comhaire-Sylvain and Lefebvre would have it, relexification.

Nonetheless, the power of the filtering effect of African languages should not be underestimated. In HC possessive determiners are also postposed:

chat mwen yo   Fr. 'mes chats, les chats à moi'
    My cats, those cats of mine.

Although the HC construction may be modeled on the vernacular constructions *les chats à moi* or *mes chats à moi*, the influence of the African model undoubtedly played a determining role in the development of the noun determiner system of HC. For example, in both HC and Ewe, the definite article appears at some distance from the noun it modifies, for example, at the end of a relative clause:

> HC   oto li vann mouen *an* 'the car which he sold me'
>   car he sold me *DEFINITE*
>   Fr. '*la* voiture (l'auto) qu'il m'a vendue'
> Ewe evu si wòdra nam *la*
>   vehicle which he-sold to-me *DEFINITE*

The marking of definiteness on clauses represents a deeper level structural model than the postposition of noun determiners, and its African origin appears undeniable.

The importance of also comparing Creole to regional varieties of French that were transported to the colonies is demonstrated by the LC interrogative pronoun *kofè* (*cofè*) 'why' that M. Roy Harris traces to the combination 'what' + 'make' of the Kwa languages and Yoruba. To strengthen the case, he points out that it is also reflected in Atlantic English-based Creoles, *wa mek* in Jamaican Creole, and *mek* in Gullah. However, Harris also finds the combination *quoi* 'what' + *faire* 'make' in the western French dialect Saintongeais, whose influence on Cajun French via Acadian French has been established, as well as in Cajun French, for example, *Quoi faire vous dit ça?* 'Why do you say that?' [15]

A syntactic feature of French-based Creoles for which a stronger case can be made for an influence from African languages is that involving serial verbs or "serialization." In serialization, the meaning of the combination of verbs cannot be derived from the individual meaning of its constituent parts. One of the verbs, usually a verb of motion, adds a nuance to the main verb. For example, in the HC combinations *mennen ale* '[to lead] + [to go]' = 'take someone away', *pote ale* '[to carry] + [to go]' = 'to carry away', *pote vire* '[to carry] + [to turn]' = 'to bring back', the second verb, the verb of motion, indicates the directionality of the action and thus functions like an adverb in French. In another type of serialization, the verb *ba* 'to give' carries the benefactive meaning and functions like the English preposition 'for' or the French *pour*. This is similar to *na* in Ewe:

> HC   M kuit manje *ba* ou.   'I cooked the food for you'; I cook food
>   give you

Fr   J'ai cuit la nourriture (le manger) pour toi.
Ewe   meda nu *na* wo   I-cook food give you

A third type of serialization in HC takes the form of lexicalized combinations that are best treated as idiomatic combinations rather than serial verbs proper: *mòde soufle* '[bite + blow (as does a rat)] to act as a hypocrite', *rete pran* '[stay + take, endure] to tolerate', *mache bwete* '[walk + limp] to limp'.

The fact that serialization occurs in a wide variety of languages of the world, those of Papua New Guinea and East Asian languages like Mandarin, Thai, and Vietnamese, as well as the Kwa and Benue-Congo languages of Africa, has led some Creolists, notably Derek Bickerton, to postulate that it is a manifestation of a language universal whose appearance in creole languages stems from the special situation of language contact that spawned them.[16] But this account does not explain why serialization appears to be absent from the Indian Ocean Creoles whose slave populations did not originate in regions of Africa in which Kwa and Benue-Congo were spoken.[17] It also should be noted that the French input provided a target that could be reinterpreted in light of African serialization: combinations such as *il vient manger* in which *venir* serves as the directional pivot for the focal verb *manger*.

For the late French Africanist Gabriel Manessy, syntactic differences between serialization in these African languages and those of Atlantic Creoles suggest that the presence of this feature in the latter languages does not reflect direct transfer or relexification but rather the slaves' superimposition on the input of a cognitive mode, a particular manner of structuring experience characteristic of a large area of Africa.[18]

Many aspects of creole culture such as music, folklore, and food have their roots in the slaves' native cultures, but the evidence that linguistic patterns were transferred as directly is not overwhelming. However, this is not to deny any African influence. A dozen years ago, when talking about the Creole of his island at the annual meeting of the American Association of Teachers of French in Fort-de-France, the great Martinican writer Aimé Césaire gave what stands as the most profound statement about the African element in Creole: "The body of the creole language is French, but its soul is African."[19] The mistake many linguists have made is to equate the soul of a language with its grammar. Hall comes closer to the truth when she points out that members of the Louisiana Creole community, which includes whites as well as blacks, share speech rhythms and intonation and ways of using language, such as the use of proverbs.[20] It is perhaps these aspects of language and language use and a particular type of cognitive organization underlying syntax and semantics, all of which have received scant attention from linguists, that constitute the soul of Creole, and it is there that the permanence of African modes of expression and communication might be sought.

The nonpreservation of African languages constitutes another puzzling aspect of plantocratic society from a linguistic point of view. In some colonies, such as Saint-Domingue, the slaves constituted the overwhelming majority of the population—more than 90 percent of the approximately 500,000 inhabitants at the end of colonial rule. The high death rate and low birth rate in the servile population required constant importation of new slaves. For example, in Surinam, an estimated 200,000 Africans were imported between 1650 and 1815, but only 36,000 remained in 1853. Father Labat estimated a 33 percent loss after six years among slaves engaged in construction and agriculture in colonial Martinique; according to Gabriel Debien, the Cottineau sugar plantation in Saint-Domingue had to renew 75 percent of its 150 slaves in the thirteen years between 1765 and 1778.[21]

Two additional factors that conspired to maintain low rates of reproduction among the servile population were the low proportion of children and the abortive practices of female slaves. For example, on the Ramire plantation in Cayenne in 1690 only 6 of the 104 slaves were children. In the minds of plantation owners the prized acquisition was the *pièce d'Inde*, a six-foot man between eighteen and thirty years old. As is demonstrated by current immigration patterns in the United States, the constant renewal of an immigrant group helps to preserve the functional use of its language and guarantees its maintenance. The constant resupplying of new slaves, the bossales, should have helped maintain the African languages as a means of communication and expression within subgroups of the slave population.

The formation of maroon communities would seem to have created a favorable environment for the maintenance of the native tongues of the escaping slaves. But, with the exception of the Coromantin maroon kingdom in Jamaica, where Twi was the primary everyday language, creole languages served as the dominant vernacular for these groups.[22] The Bush negroes descended from slaves who had fled to the jungle from the plantations established in Dutch-governed Surinam by Portuguese Sephardic Jews founded the most autonomous maroon communities. Yet their languages, Saramaccan and Djuka, which though distinct from Sranan, the English-based creole language produced in the coast plantations, were Creoles that do not appear to be particularly more Africanized than other Atlantic English-based Creoles.[23] It seems that, perhaps with the exception of the Coromantins, the maroon groups did not intend to create African communities in the New World. The Bambara insurgents who allied themselves with Amerindians to wipe out the French settlement in Pointe Coupée, Louisiana, planned to seize control of the colony, enslave the other servile groups, and substitute black for white power.[24] Presumably, they would have maintained Creole as the language of communication along with other colonial institutions, just as the leaders of the slave revolt in Saint-Domingue reestablished the colonial plantation system and maintained French, the prestige language of the former colony, as the language of administration and education.

It is generally held that plantation owners carefully separated slaves from the same ethnic group in order to prevent revolts. Although this policy was recommended by the trading companies and colonial officials, it proved to be counterproductive and was not followed by plantation managers. For members of the same work teams (*ateliers*)—especially those entrusted with cultivation and work in sugar mills (*grands ateliers*)—to work effectively together, they needed to communicate. For that reason, plantation managers strove for homogeneity in the work force and selected slaves from the same *nation*. In addition, there developed stereotypic notions about characteristics of the members of various nations and their suitability for certain tasks: the Senegals and Minas made good domestics, the Aradas excelled in agriculture, and the Congos were hard working and docile.

The various aspects of the plantocratic system discussed so far suggest that African languages were used in the colonies as long as the slave trade continued. There exists plentiful evidence attesting to the use of these languages among the slaves. Walter Rodney states that in Brazil up to the beginning of the nineteenth century, Kumbundu, a Bantu language from Angola, and Yoruba were more widely spoken by the slaves than Portuguese. Labat relates that he learned what he terms Arada (undoubtedly a dialect of Ewe) in order to communicate with *bossale* slaves. Finally, Marcel d'Ans describes how in 1812 Pétion had soldiers (Ibos, Congos, Aradas) stationed on the ramparts of Port-au-Prince address the besieging soldiers of Christophe in African languages to urge them to join him.[25]

African languages were also maintained because their use was an integral part of the *seasoning* process, the progressive acculturation and socialization of the *bossale* slaves. Following a custom that was part of slavery in Africa, these slaves were entrusted to the care of older acculturated slaves who, among other things, transmitted the rudiments of religion in a shared African language. Debien cites a directive sent by a certain Stanislas Foäche to the managers of absentee-owner plantations that he administered in which he stresses the importance of nurturing in the seasoning process, which, according to him, lasts a full year.[26]

Another puzzling aspect of the linguistic situation of the plantocratic society is the absence of *pidgins,* that is, rudimentary languages used as vehicular languages by groups speaking different languages. According to Manessy, Mandingo traders had gone deep into the West African forests since the Middle Ages and used a pidginized form of their language, related to present-day Dyula.[27] Other vehicular languages existed in Africa before the arrival of European traders: Kissour (a variety of Songhay) in the Niger valley, Bambara and Soninke on the Upper Senegal River, and Kituba and Monokituba in the Congo.

Slaves remained up to several months in the factories or on the ships awaiting a full human consignment before they set out on a sea crossing that could last up to four months. Several Creolists, notably Goodman and McWhorter, do in fact trace the origin of the Atlantic Creoles to pidgins acquired in Africa by slaves.[28] Manessy, however, rejects this view by arguing that although pidgins such as Tok Pisin develop among indentured laborers, they are excluded in plantocratic societies by the very nature of slavery in Africa. The late Africanist points out that many of the slaves exported to plantation colonies had already experienced slavery as governed by African norms.[29] Upon being removed from their own group either by force or transaction, slaves lost their original social status and expected to be socialized into the dominant group. In particular, they had to learn the language of their masters, just as the child learns to speak, and they expected to be entrusted into the care of an older slave whom they respected as they would their father. The seasoning the plantation slaves would undergo after the sea voyage mirrored the socialization into a new African group, as did some of the practices of the slave trade: the shaving of the head, nudity, a new set of clothing, baptism, and a new name.

One distinctive feature of the plantocratic linguistic situation in the French colonies, as opposed to the English ones, for example, was the acquisition and use of Creole by the dominant European group. There are numerous statements by contemporaries that indicate its generalized use among the Creoles, that is, all inhabitants born in the islands. Moreau de Saint-Méry, who described himself as a *Créole* born in Martinique, characterizes it as the general vernacular of

Saint-Domingue: "It is in that language . . . that Creoles [of all colors] like to converse and the Negroes do not use any other [language] among themselves."[30] A foreign visitor, the Swiss Girod-Chantrans, was scandalized upon hearing the daughters of the best families of the colony use in ordinary conversation what he considered to be an uncouth jargon invented for the use of the blacks. The nostalgic anonymous Saint-Domingue refugee who, in Philadelphia, edited the song and light verse compendium *Idylles et chansons ou essais de poésie créole* stressed that the language was spoken by blacks, Creoles, and most of the inhabitants of the American islands. That a mastery of Creole serves as a symbol of colonial, versus metropolitan, identity is suggested by Moreau de Saint-Méry's assertion that it could never be acquired fully by outsiders. The generalized use of Creole as the colonial vernacular is reflected in its retention as the private language by present-day white speakers in Louisiana and the island of Saint-Bart.[31]

Dany Bébel-Gisler argues that Creole, together with other cultural phenomena such as dancing, represents a pocket of the slaves' resistance against total acculturation.[32] Mervyn Alleyne attributes this resistance to the field slaves who, unlike their house slave brethren, enjoyed little social intercourse with Europeans. For him, there developed among field slaves and those who identified with them a group consciousness expressing itself by "positive refusals to become totally acculturated to the European way."[33] In the linguistic domain, these refusals could take the form of the preservation of African languages or the development of a variety of Creole distinct from that used by the whites.

In the literature on early stages of French-based Creoles there are allusions to coexisting varieties situated on a continuum ranging from that most distant from French, *le gros créole*, to that which shares many features with it, *le créole de salon*.[34] This continuum corresponds to the one existing today between *kreyòl rèk*, spoken by rural monolingual Haitians, and *kreyòl swa*, the frenchified variety found among urban bilinguals.[35] The few available texts from the late Saint-Domingue colonial period do not reflect the distinction between *gros créole* and *créole de salon*. In any case, the range of genres represented is too narrow; these texts consist of either light verse (e.g., *Idylles et chansons ou essais de poésie créole*) or official proclamations ostensibly translated from French:

Proclamation officielle, Novembre 1801 (17 Brumaire An 19)
    Read this proclamation that the First Consul, Bonaparte, sends for your attention, You will see that he wishes that Negroes remain free. He is going to maintain trade and agriculture, because you should know

that without that the colony cannot prosper. He will fulfill his promise; it's a crime if you have doubts about what he promised you in his proclamation.[36]

The only text that represents speech is a one-act play authored by Christophe's secretary and court poet, Juste Chanlatte, comte de Rosiers, to celebrate a visit by the king to Cape Haitian, *L'Entrée du roi dans sa capitale en janvier 1818.* Chanlatte displays remarkable linguistic virtuosity by portraying various social categories with different speech varieties: bourgeois and noble characters are made to speak French, a British officer a foreigner's broken French, and the two main protagonists, the maid Marguerite and the smith Valentin, Creole. In the extract below, Valentin describes the song he intends to compose in honor of Christophe to his lover Marguerite and then responds to Marguerite's reproaches:

> We are so consumed with desire and impatience that I think that we are all going to lose our minds; and my heart is throbbing, it's delirious, just like the first time that my eyes met yours . . . it's quite a composition he is going to compose in his head, so much do I want the birds in the woods to stop singing so that they may hear me sing. . . .
>
> . . . You are always reproaching me reproaches and it breaks my heart. You have already filled your head with a thousand wild dreams, a thousand fictions that have neither head nor tail. Hey! How am I able to forget Marguerite, that beautiful young girl who gave me her heart and her hand? No, my dear friend, that's not possible, I'll always love you.[37]

Interestingly, when Chanlatte represents Valentin's song, to signal the shift from the informal to the formal style, he does not switch to French or a more frenchified variety of Creole—the so-called *créole de salon*—but he imitates the dialect of Molière's peasant in Don Juan: "God! What a day! Oh! What a show! And what delicious pleasure! To our eyes it's like a miracle. So beautiful, good, gracious are they. We're going to see our Monarch, our Monarch and our Queen. The beautiful little crown prince, and his sisters too." [38]

From a linguistic perspective, slavery in the Francophone world was characterized by the emergence of a new language, Creole. Although it does represent the attempt on the part of foreign learners to acquire vernacular and dialectal varieties of French, Creole is not a reduced language formed by superimposing African grammar on French lexical items. In its early manifestations, it was akin to the highly variable approximative forms of French devised by immigrant workers with limited access to native well-formed speech. As it became the main medium for communication on the part of the servile population of plantocratic societies for interacting both with French speakers and with fellow Africans, Creole underwent a dynamic process of restructuring and complexification, as well as lexical enrichment. At the lexical level, the French contribution to Creole is readily observable. As is the case with all overseas varieties of French, however, Creole shows numerous differences from SF traceable to vernacular or dialectal sources, to internal creation, and to borrowing from other languages, some of which were transmitted through the intermediary of what may be termed Colonial French, a type of French that was also highly variable. At the grammatical level, the source of particular creole features cannot be readily determined. Most of the function words are of clearly identifiable French origin, although their structural role and their meaning reflect convergences between those of vernacular or dialectal French and African languages, incorporation of African features, or, as is the case for most of them, original creations. In their present form, the phonological, grammatical, and semantic systems of Creole are as well integrated and adequate as those of other natural languages.

Interestingly, it appears that in French plantocratic societies, Creole assumed the function of vernacular shared by all social subgroups of these societies, and it came to mark colonial as opposed to metropolitan identity. Today, the various French-based Creoles, although they are still called Creole (*kreyòl*) by their speakers, are associated with territorial identity: Guadeloupean, Mauritian, Seychellois, and so on. Everywhere, however, they remain the low language in a diglossic situation, where Standard French or a local variant of it conserves its status as the dominant language suitable for administration, education, and belles lettres. In some areas, such as Mauritius, the Seychelles, and the British-administered West Indies, French has ceded its dominant place to English, but its diglossic relationship with Creole remains. Finally, in the English-dominant regions, notably Dominica and Saint-Lucia, Creole, labeled *patois*, is losing ground as the main vernacular to a creolized form of English.

The Seychelles and Haiti represent a special case, for the governments of these two countries have formally recognized Creole as an official language. The vernacular, endowed with an autonomous standard orthography, is competing with French (and in the case of the Seychelles, with English) in domains of language use heretofore reserved for the dominant language: administration, education, the media. Whether Creole will free itself from the diglossic yoke depends not on its level of development (codification, lexical enrichment, stylistic expansion, etc.) but on social and political factors. In the case of Haiti, the future status of Creole is intimately linked to the empowerment of the monolingual and impoverished rural and urban masses. The fact that language situations are never simple is demonstrated by the potential differentiation of Creole into a variety associated with the politically and economically powerful bilingual group *kreyòl swa* and another spoken by the masses, *kreyòl rèk*. Potentially, a tripartite diglossic situation might develop in which French shares the high status with *kreyòl swa*, and the masses continue to remain linguistically disenfranchised or enslaved by the continued low status ascribed to their vernacular.

NOTES

Grateful acknowledgment is made to Deborah Piston-Hatlen, who assisted in preparing this essay for publication. All translations from French and Haitian Creole are the author's.

1. William Morris, ed., *The American Heritage Dictionary of the English Language* (New York: American Heritage, 1969).

2. Suzanne Comhaire-Sylvain, *Le Créole haïtien: Morphologie et syntaxe* (Port-au-Prince, Haiti: by author; Wetteren: DeMeester, 1936), 8.

3. Robert Chaudenson, *Des Isles, des hommes, des langues: Langues créoles, cultures créoles* (Paris: L'Harmattan, 1992).

4. On the basis of persuasive comparative evidence involving a creole English that developed in Surinam and a Jamaican offshoot of that language (Maroon Spirit language), as well as sociohistorical facts, John McWhorter, "It Happened at Coromantin: Locating the Origin of the Atlantic-Based English Creoles," *Journal of Pidgin and Creole Languages* 12, 1 (1997): 59–102, proposes a more powerful monogenetic (diffusionist) theory for the genesis of English creoles spoken today in Africa and the New World. He hypothesizes that these languages originate in a pidginized version of English spoken in the 1630s by castle slaves in the English fort of Coromantin in the Gold Coast of the Guild of Guinea. How exactly the pidgin was transported across the Atlantic remains problematic, however.

5. The proponents of this nomenclature refer to the general pattern of naming a language by the name of inhabitants of a country: French, the language of the French; German, the language of the Germans. There are, however, some notable exceptions involving both monolingual and multilingual countries: Spanish in the various Latin American countries; English in the United States, Canada, New Zealand, Australia, and South Africa; French and Dutch (Flemish) in Belgium; Wolof, the principal language of Senegal.

6. Hall, *Africans in Colonial Louisiana*. Both terms referring to *Hibiscus esculentus*, whose mucilaginous green pods are used in Louisiana creole cuisine, derive from African loanwords: *okra* presumably from Igbo *nkruma* and *gumbo* from Western Bantu.

7. Lucien Adam, *Les Idiomes négro-aryen et malayo-aryen* (Paris: Maisonneuve, 1883).

8. Elodie Jourdain, *Du Français aux parlers créoles* (Paris: Klincksieck, 1956), xxii.

9. According to the noted pioneer of pidgin and creole studies, Robert A. Hall Jr. (personal communication cited in John A. Holm, *Pidgins and Creoles* [Cambridge: Cambridge UP, 1988], 1, 37–38), Comhaire-Sylvain included this oft-quoted conclusion at the express request of her University of Paris (Sorbonne) doctoral dissertation director, the French Africanist Lilias Homburger. Presumably, she herself did not hold to such a strong relexificationist position.

10. For example, Claire Lefebvre, "Relexification in Creole Genesis: The Case of Haitian Creole," in *Substrata versus Universals in Creole Genesis*, ed. Peter Muysken and Norval Smith (Amsterdam: John Benjamin, 1986).

11. Nonetheless, there are, at the lexical level, calques modeled on African patterns, for example, *dlo bouch* "saliva [water mouth]," *dlo je* "tear, teardrop [water eye]."

12. Claude Favre de Vaugelas, *Remarques sur la langue française* (1647; reprint, Paris: Ivrea, 1996).

13. Ferdinand Brunot, *Histoire de la langue française des origines à nos jours*, 9, in *La Révolution et l'Empire* (Paris: Armand Colin, 1967), 207.

14. Revon Reed, *Lâche Pas La patate: Portrait des Acadiens de la Louisiane* (Montréal: Editions Partis Pris, 1976), 201.

15. M. Roy Harris, "Cofè 'pourquoi', un africanisme parmi d'autres en créole louisianais," *Revue de Louisiane/Louisiana Review* 2, 2 (1973): 88–102.

16. Derek Bickerton, *Roots of Language* (Ann Arbor, Mich.: Karoma, 1981).

17. The presence of serial verbs in the Indian Ocean (Isle de France) French-lexifier Creoles is a moot point: see the discussion con and pro between Chris Corne, Deirdre Coleman, and Simon Curnow, "Clause Reduction in Asyndetic Coordination in Isle de France: The 'Serial Verbs' Problem," and Derek Bickerton, "Why Serial Verb Constructions in Isle de France Creole Can Have Subjects: A Reply to Corne, Coleman, and Curnow," in *Changing Meanings, Changing Functions*, ed. Philip Baker and Anand Syea (London: U of Westminster P, 1966), 129–69.

18. Gabriel Manessy, *Créoles, pidgins, variétés véhiculaires* (Paris: CNRS Editions, 1995), 184–85.

19. "Le créole est une langue dont le corps est français mais l'âme africaine." My recollection of this notable statement was corroborated by a participant at the Conference on Slavery in the Francophone World, A. James Arnold, who was present at that AATF meeting.

20. Hall, *Africans in Colonial Louisiana*, 188.

21. Jean-Baptiste Labat, *Nouveau voyage aux isles de l'Amérique* (1722; reprint, Paris:

Phébus, 1993); Gabriel Debien, *Plantations et esclaves à Saint-Dominigue* (Dakar, Senegal: Université de Dakar, 1962).

22. Mervyn C. Alleyne, *Syntaxe historique créole* (Paris: Karthala, 1996).

23. McWhorter, "It Happened at Coromantin."

24. Hall, *Africans in Colonial Louisiana.*

25. Walter Rodney, "Africa in Europe and America," in *Cambridge History of Africa* (Cambridge: Cambridge UP, 1975), 4, 578–622; Labat, *Nouveau voyage;* Marcel d'Ans, "Essai de socio-linguistique historique à partir d'un témoignage inédit sur l'emploi des langues, notamment africaines, en Haïti au cours de la guerre de libération et des premières années de l'Indépendance," *Etudes créoles* 19, 1 (1996): 110–24.

26. Debien, *Plantations,* 126.

27. Gabriel Manessy, "Réflexions sur les contraintes anthropologiques de la créolisation: De l'improbabilité du métissage linguistique dans les créoles atlantiques exogènes," *Etudes créoles* 19, 1 (1996): 61–71.

28. M. F. Goodman, *A Comparative Study of Creole French Dialects* (The Hague: Mouton, 1964); McWhorter, "It Happened at Coromantin."

29. Manessy, "Réflexions sur les contraintes."

30. Médéric Louis Elie Moreau de Saint-Méry, *Description topographique, physique, civile, politique et historique de la partie française de l'isle de Saint-Domingue,* (1797; reprint, Paris: Société de l'Histoire des Colonies Françaises, 1958), 82–83.

31. Justin Girod-Chantrans, *Voyage d'un Suisse dans les diverses colonies d'Amérique pendant la dernière guerre* (Neuchâtel, Switzerland: Imprimerie de la Société Typographique, 1795); *Idylles et chansons ou essais de poésie créole, par un habitant d'Hayti* (Philadelphia: J. Edwards, 1818); Moreau de Saint-Méry, *Description,* 83.

32. Dany Bébel-Gisler, *La Langue créole, force jugulée* (Paris: L'Harmattan, 1976).

33. Mervyn C. Alleyne, "Acculturation and the Cultural Matrix of Creolization," in *Pidginization and Creolization of Languages,* ed. Dell Hymes (Cambridge: Cambridge UP, 1971), 169–86.

34. Alleyne, "Acculturation."

35. Dominique Fattier, "De La Variété rèk à la variété swa: Pratiques vivantes de la langue en Haïti," in *Conjonctions* (March 1984): 39–51; Albert Valdman, "Les Créoles français entre l'oral et l'écrit," *Proceedings of the Freiburg Symposium on Creole Literacy,* ed. Ralph Ludwig (Tübingen, Germany: Gunter Narr Verlag, 1989), 43–63.

36. Serge Denis, ed., *Trois Siècles de vie française: Nos Antilles* (Paris: Maison du Livre Français, 1935), 7–8: *"Lire proclamation primié Consul Bonaparte voyez pour zote. Zote à voir que li vélé nègues resté libre . . . Li va mainteni commerce et culture, parce que zote doit conné que sans ça, colonie pas cable prospéré. Ça li promé zote li va rempli li fidellement; se yon crime si zote té douté de sa li promé zote dans Proclamation à li."*

37. Juste Chanlatte, Comte de Rosiers, *L'Entrée du roi en sa capitale en janvier 1818* (Cap Haïtien, Haiti, 1818; reprint, *Le Nouveau Monde: Supplément du dimanche,* August 19, 1979 [Port-au-Prince, Haiti], 6–13): *"A force nou brûlé d'envie et d'impatience,*

mo craire tête à toute monde va tourné folle; quant à coeur à moé li après palpité, li dans délire tant comme prémié fois gié à moé té contré quienne à toé . . . n'a pas pitit composé li va composé dans tête à li, tant mo vlé toute zoizeaux pé dans bois pou io tendé mo chanté. . . .

. . . Toujours comme ça to faire mo reproches qui chiré coeur à moé. Avla dijà to forgé dans tête à to mille chimères, milles imaginations qui pas gangné ni queue ni tête. Eh! Comment mo capable blié Marguerite, belle pitit fille cilala qui ba moé coeur à li aqué main à li? non, cher zami moé, ça pas possibe, mo va aimé toé toujours."

38. Chanlatte, *L'Entrée du Roi*, 8: *"Bon Dieu! queu jour! ah! queu spectacle! Et queu plaisir délicieux! A nos yeux cé comm'un miracle. Tant ils sont biaux, bons, gracieux. J'allons voir not'Monarque, not'Monarque et not'Reine. Le biau pitit Dauphin, ses soeurs itou."*

From the Problematic Maroon
to a Woman-Centered Creole Project
in the Literature of the French West Indies

A. JAMES ARNOLD

THE MYTH OF THE HEROIC MAROON

Nowhere in the Caribbean is the literary topos of the maroon more prominent than in Martinique. However, in few places in the Caribbean were maroon communities less historically significant than in Martinique. Nonetheless, from Aimé Césaire's *Et Les Chiens se taisaient* in 1946 to Edouard Glissant's *Le Quatrième siècle* in 1964, the figure of the heroic maroon was elevated to the position of unique founder of a culture of resistance to the plantation.

As late as 1981, in *Le Discours antillais,* Glissant bemoaned the absence of the heroic maroon at the center of popular culture in Martinique.[1] Other commentators have pointed out that in the popular culture the maroon does have a role, but as a demonized figure, a bogeyman. Mothers are likely to threaten their children: "Don't go out at night. Spirits will come for you; the maroons will take you away."[2] What does this divorce between the popular culture and the culture of the elite signify? Why have the foremost literary figures of Martinique sought to impose an image that contradicts the popular culture of the French West Indies? And why do fictional and dramatic representations of the heroic maroon contradict what the historical record demonstrates so convincingly?

In a remarkably detailed recent study, Richard D. E. Burton has demonstrated that the phenomenon of *grand marronage,* quite important in Martinique during the first century of colonization when Europeans were less numerous and the island was less settled, had nonetheless declined significantly by 1763; by 1784, on the eve of the French Revolution, there were no more than 282 maroons out of a slave population of 68,396 on the island.[3] By 1815, there were no longer any organized groups of maroons in Martinique at all.[4]

Numbers don't tell the whole story, of course. The negritude ethos embodied in Césaire's Rebel in the 1946 lyric tragedy *Et Les Chiens se taisaient* represented the escaped male slave as a heroic figure in revolt against the plantation system.[5] Glissant goes Césaire one better: his original maroon was a newly arrived African who successfully took to the hills before he was ever subjected to the regime of the plantation.[6] In the first phase of his career, Glissant effectively articulated a theory of Martinican culture based on a strict separation of maroon resistance opposed to servile submission. In the case of both Césaire and Glissant, however, the ideological overdetermination of the maroon myth is evident in the representation of this idealized heroic male figure as entertaining no ongoing relations with the plantation. This representation of the maroon does not square at all with the historical record. Burton has summed up the available data so well that, for present purposes, I need cite only the points that are central to my argument:

1. Maroon communities in Martinique (and Guadeloupe) always existed in a state of symbiosis with the plantation proper, depending on it for trade and for women.

2. Maroon communities represented a conditional refusal of the plantation, rather than the categorical, absolute refusal required by the myth of the maroon from Césaire to Glissant.

3. From the time the plantation system stabilized in the eighteenth century until the abolition of slavery in 1848, maroon communities were creolized in their customs, mores, and language. They were not, and could not be, vectors of African, as opposed to creole, values, although the exact nature of their creolization was, of course, different from that pertaining in slave society on the plantations.[7]

There is still more embarrassing evidence that undermines the myth of the heroic maroon as founding ancestor of a culture of resistance. It was not at all uncommon for maroon groups throughout the Americas to enter into compacts with the planters, who guaranteed the relative autonomy of the maroon communities on the condition that their leaders return any new runaways to the plantations. These agreements effectively made the maroon leaders feudal vassals of the plantation owners and an extension of the island's police. Such compacts remained in force as long as organized maroon communities and the institution of plantation slavery coexisted in the Lesser Antilles. Far from being independent of the plantation system, then, the maroon communities served to guarantee the property rights of slaveholders by keeping plantation slaves in bondage. Maryse Condé addressed this problem toward the end of her novel *Moi, Tituba, sorcière . . . noire de Salem* in 1986.[8] There has been very little commentary on the importance of this plot device, which constituted a frontal attack on the myth of the maroon as cultural hero in the Lesser Antilles.

In his analysis of Glissant's fiction, Burton focused on the original binary opposition between the descendants of those who refused slavery (the Longoué clan) and those who submitted (the Béluse descendants), demonstrating how Glissant initially constructed a symbolic geography of his fictional Martinique: the hills (*les mornes*), which signify freedom, are the domain of the maroons; the plain, where the plantation is located, signifies submission (*le décor consentant*). Burton points out that this binary opposition in Glissant's novels has often been noted; he then works a significant variation on its connotations: the plain is feminine and matriarchal, whereas the hills are masculine and patriarchal.[9] Burton unfortunately systematizes these binary oppositions throughout Glissant's fictional *oeuvre*, which constitutes a multigenerational saga spread over centuries of colonial history. He reads all of Glissant's fiction through this rigid grid; consequently, he is unable to grasp the evolution of Glissant's thought, from *Le Discours antillais* to *Poétique de la relation* (1990) to *Introduction à une poétique du divers* (1996). Burton's reading of Glissant's latest novel, *Tout-Monde* (1993), highlights the weaknesses in his critical model by denying significance to Glissant's manifest postmodern play and postcolonial engagement with his subject.

It may well be that these same binary oppositions structured the plot of *La Lézarde*, Glissant's first novel (1958). How else can we understand why Valérie, daughter of the plain, must be torn apart by the dogs owned by her fiancé, Thaël, when she ascends the *morne* to live with him toward the end of the novel. Ne'er the twain shall meet, it would seem, at this early point in Glissant's aesthetic. J. Michael Dash is a much more subtle, and finally superior, reader of Glissant's later novels. Whereas Burton reads *Mahagony* (1987) as the agonistic tale of paired maroon heroes in the past and the narrative present,[10] Dash calls our attention to the fundamental role of the "women who . . . had maintained the strength, allowed the survival, who had amassed enough energy to preserve plants" and thereby transmit the culture to the next generation.[11]

In this same novel Dash foregrounds the role of the storyteller: "*Mahagony* is also about a succession of storytellers who keep the dream alive. . . . They include those who gather data like Mathieu and Ida, those who use their literacy to subvert like Hégésippe and the 'chroniqueur', those who simply tell stories, like Longoué, Lanoué, Mycéa and Eudoxie."[12] Nearly half of these storyteller figures in Glissant's novel are women, as Dash points out. Burton is silent on this subject, as are the creolist writers whom he follows in his model of cultural transmission. In 1994 I demonstrated the gratuitous masculine gendering of the storyteller figure in the work of the Martinican Creolists.[13] The final section of this article proposes the work of Dany Bébel-Gisler as a useful and necessary response to the creolist vision of cultural transmission.

CREOLIST RECONFIGURATIONS OF ETHNICITY, GENDER, AND CLASS

At this point it is desirable to comment on Burton's strategy in *Le Roman marron: Études sur la littérature martiniquaise contemporaine,* which is part of a larger project of masculinist gendering of culture in Martinique. Burton pushes to the extreme the binary oppositions he finds in Glissant's early work so as to represent him as an unrepentant supporter of the myth of the heroic maroon, elements of which undeniably exist in Glissant's fiction. Burton's overarching goal, however, is to show that the Martinican creolist writers, principally Patrick Chamoiseau and Raphaël Confiant, have transcended the binary oppositions embraced by Glissant and have abandoned the myth of the heroic maroon. To more effectively highlight the presumed superiority of Chamoiseau and Confiant as novelists, Burton has stressed the continuities with Césaire and negritude in Glissant's work, rather than his gradual abandonment of negritude's binary oppositions. The resultant reading of the inheritance of plantation slavery relegates Glissant to the past, whereas the Creolists are presented to us as the wave of the future. This is at best a tendentious reading of the conflict that separates Glissant from Chamoiseau and Confiant. At worst it is a serious distortion of the significance of Glissant's later fiction, and it obscures the reification of gender and ethnoclass roles in creolist fiction and autobiography.

At issue here are the implications of the representation of plantation slavery and its aftermath in the recent work of novelists from Martinique and Guadeloupe. I submit that it is the Creolists, rather than Glissant, who in their fiction have created a commodified post-emancipation Martinique designed to titillate consumers in Europe and North America. Indeed, I have argued elsewhere that their aesthetics results in an exoticized version of cultural dependence upon France. The present contribution to this debate is the third in a series. At a conference on (Un)Writing Empire in 1994 at Leiden University, I extended the argument on the gendering of culture by the Creolists from the fiction of Chamoiseau and Confiant to their personal memoirs, which had recently been published in Paris.[14]

Confiant has created a particularly static representation of the society that evolved in the towns in the wake of emancipation in the French West Indies in 1848. Whereas Glissant in the 1980s and 1990s has been attentive to showing creolization as an ongoing, open process that he theorizes as *la relation* (relating), Confiant has reified the social stratifications and divisions between and among ethnoclasses that resulted from the emancipation of the slaves and the introduction of East Indian indentured labor in the late nineteenth century. This is especially evident in his representation of sexuality, which is the locus of cultural conflict in the work of the Creolists. Once one looks beyond the carnivalization of language—the creation of a mesolect to give non-Creole speakers the illusion that they are reading Creole—what one finds is a remarkably harsh and misogynistic assignment of gender roles. Prostitutes accept clients based on their ethnoclass and the notions of *bienséance* (social propriety), if one may call it such, that exist between racially defined groups in Martinique. This places such stock characters as the *Syrien* (the Levantine merchant) and the *coulie* (the descendant of South Indian indentured laborers) at a serious disadvantage in the sexual marketplace. Confiant creates comic scenes using the misadventures of such characters, who are shown to be not fully integrated into creole society. It is true, as Burton argues in *Le Roman marron*, that Chamoiseau and Confiant have moved the plot of their fiction away from the *mornes*, or hills, to the towns and that the fictional maroons are no longer the protagonists of the novel. Their descendants are present, however, and they invariably play a determining role in the plot. These are the *majors* dear to both Chamoiseau and Confiant; in Trinidad this same stock character has been called the Bad John. In Trinidad as in Martinique he is a marginal character whose refusal to work remains the hallmark of his social identity. This refusal to work, represented as the revolt of the lumpenproletariat, ties him functionally to the maroons of the past. The Trinidadian novelist Earl Lovelace problematizes the plight of the Bad John in his novels *The Dragon Can't Dance* (1979) and *The Wine of Astonishment* (1982), showing the progressively dysfunctional nature of his behaviors in urban society. Not so the Martinican Creolists, who exoticize these stock characters. In Confiant's fiction as well as his

autobiography—which are voluble on the subject of heterosexual coupling—
these *majors* are universally feared by men and women alike. They take women
more or less brutally on the roadside or in the cane fields. They are effectively
rapists in the many cases fictionally created or recalled by Confiant from his
youth. Over against this vile behavior by the blackest of his male characters, he
invariably sets the more civilized style of mulatto lovemaking. In Confiant's
autobiography we read that "godfather Salvie, the mulatto, always used charm
and roguish tricks whereas the maroon preferred to ravish the first isolated female that chance put in his way." [15] The homology between the maroon of the
past and the *major* in the fictional present is made linguistically explicit in this
passage.

   Caribbean fiction has typically used a more or less specific ethnoclass position to focalize the narration. The negritude ethos reacted against the superior
class position of mulattoes who had long dominated the literature written by
people of color in the region. Since World War II we have come to expect an
Afro-Caribbean worldview and fictional focalizers who organize and express
it. The creolist movement in Martinique is unique in this respect as well. As the
sexual anecdote cited above illustrates, the blackest segments of the population
are depreciated in their manners and mores in favor of lighter-skinned Martinicans. More specifically, it is the ethnoclass known as *chabins* (red, in U.S.
terminology) that focalizes both the fiction and the autobiography of a writer
like Confiant. Passages of *Ravines du devant-jour* are positively obsessed with
whiteness. To reinforce his identification with his own ethnoclass, the *chabins*,
Confiant writes: "Your mother is very beautiful. . . . Her white *chabine* beauty
dazzles the black folks." [16]

   In her contribution to this volume, Marie-José N'Zengou-Tayo notes this
same preoccupation in Confiant's novel *Eau de café*. My argument comple-
ments hers in problematizing the special racial perspective developed by Confiant, who expatiates on the subject of the *chabin*. Indeed, at the age of six,
Confiant discovered that to be a *chabin* was to be neither black nor white: "The
word petrifies you for the first time in your life: *chabin!* Ordinarily it is pronounced with gentleness by those around you, although you have been sur-
prised to discover that this word is always used to describe you, whereas *black*
or *mulatto* are used habitually for people of those complexions. You vaguely
sense that to be red is to be a separate category of being. Black and not black,
white and not white at the same time. However, you haven't yet realized the extent of the distance that your skin and hair color creates between ordinary folk
and you." [17]

The *chabins* even benefit, if that is the word, from a separate category of curses that is reserved exclusively for them: "Evil race of *chabins!* Sour-haired *chabin!* Guinea-hen-spotted-face *chabin!* Ripe-banana-spotted *chabin!* Get the hell out of here; *chabins* are an evil race that God should never have set on this Earth!" [18]

There are many more similar examples in this extraordinary memoir of early childhood that elucidates Confiant's ideological position. Perceiving his own ethnoclass in terms of exclusion—neither black nor white and not mulatto either—Confiant elaborates a vision of the nation that is similarly exclusionary. As he casts his gaze back over the history of Martinican society since emancipation, his imagination encounters the sort of rigid, ethnically determined divisions that characterized the Caribbean according to the segmented-society model once prevalent in the social sciences. It is a pessimistic vision of creole societies that sees ethnoclasses as forever in opposition to one another. This negative, exclusionary vision informs the astonishingly static representation of Martinique that recurs throughout Confiant's novels, and to a considerable extent Chamoiseau's as well. A decade ago in their manifesto *Eloge de la créolité* (1989), Jean Bernabé, Chamoiseau, and Confiant confidently declared, "Because of its constituent mosaic, Creoleness is an open specificity." [19] At the time, readers were prepared to look at the mosaic metaphor as a positive representation of the *socius*, of the creole nation. The mosaic, it was presumed, would realize the unity in diversity that has been institutionalized in the official ideology of a number of independent Caribbean countries since the 1960s.

What is the evidence in the fiction and autobiography that Chamoiseau and Confiant have published in the past decade? To play on the mosaic metaphor, we have been shown the sharp divisions between the constituent shards, or fragments. Far from bonding the fragments into a strong, unified whole, Chamoiseau and Confiant's *oeuvre* offers a vision of separate ethnoclasses that are further divided by rigidly defined gender positions. The subject positions attributed to men and women in Chamoiseau's and Confiant's fiction and autobiographies ultimately serve to push to the limits of creole society all those latecomers—in Kamau Brathwaite's terminology—who gradually entered the Caribbean after emancipation: East Indians, Levantines, Chinese. The case of René Coulie in *Eau de café*, discussed elsewhere in this volume by Marie-José N'Zengou-Tayo, is exemplary. More instructive, although more shocking in its misogynistic intent, is the phrase attributed in *Ravines du devant-jour* to Confiant's aunt Emérante. Speaking of the undesirability of sexual relations between black creole men and East Indian women, aunt Emérante claimed, "Anybody who rubs against them, gets cut!" To which Confiant adds in his own voice that East Indian women are "engagement-breakers, seducers of boy-friends, stealers of fiancés, and first-class kinky women, although their cunt hairs are sharp as razor blades (*des briseuses d'épousailles, des détourneurs de con-cubins, des voleuses de fiancés, des vicieuses de première catégorie, bien que les poils de leur coucoune soient effilés comme la lame du rasoir*)." [20]

Finally, the construction of masculinity by the creolist writers involves much more than gender position in the usual sense. (It is true, of course, that this vision serves to keep women down or at least in the missionary position.) This ideologically determined conferral of (sexual) power on specific groups of creole males serves to reinforce the segmented-society vision of Martinique, both under slavery and today.

A WOMAN-CENTERED CREOLE PROJECT

One year before Maryse Condé's *Tituba* appeared, Dany Bébel-Gisler published *Léonora: L'Histoire enfouie de la Guadeloupe*. As I have shown elsewhere, *Tituba* challenged the myth of the heroic maroon. *Léonora*, which has not yet received the attention it manifestly deserves, was the first *testimonio* or testi-monial fiction to emerge from the French West Indies. Conceived on a model similar to Rigoberta Menchú's book written with Elisabeth Burgos-Debray, *Léonora* constitutes a woman-centered vision of creole language and culture in Guadeloupe in the interests of national independence.

Dany Bébel-Gisler is a researcher trained in the social sciences and attached to the French equivalent of the National Science Foundation (CNRS) in Paris. As an anthropological project, *Léonora* constituted field work of the sort done by the new cultural anthropologists who come to terms with their involvement in the project. The book, which Bébel-Gisler has called a novel, was edited by the author from audio tapes amassed from a long series of interviews with her subject, who was in her mid-sixties when the book was published. The narra-tive engagingly relates the stages in the life of a woman born in 1919 to poor agricultural workers in the countryside, for whom French, learned at school, was a foreign language. World War II, resistance to Vichy France and its rep-resentatives in Guadeloupe, and the change from colonial to departmental sta-tus in 1946 are all narrated from the limited perspective of this woman, whom we observe as she grows in understanding of the world around her, coming to political consciousness well into her middle years.

Many of the concerns of the Martinican creolist writers are in evidence in

Léonora: promotion of the creole language, concern for folk traditions and their transmission, relations between the sexes. Bébel-Gisler's treatment of these subjects, however, recenters them in a number of important ways. Léonora relates her own struggles with French as the prestige language in Guadeloupe and the way in which the schools were used to render inferior the mother tongue of Guadeloupeans, both in her own and her children's experience. Although Bébel-Gisler runs an alternative school that uses Creole to teach children who have had difficulty in the state-run schools, her text in *Léonora* expresses a much more flexible attitude toward the need for French than do the novels of the creolist writers.

The focus of *Léonora* shifts from the rural villages surrounding the cane fields to the capital, Pointe-à-Pitre, and back again several times in the course of Léonora's life story. In the early chapters the reader learns how black creole children and the children of East Indians mingled in the schools, at play, and in funerary rituals in the countryside. Bébel-Gisler shows us the ongoing creolization process that was already breaking down the cultural differences between these two groups before World War II. She does so, however, in a matter-of-fact way that points up both continuing conflict between the groups and mutual misunderstandings that mediate their culture differences. The contrast with the program of the Martinican Creolists is striking on this point. Confiant's novel *Commandeur du sucre* (1994) is itself an ethnographic fiction concerned with reconstructing a typical crop season on a sugar plantation in Martinique in 1936 (when the historical Léonora would have been seventeen years old). In his vision the post-emancipation roles of white plantation owners, mulatto overseers, and black laborers remain rigidly stereotyped in terms of ethnoclass, with the Indians or *coulies* remaining marginalized throughout the story.

The woman-centered vision of *Léonora* comes through most clearly in the chapters on child rearing, those devoted to her own childhood as well as those in which she relates her child-rearing practices. Sexual relations are not neglected by Bébel-Gisler, but they are subordinated to Léonora's role as daughter, then as mother and grandmother. The reader comes away from *Léonora* with a fundamentally different sense of the roles of men with respect to women. Men are represented as longtime *concubins* as well as husbands and indifferent fathers; Léonora herself had six children by her husband before they were married. The sexual exploits of men that constitute the staple of Martinican creolist fiction are related by Leonora in terms of the necessity of rising in the middle of the night to prepare a meal for her man, who has just returned from another woman's bed. If she refuses or resists this tyrannical behavior, she runs the risk of a beating.[21] The greater problem from the wife and mother's standpoint, however, is the impoverishment of her children that the man's financial support of his outside woman causes. Bébel-Gisler shows Léonora engaging in labor outside the home in order to supplement the male provider's income, which no longer suffices to feed her children. Creole language and culture are directly related to economic realities by Bébel-Gisler and always from a woman-centered perspective that grounds the narrative in the history of the family over three generations.

Bébel-Gisler draws Léonora out on her role as a performer of folktales and riddles at wakes and other ritual events. This narrative strategy might seem unexceptional were it not for the fact that the Martinican Creolists have reserved this role in slave and post-emancipation West Indian society exclusively for men, as pointed out in my 1994 article. Thus *Léonora* serves as a necessary gender corrective in the area of transmission of traditional culture as well.

Finally, it is the growing role of Léonora as an agent of change in labor relations in rural Guadeloupe in the 1970s, when she was already a grandmother, that throws Bébel-Gisler's book into sharpest relief with respect to the production of the Martinican Creolists. Only Chamoiseau's *Texaco* (1992) has given a somewhat analogous role to a female narrator; but Marie-Sophie Laborieux in Chamoiseau's novel is engaged in a rearguard action against the inevitable process of modernization of the urban slums around Fort-de-France. Léonora, converted to social activism by a liberation theology priest who encouraged the women of his parish to raise their social and religious consciousness in the creole language, participated in labor union activities on the large sugar plantations in her neighborhood, where her husband was employed as a supervisor. Bébel-Gisler has edited her "novel" in such a way that the sharp focus on strike activity, the opposition of the government and the presence of paramilitary security forces (CRS) specially flown in from the Metropole, Haitian scab laborers in the cane fields, and the hunger strike of Father Chérubin Céleste (the liberation theology priest), all combine to bring the narrative to a climax worthy of well-plotted fiction.

Bébel-Gisler's narrative in *Léonora* is committed to the proposition of political independence for Guadeloupe in a way that the fiction of the Martinican Creolists is not, although they are nominal supporters of independence. Bébel-Gisler chose to portray a representative woman of the people, Léonora, in whose story readers could believe. She has embedded the fate of the creole language and culture deeply in a story whose veracity is authenticated by the simple, honest questioning of the first-person narrator. The careful documentation and abundant notes that accompany Bébel-Gisler's text have already caught the attention of other social scientists, as Arlette Gautier's use of *Léonora* demonstrates. The literary establishment has largely boycotted the book.

Now that the first flush of enthusiasm for the Martinican creolist writers has passed, is it not time to attend seriously to this other creole project in the French West Indies?

NOTES

1. Edouard Glissant, *Le Discours antillais* (Paris: Seuil, 1981), 104. The articles published in *Le Discours antillais* date from the 1970s. Over the succeeding decade Glissant would gradually abandon this position.

2. Dany Bébel-Gisler, *Léonora: L'Histoire enfouie de la Guadeloupe* (Paris: Seghers, 1985), 13. All translations are the author's unless otherwise indicated.

3. Richard D. E. Burton, *Le Roman marron: Études sur la littérature martiniquaise contemporaine* (Paris: L'Harmattan, 1997), 59–63.

4. Léo Elisabeth, "La Société martiniquaise aux XVIIe et XVIIIe siècles, 1664–1789" (state doctoral thesis, Université de Paris I, 1988, Part I, section 2), 162–163.

5. Aimé Césaire, "Et Les Chiens se taisaient," in *Les Armes miraculeuses* (Paris: Gallimard, 1970), 73–154.

6. Edouard Glissant, *Le Quatrième siècle* (Paris: Seuil, 1964).

7. Burton, *Roman marron*, 59–63.

8. Maryse Condé, *Moi, Tituba, sorcière . . . noire de Salem* (Paris: Mercure de France, 1986). I addressed the question of Condé's critique of the maroon myth in "Poétique forcée et identité dans la littérature des Antilles francophones," in *L'Héritage de Caliban*, ed. Maryse Condé (Pointe-à-Pitre, Guadeloupe: Jasor, 1992), 26–27.

9. In Glissant's novel *Le Quatrième siècle*, the son of the first Longoué, Liberté, is killed by the son of the first Béluse, Anne, "whose androgynous given name [Anne] embodies his straining between the feminized, not to say matriarchal, world of the plain and the highly masculine and patriarchal world of the heights"; Burton, *Roman marron*, 72.

10. Burton, *Roman marron*, 91–98.

11. J. Michael Dash, *Edouard Glissant* (Cambridge: Cambridge UP, 1995), 172.

12. Dash, *Glissant*, 172–73.

13. A. James Arnold, "The Erotics of Colonialism in Contemporary French West Indian Literary Culture," *New West Indian Guide* 68, 1–2 (1994): 5–22. Maryse Condé and Madeleine Cottenet-Hage included an earlier text of the article in their *Penser la créolité* (Paris: Karthala, 1995), 21–40, under the title "The Gendering of *Créolité:* The Erotics of Colonialism." Edward Kamau Brathwaite and Timothy Reiss have reprinted

the text of my *NWIG* article in their special issue of *Sisyphus and Eldorado: Magical and Other Realisms in Caribbean Literature*, 11, 3–12.1 (1996): 360–89.

14. A. James Arnold, "*Créolité:* Cultural Nation-Building or Cultural Dependence?" in *(Un)Writing Empire*, ed. Theo D'haen (Amsterdam: Rodopi, 1997), 39–50. The first article in this series is cited in the preceding note. Chamoiseau's memoir of childhood is *Antan d'enfance, haute enfance* (Paris: Gallimard, 1993). Raphaël Confiant's memoir is *Ravines du devant-jour, Haute enfance* (Paris: Gallimard, 1993), 96.

15. Confiant, *Ravines*, 96.

16. Confiant, *Ravines*, 15.

17. Confiant, *Ravines*, 34–35.

18. Confiant, *Ravines*, 34.

19. Jean Bernabé, Patrick Chamoiseau, and Raphaël Confiant, *Eloge de la créolité*, bilingual ed. trans. Mohammed B. Taleb-Khyar (Paris: Gallimard, 1993), 89.

20. Confiant, *Ravines*, 80.

21. France Alibar and Pierrette Lembeyre-Boy, in their *Le Couteau seul: La Condition féminine aux Antilles* (Paris: Editions Caribéennes, 1981), report that fully three-quarters of French West Indian women report being beaten by their domestic partners. In her chapter "Women from Guadeloupe and Martinique," in *French and West Indian: Martinique, Guadeloupe, and French Guiana Today*, ed. Richard D. E. Burton and Fred Reno (Charlottesville: UP of Virginia, 1994), 119–36, Arlette Gautier cited Bébel-Gisler's *Léonora* in support of these sociological data.

Exorcising Painful Memories
Raphaël Confiant and Patrick Chamoiseau

MARIE-JOSÉ N'ZENGOU-TAYO

Nearly a century and a half after emancipation, the issue of slavery is still a burning one in the French Overseas Departments. As evidence, one has only to read the polemic articles written recently in *Antilla* about the celebration of May 22, 1848, versus April 27, 1848.[1] The two articles give an interesting insight into Martinican writings about society and history because they show how sensitive Martinican intellectuals are on issues pertaining to slavery and emancipation. They also confirm Beverley Ormerod's comments about Michèle Lacrosil's *Demain Djab-Herma* and Joseph Zobel's *Rue cases-nègres,* and we could extend her analysis to most Caribbean writings about slavery: "Characters of every class and skin shade still retain ancestral memories of the estate hierarchy with its privileges and its disparities, and their behavior is very largely determined by traditional responses."[2] Ormerod identifies slavery as an important element helping to understand French Caribbean literature. According to her, it was associated with the trauma of uprootedness: "Slavery was the starting-point of alienation, loss of pride in one's race and of confidence in oneself. The cruelties of the colonial era and the harsh realities of the present have served to perpetuate this state of alienation."[3]

Attitudes toward slavery vary between amnesia and protest in French West Indian writing. In their 1989 work *Eloge de la créolité,* Jean Bernabé, Patrick Chamoiseau, and Raphaël Confiant defined a new literary program, *créolité,* aiming at establishing "true" creole literature. Among the first items of their agenda, we note the reassessment of Martinican official history. "Between the currents of the history of France, between the great dates of the governor's arrivals and departures, between the beautiful white pages of the chronicle (where the bursts of our rebellion appear only as small spots), there was the obstinate progress of ourselves. *The opaque resistance of maroons allied in their disobedience. The new heroism of those who stood up against the hell of slavery, displaying some obscure codes of survival, some indecipherable qualities of resistance, the incomprehensible variety of compromise, the unexpected syntheses of life.*" [4]

The two italicized sentences catch our attention because they define a new approach to slavery and *marronage*. The characterization of maroons' resistance as "opaque" and the slaves' lives as heroic gives us a reading guide for examining maroons' and slaves' representation in the fictions of the *créolité* movement. We have to note the paradox expressed in the use of "heroism" for attitudes and strategies of survival that are all but heroic. Similarly, the definition of maroons' resistance as "opaque" suggests a new assessment of *marronage* and maybe a hint at the ambiguity of their role in the plantation history. As we should read "opaque" with the connotation Glissant gives it, we could read their analysis as a signal of the misunderstanding lingering between the descendants of the maroons (the people from the hills) and those of the new freedmen (the people from the plains).

In addition, their claim of modernity points out the awareness that presides over the act of writing in their work. I would go even further and argue that the writings of the *créolité* movement are postmodern because of their theoretical awareness and decision to write against the backdrop of the various cultures of the world. By denying absolute authority to western culture, by assuming the flaws of their society, they set out to produce books that undermine and reverse the hegemony of western culture. [5]

It is in the light of these statements that I would like to examine Confiant's *Eau de café* as well as Chamoiseau's *Texaco* and *L'Esclave Vieil Homme et le molosse*. These three novels are part of the *créolité* project of reassessing and recapturing the Martinican past. How do these writers deal with this part of their history that would be different from their predecessors?

Most French Caribbean fictions have at one time or another dealt with the issue of slavery. The negritude and postnegritude writers introduced the topic in their poetry, drama, and fictions. Long before *Eloge de la créolité*, they had tried to recover from the (voluntary) amnesia on the matter that characterizes the region. Most presented slavery as a humiliating experience. However, they acknowledged the fact that it led to survival behavior based on a double discourse. In Maryse Condé's *Moi, Tituba, sorcière . . . noire de Salem*, John Indian typifies this survival strategy. In Simone Schwarz-Bart's *Pluie et vent sur*

Télumée miracle, Reine-sans-nom warns Télumée and invites her to become a double-sided drum in order to cope with life and deal with the Desaragne family (the whites, or *békés*, for whom she works). Edouard Glissant's *Le Quatrième siècle* offers an original approach to slavery and the plantation world in which past and present are confronted as well as the viewpoint of the three protagonists of the plantation society, the *béké*, the maroon, and the slave.[6]

Chamoiseau's and Confiant's fictions examine slavery always as a backdrop against which present time is analysed. Therefore, its evocation alternates in a counterpoint with that of contemporary Martinique. The influence of Glissant's thought is strongly present in Chamoiseau's fictions. The latter's most recent novel, *L'Esclave Vieil Homme et le molosse*, contains inserts of Glissant's work, which highlights the "relation" between the writings of the two authors. Though Confiant acknowledges Glissant's ideological influence, it is difficult to identify any trace of it in his fictional works.

In the work of Confiant, slavery is evoked occasionally while he retraces the lineage of a protaganist. The experience of slavery is what establishes a link between the *békés* and the descendants of the slaves. Confiant is more interested in portraying the urban life of the lumpenproletariat than the plantation life. In *Eau de café*, the narrator/author investigates the death of Antilia, a young woman adopted by her godmother. However, from time to time, the past is evoked, and memories of slavery are used to explain the actual behavior or existing relationships between his characters. The maroons are represented through Julien Thémistocle, who is proud of his ancestry. He defies the rural police by boasting of his origins: "I am a maroon. The last of the maroons who made you eat your crushed souls in the Morne Jacob woods."[7]

This statement will earn him the admiration of the villagers, who consider him a "popular hero." The *békés*, on the other hand, are associated with the experience of slavery as torturers: "The *béké* is a Luciferian race! The old communist [Thimoléon, the cabinet maker] thundered forth. Since they landed in this country, they never stopped tormenting people. . . . When is this disorder going to stop, hey?" (37).

Slavery and post-emancipation policies are blamed for various problems encountered by black and colored Martinicans, and the issue of language appears to be one problem. The supercilious respect of Martinicans for the French language is justified through the limitations imposed on the new freedmen. On several occasions, the narrative voice acknowledges also the respect and admiration of his fellow citizens for "beautiful language": "It is because when slavery ended—it was less than a century ago, I tell you—the whites did not accept our children in their schools and patronizingly taught us only few words of their languages. They thought they could keep us down into poverty in doing so. They underestimated the creole negro, though" (93).

Similarly the etymology of some words is traced back to the period and attributed to the master-slave relationships. In the case of words coined to give account of the mixing of various ethnic groups in the colony, Thimoléon is the one who explains the origins of *chabin* and recalls that of *mulâtre*. "Do you know the origin of the word *chabin?* It refers to a race of sheep with yellow fleece that is found in Normandy. Exactly the same as mulatto that comes from 'mule'! Your fathers, the white men, threw you back in the pure animal reign, you, the sons the negress slaves bore them. Never forget this, old pal. You don't need however to keep any kind of grudge. What is done is well done" (180). There is no such etymology in the French *Petit Larousse* or *Petit Robert*. The Allsop's *Dictionary of Caribbean English Usage* (1996) gives the etymology from the Cotgrave's *Dictionnaire* (1611): "The sheepe of Berry (whose wool is verie thicke, and as long as goats haire)." In France this type of animal was once thought to be a cross between a sheep and a goat, and the notion of a thick-haired cross-bred animal (cf Fr. *mulâtre* < *mulet*) was transferred to this particular type of negro "half-breed." Thimoléon explains also the origin of *l'estravail* created on the model of *esclavage* by the technique of the *mot-valise* (portmanteau word), and he justifies the apparent disinterest of Martinicans in hard work as the result of this association between work and slavery: "And when there was no more meat and vegetables in the hills and the yard behind our huts turned into a desert, one could swear that slavery had been reestablished. In Macedoine, people repeated *l'estravail* stubbornly as if to remind themselves that it was a period of endless sweating" (188).

Slavery is present through legends and superstitious beliefs, as the episode of the jar of gold coins reminds us. Stories of jars full of gold coins and killings of slaves beside them are perpetuated in the contemporary imagination. Thimoléon uses de Cassagnac's jar as a bargain instrument because he wants to convince Passionise, a prostitute, to seduce René Couli, the Tamul priest, on the eve of an important ceremony (142). In fact, Thimoléon tricks Passionise since there is no jar when she comes back to receive her payment. She learns that the jar had moved along:

The *béké* of Cassagnac's jar of gold coins? She said incredulously. But how come it is here? People say that it is buried somewhere beneath at the Seguineau Plantation?

—Ha! Ha! Ha! You, poor idiot, . . . Gold jars travel underground, girl,
especially those beside which the békés interred the slaves who had just
buried them. (142)

Confiant's story asserts the importance of name and lineage as making the
difference between the *békés* and the blacks: the *béké* can assert his right to the
property by retracing his family tree. By keeping the memory of his genealogy,
he can assert his authority upon those who cannot go very far back. When de
Cassagnac addresses Julien Thémistocle, he questions this ability: "Do you
know your father's father? And then, your father's father, did he know his own
father?" (227). Julien's attempt at answering is swept away by this final declaration: "You, negroes, you are nobody's children" (228).

The descendant of the maroon is shaken as he realizes that he had nothing to
claim as an intangible proof of his genealogy except for the infamous fleur-de-
lis stamp on his grandfather's shoulder, which branded him as a captured maroon (230). The text confirms the link between naming and slavery. "Not a
week would go by without seeing him laugh at someone's name and take the
opportunity to boast about his own name. According to him his 'title,' Thémistocle, had been imposed—after a hard-fought struggle—on the 'whites-
from-France' who were in charge of establishing a civil status register in the
aftermath of Emancipation" (293).

Memory of slavery is anecdotal in Confiant's work. Contrary to Glissant or
Chamoiseau, there is no attempt at reconstituting this period of Martinican history as such. Indeed, one protagonist (Thimoléon) acknowledges the fact that
Afro-Martinican history always needs to retrace its steps to the arrival of the
first slave ship. "The problem with the negro is that to understand the texture
of his life, you have to go far back to the first who landed or nearly. The story
of the white islander is simpler: it starts and ends with himself as if his greatness
was self fulfilling" (363). Nevertheless, the selected references to slavery seem
more to confirm stereotypes about Martinicans than to shed a new light on their
unofficial / silenced history.

In the two selected texts of Chamoiseau, *Texaco* and *L'Esclave Vieil Homme
et le molosse,* the issue of slavery is approached differently. First, the influence
of Glissant's work and thought is openly acknowledged, and in the second
novel the writings of the two authors alternate in a sort of dialogue.

In *Texaco,* Marie-Sophie Laborieux tells the story of the descendants of
slaves from the nineteenth century to the twentieth century, covering a period
of approximately one hundred and sixty years. The account concerning slav-

ery covers pages 43 to 155 of the section entitled *Temps de paille*. Through the story of her father, Esternome, the narrator relates the experience of slaves during the twenty-five years preceding the Emancipation Act and its enforcement in the colony.[8]

From the very beginning, Marie-Sophie hints at the silence surrounding this period. Her father would not talk to her about the period though he and his wife would whisper stories to each other (44). One can see from this comment how the new freedmen deliberately blocked the memory of the next generation so that the children would not remember their parents' painful experiences. This voluntary amnesia was accompanied by the forgetting of Africa, African languages, and customs. Even before emancipation, creole slaves did not speak the languages of their ancestors though Africans were living in their midst (134).

Slavery did not destroy human feelings among the slaves. It did not prevent people from falling in love, as described in the relationship between Esternome's father and mother (50–51). However, a password circulated forbidding reproduction. In contrast with the maroons, who seemed completely cut off from the slave population, the author focuses on the presence of *mentôs* (men of strength) among the slaves. These hidden leaders ruled the plantation through their supernatural powers. They did not try to take over the plantation but hampered its management, causing severe losses and damages to the *békés* (45–46). As a result, repression increased, and the *békés* devised other forms of torture to retain control of their property. However, sabotages went on unabated (46–47). Esternome invites us to reassess the condition of the field slaves in opposition to the maroons: "The field negroes walked toward freedom through paths that were rougher than the maroons'. More difficult, I would say, as their struggle included the risk of falling down in the deepest pit, the one in which you accept without protest what you have been turned into. The maroons withdrew from battle but the field negroes remained in line. They tried as best as they could to stay at the surface of the mud, . . . holding, holding on firm and sanding your heart at the core with freedom, without waving your arms about" (95).

Esternome's life reveals the contradictions of slavery. The first slave child to be born on a plantation, Esternome had a special status and therefore did not experience the hardships of the field slaves, though he witnessed them. For saving his master's life, he benefited from *liberté de savane*, which means partial freedom to go as he pleased. He was able to gather firsthand information on emancipation and to spread the news on the plantations.

It is interesting to note that Chamoiseau chose to retrace the last years of slavery. He shows the dereliction of the plantation economy and the change in the atmosphere. He also describes the hope raised by the campaign for emancipation. A new form of *marronage* was taking place as slaves fled to the British colonies, since emancipation in the British islands dated from 1838 (105). He also shows that slaves received information on the political events taking place in France: they heard about the 1848 revolution and the advent of the Second Republic. Schoelcher's campaign for emancipation was known, but slaves did not wait passively for it to be conferred upon them. Here, Chamoiseau challenges the official history that created the myth of freedom being granted to submissive slaves. He suggests that the slaves claimed their rights as soon as they knew about these rights (95–117). As they kept watch for the arrival of the official decree, they started to organize a new order by dividing the properties. "Already on the plantation many impatient negroes improvised themselves as land dividers. With Mahaut ropes, they measured the fields with new canes, going up to the hills and then to the Great-House. However their rigorous shares would leave a respectable expanse around the latter. Each divider would then allot the land feverishly. . . . An interesting word was 'citizen'" (126).

Through Marie-Sophie's account we are made aware that the post-emancipation period was pregnant with revolutionary promises ("citizen" recalls the 1789 Revolution; the fair division of land is a sign of socialist ideas of "access to property for all.") It reveals that the former slaves (or newly freed) wanted to work for themselves and not for a master. It also tells about the aborted attempt made by the slaves to appropriate the land (completing the creolization process and gearing toward some form of nationhood). The narrative poem "Le Nouteka des mornes" is the account of this attempt at conquering a soil they landed on as unwilling migrants and improbable conquerors (140–50).

With emancipation, the former maroons lost their prestige and became symbols of backwardness. Their isolation and refusal of the plantation order ceased to be admired and instead indicated resistance to progress. They became "exotic" reminders of the African origins—but with the connotation of "savagery." "We met some maroons. Their huts were nested in the ferns. Those maroons were stern, withdrawn from the world too, they were different. As time went by, they had remained in spirit in the country of beyond. To see them appear was disquieting. They wore loin cloths, carrying spears and bows. They showed off some kind of bracelets carved in bamboo wood, feathers of John Crow, earrings, and streaks of ashes on their faces" (142).

This description of the maroons borrows a lot from the popular imagery (the French *image d'Épinal*) of the African native/savage as portrayed in the nineteenth-century popular magazines. The stereotype is obvious, as the description presents them geared in full regalia, which would be unlikely if they were going about their day-to-day activities. Nevertheless, the lack of communication and fraternity between the old maroons and the new freedmen reflects their antagonistic worlds. It also suggests the dichotomies they represent: "resistance and endurance, engagement and alienation, self-determination and domination."[9] As Chamoiseau states, "Among these early rebels, there was no kindness for us, not a friendly sign, nothing to hope for but contempt" (142).

Two other protagonists of the colonial society are present in Esternome's account of the pre-emancipation period: the urban *békés* and mulattoes (or freedmen). They represent a "fascinating" (82) world, for they give Saint-Pierre its rhythm. We learn about the competition between the *békés* and the wealthy mulattoes. The narrator presents the mulattoes' social advancement as the result of a political strategy. By aquiring knowledge they were able to take advantage of the political changes taking place in the *Metropole* or Continental France (82–83). Their ambition and their readiness to occupy the forefront of all political struggle made them the support of the colonial administration at the expense of the *békés*. As a result, they will be instrumental in the campaign for emancipation.

The urban space seems to offer a certain freedom of movement even to slaves coming from the plantation to sell the food they grew to the marketplace (91–94). Paradoxically, field slaves used the example of the freedmen as a guide for dressing and behavior in town, though they were envious. Through Esternome's story we can see the emergence of class and color rivalry as we observe mulattoes imitating the *békés*, the free blacks imitating the mulattoes, and the slaves imitating the free blacks. An alienating ladder of social values based on color and appearance established itself in the pre-emancipation period, which exists even today despite the works of the negritude movement, Glissant, and the contemporary writers of the *créolité* movement.

Five years after *Texaco*, Chamoiseau published a short novel, *L'Esclave Vieil Homme et le molosse*.[10] This 1997 novel openly written to demonstrate the "relation" between Chamoiseau's and Glissant's work asserts the need for a reassessment of the time of slavery. In its opening lines we read: "We are not interested in stories about slavery. There is not much literature on this topic. However, here in these bitter lands of sugar, we feel ourselves drowned in these entangled memories that embitter us with both their lapses and howling presences. Each time our discourse tries to construe itself, we have to turn toward this area as if we were caught in the axis of a spring, the continuous gush of which is still unable to quench the inextinguishable thirst that we have in us" (17–18).

Although Chamoiseau's statement could be read as displaying a limited knowledge of Caribbean literature and historiography, we should examine this affirmation against the background of Martinican social history. Chamoiseau speaks here for the Martinican middle class ("we"), a middle class that looks only toward the *Metropole* and that despises and silences its past. Nevertheless, he acknowledges the importance of the experience of slavery as the foundation for Caribbean writings.

L'Esclave Vieil Homme et le molosse can be read as the archetypal story of the plantation system. Such an interpretation is induced mainly by the anonymity of the protagonists, the absence of geographical landmarks, and the use of the present tense (17–20). The short nominal sentences that describe the setting and recall the beginnings of the plantation help to convey this feeling of scattered memories and the inability to make any sense of the slave economy: "The plantation is small yet every bit of its memory goes far back in the dust of time. The bite of the chains. The lash of the whip. The screams. Blasting deaths. Starvations. Decimating tiredness. Exile. Deportations of different populations which are forced to live together without the moral values and laws of the old world" (20).

Characteristic of the slave society is the dehumanization of the slaves but also of the slaves' master. Against this background, the anonymous slave "Old Man" stands as the example of silent resistance, a voluntary withdrawal that makes him almost invisible on the plantation. Chamoiseau's slave protagonist refuses to play any part in the system (22–24). He offers a kind of "opaqueness" to both the other slaves and the *béké* as time and life seem to pass by him. There is something mechanical about the way he goes on working and living on the plantation (23). However, despite his passivity and anonymity, the slave Old Man seems to dictate the rhythm of the plantation. He is a reassuring presence even if he goes unnoticed: "Sometimes, the master's watchful eyes are unable to recognize him among the machines as they seem to move all by themselves; however, the master leaves with the feeling that he is somewhere—this feeling is reinforced by the proper smell of the fresh sugar and the smooth humming of the turbines" (22).

The slave Old Man always resisted the temptation of *marronage:* running away from the plantation is presented as an impulse (*la décharge*, the jolt, 38) that generally affects young or newly arrived slaves. In the case of Old Man, he does not consider his departure from the plantation as "running or going away" but just as "going" (49). The relevance of this distinction is marked in the novel by the knowledge of his forthcoming death and by the lack of preparation surrounding his departure (49).

Old Man's flight from the plantation is described as a way to recover one's humanity in order to die as a human being and not as cattle. Despite the risk and the fact that he does not stand a chance, Old Man runs away. As soon as he reaches the woods, he feels different. In fact, the three protagonists involved (the slave, the hound, and the *béké*) will never be the same after the hunt. The most interesting aspect of Chamoiseau's novel is that hunted and hunters undergo a tremendous change in terms of self-awareness. In the case of the slave, running in the woods restores his subjectivity. From the forced invisibility and reification process at work on the plantation, his self emerges as "I." As he runs blindly in the wood, overwhelmed with terror and knowing that he is running toward his death, the Old Man becomes aware of his "self": "He had to listen to himself in some unknown areas, to isolate his heart beats, thumping louder than ever" (59).

He is born again symbolically after a narrow escape from death in the quicksands of a spring (79–81). The episode plays on the symbolic value of death and rebirth and the imagery of the mud and water as the primal elements presiding at the birth of humankind (myths of creation from mud and clay and of spring water as the Christian symbol of baptism). The experience of death coincides with the intrusion of the author/narrator as "I" in the story (80) acknowledging his inability to comprehend such an intimate experience. Once Old Man has survived, he can say "I" because he can identify and "describe" his surroundings. The following sequence is then told using the first person narration to retrace the experience of the new maroon in the woods (82–94).

The hunt in the woods also affects the hunters (the *béké* and his hound). The hound is presented as a "monster" (31, 39) at the beginning of the story. He shared the experience of the middle passage only to be turned from an ordinary dog into an indefinite animal (nobody agrees on his description, 32–33). The color of his hide changes depending of the witness's relationship with him: the sailor on the boat saw him as black with a white spot between the eyes, inverting the initial description from white with a black spot between the eyes; the slaves saw him as totally black; the hunted ones saw him as red or red orange like a burning heart. Though the text does not elaborate on the constant shift in the description, we can recognize the implicit symbols of the devil and inferno in the slaves' vision of the hound. This perception contributes a supernatural element to the function of the hound in the plantation system. In addition, the feeding of this hound is surrounded with magic practices: "The master-*béké* fed it with strange food prepared, above all, in deep secret: fresh raw meat; bones with their burning marrows; bloody and fleshy mixtures he blended himself in a Carib warrior's skull. People say that he ground wasps in it, with hot pepper, humming birds' heads, snakes' oil, powders from the bones of rabid men, hair of mad *chabines,* brains of big *balaous* and bones of big swordfish. The hound gobbled it all up voraciously with more stubborness than appetite" (38).

The terror created by the hound tells about the extent of the master's power since he is the one who uses witchcraft in order to assert his (evil) power over the slaves. Nevertheless, after the hunt, the animal that comes back to its master is absolutely different, almost tamed (125). The change in the animal occurred after it fell down in the spring and nearly got caught in the quicksand (104–7, 120). The resistance of Old Man and his transformation after surviving the spring disturb the hound to such an extent that he loses his ferocity by the end of the hunt. When he finally meets Old Man, he is unable to attack the slave (125).

The *béké* is also transformed as he tracks Old Man. During his search to win back his slave, the master is constantly crying (99). Chamoiseau gives a symbolic value to these tears because they signal, as did the spring for Old Man, the return of some humanity in the *béké.* The hunt turns into self-introspection and gives the opportunity of self-assessment, not as an individual but as the representative of the colonists. The master is confronted with his deeds, not as an individual but as the representative of the white planters. As he remembers the different steps of the island colonization (95–96), he is forced to question the choice of slavery as a means of labor exploitation and must admit his own dehumanization (l22).

The experience of slavery has shaped Caribbean societies and still dictates behaviors that have apparently nothing to do with the actual period. Martinican literature is no exception. It is as if an invisible wound were still bleeding in the memories of the descendants of masters and slaves alike. While Confiant resorts to derision and anecdotes to neutralize the past, Chamoiseau tries to explore it in depth, no matter how painful it may be. It is through this wound that major creative works of the region have emerged, and Chamoiseau's *L'Esclave Vieil Homme et le molosse* expresses this poetically (129–34). The quest for history and for identity, the need to control the Caribbean space, all the major themes in Caribbean literature stem from that original wound. It is even more true of the French Caribbean Islands (and of Martinique more than Guadeloupe) because of their ambiguous status of departments or neocolonies.

NOTES

1. *Antilla*, no. 733 (June 7, 1997): 15–20. Dossier 22 Mé (May).

2. Beverly Ormerod, *Introduction to the French Caribbean Novel* (London: Heinemann, 1985), 58.

3. Ormerod, *Introduction to the French Caribbean Novel*, 2.

4. Jean Bernabé, Patrick Chamoiseau, and Raphaël Confiant, *Eloge de la créolité*, bilingual ed. trans. Mohammed B. Taleb Khyar (Paris: Gallimard, 1989), 100. Emphasis added.

5. Bernabé, Chamoiseau, and Confiant, *Eloge de la créolité*, 100–106.

6. Maryse Condé, *Moi, Tituba, sorcière ... noire de Salem* (Paris: Mercure de France, 1986); Simone Schwarz-Bart, *Pluie et vent sur Telumée miracle* (Paris: Seuil, 1972); Edouard Glissant, *Le Quatrième siècle* (Paris: Seuil, 1964).

7. Raphaël Confiant, *Eau de café* (Paris: Livre de Poche, 1993), 32.

8. Patrick Chamoiseau, *Texaco* (Paris: Gallimard, 1990).

9. Barbara J. Webb, *Myth and History in Caribbean Fiction: Alejo Carpentier, Wilson Harris, and Edouard Glissant* (Amherst: U of Massachusetts P, 1992), 52.

10. Chamoiseau, *L'Esclave Vieil Homme et le molosse* (Paris: Gallimard, 1997).

FOUR

Legacies

From the Plantation to the Penitentiary
Chain, Classification, and Codes of Deterrence

JOAN DAYAN

A convicted felon, whom the law in its humanity punishes by confinement
in the penitentiary instead of with death . . . is in a state of penal servitude
to the State. He has, as a consequence of his crime, not only forfeited his
liberty, but all his personal rights except those which the law in its humanity accords to him. He is, for the time being, the slave of the State.

Ruffin vs. Commonwealth, 62 Va. (1871)

In November 1932 the film *I Am a Fugitive from a Chain Gang*, starring Paul
Muni, was released. According to film historians, the reform of the southern
chain gang system can be attributed to the public reaction generated by this
movie. Although the Georgia Department of Corrections argues that the chain
gang was abolished by the late 1940s, the practice of chaining inmates working
on public roads continued until the 1960s. As a child growing up in Atlanta,
I remember seeing men wearing zebra stripes on the Fulton County highways.
My father warned me not to look, but I ignored him, and years later, when
I thought of the South, I thought of men shackled in the sun. Two years ago,
the sight of men in fetters on Interstate 10 near Douglas, Arizona, changed the
course of my work: what began as an investigation of chain gangs became part
of a larger project on prison, memory, and the law. Shackled in lightweight
steel chains padlocked to leather ankle restraints, the prisoners performed their
part in the correctional philosophy of Governor Fife Symington, a vision that
got him reelected: "You're going to come to prison in Arizona, you're going
to work."

Chains, incarceration, shock, three strikes, and *hard labor* are words that satisfy a public eager for the visualization of punishment and retribution. *Privilege* is a word I like to ponder. The term combines *privas* and *lex,* private and law. Law, as both the southern proslavery apologists and the Caribbean planters knew, gained sustenance from the boon of property. Divine dispensation, as well as natural advantages, stems from the possession of property, which gives one a privileged position over those who do not share that advantage. The special permissions, rights, and immunities granted have contributed to our preoccupation with making permanent our privileged instants. Today, the majority of people in favor of hard time for criminal activity experience, if only for a moment of scorn and anger, the entitlement that comes with the exclusion of or to the detriment of others.

Tired of the delimitation of privilege, the closing off of what we do when we teach and write in the academy from the places we claim to be speaking about or for, I began work in the county jail and state prison systems in Arizona. The new mechanisms of institutionalized servility that sustain order and produce obedience mark the most concerted effort since Reconstruction to create a class of citizens subordinate to and separate from those outside the walls of confinement.

Two-thirds of those incarcerated in the state prisons in Arizona are convicted of nonviolent crime, and the Maricopa County jail rate of incarceration has tripled in three years, as Joe Arpaio, "the meanest sheriff in America," announces. Social programs are slashed; new prisons are built. What one warden called the military prison complex is the fastest growing business in this country. The growth of America's prison population is more than ten times that of the general population. "Crime is increasing," an officer in Arpaio's "tent city" informed me, "so you'll never lose our job. If you want a recession proof job, get into corrections, 'cause during a recession you're sure to have more crime."

My interest in writing about changing forms of containment and incapacitation in Arizona is an extension of the historiography of control and classification I began in *Haiti, History, and the Gods,* which concluded with a discussion of two moments in the history of property and dispossession. First, in 1685 the *Code Noir,* or Black Code, was instituted to convey Louis XIV's edicts concerning the discipline and control of slaves in the French colonies. The *Code Noir* has never been published in English, resulting in three hundred years of silence about the legalization of the commerce in human flesh and genocide. Second was the systematic codification of humans, the codes of color, dress, and comportment that assured the methodological exclusion of certain folks outside the pale of human relation and empathy.[1]

Alternately defined as chattel and as real property, slaves were sometimes movable assets (part of the planter's estate) and sometimes immovable (disposed of as if real estate). What is remarkable about the Black Code is that it existed only as precepts and was rarely recognized in practice. Yet the rituals of constraint and classification that I found present in Saint-Domingue on the eve of the Revolution of 1791 are now literalized in the "get tough" rhetoric of contemporary politicians and media that, in picturing spectacles of denigration, perpetuate them while trivializing their effects. What Orlando Patterson in *Slavery and Social Death* describes as "a secular excommunication," and what we might recall in that strangest of legal fictions as "civil death," circumscribes a terrain of servitude and degeneration.[2]

I want to turn briefly to *Ruffin v. Commonwealth*, a case that provides an apt vehicle for characterizing and, more precisely, conceptualizing the status of inmates in the state prisons and county jails of the United States. The date is 1871. It is the Reconstruction South. The scene is Richmond, Virginia. Woody Ruffin, a "convicted felon," committed murder while working on a chain gang outside the county where he was convicted. What is at stake here is the power of competing analogies that redefine "rights." The judicial language of the case, though emphasizing the law's "reasonable rather than literal construction," defines the inmate as "the slave of the State." Statutory laws and regulations, as Justice Christian argues, "attach to the person of the convict wherever he may be carried by authority of law . . . as certainly and tenaciously as the ball and chain which he drags after him."

Declared civilly dead, the inmate is no longer a person, for the prison walls, like the figure of the ball and chain, circumscribe the prisoner in a fiction that, in extending the bounds, the balls and chains of servitude, becomes the basis for the negation of rights, thus reconciling constitutional strictures with slavery. The figures of containment and deprivation enunciated here as fundamental to the order and protection of society, once maintained in time as legal precedent, create the possibilities for the "walls," metaphorized by the law as if "reasonable," to ensure the "literal construction" of contemporary locales for punishment. No longer called the "hole" or "solitary," but adapting the judicial language of decorum and a vocabulary of decency and security, these places are now redesignated as "special management units," "security housing units," or "control units," engaging language in legality to the extent that the new prison

plantations are recast as "state-of-the-art facilities" for the discipline and incapacitation of those now known as "strategic threat groups."

There are certain things about personhood, about what it means to be a person, that are not lost with conviction, even if, as I argue, the Thirteenth
Amendment, read strictly, puts prisoners outside the bounds of civil rights. To
push the idea of penal forfeit further, we might reconsider the concept of civil
death in terms of its ruling metaphors: "corruption of blood" or "forfeiture of
property." The English common-law fiction of strict civil death, to be "at-
tainted" or "dead in law"—forfeiting property, as well as personal rights—
though generally rejected as a rule of American common law, was adopted by
some states.

Christian's use of civil death to legally confine prisoners even when beyond
the actual prison walls remains effective because of a working dichotomy that
construes both persons and privilege: not only the opposition between natural
(read *physical*) death and unnatural (read *legal*) death, but also the strategic
and classificatory agenda implied in the distinction between natural rights and
civil rights. One can, hypothetically, retain natural rights but still be disabled
by statutory abridgment, condemned by societal (or civilized) needs. Once the
legal terminology of blood taint or disability was surcharged with racial prejudice—handily accomplished by Christian's definition of the convict as "slave
of the State"—then the claims for personal rights become shifting and tenta-
tive, as the inmate becomes something like a synthetic or artificial slave: incapacitated, and hence barbaric.

Crucial to this project is the redefinition of terms: what might be called a semantic genealogy of slavery and involuntary servitude: words like *labor, service,* and *discipline* are key to this specification. The practice of rendering certain groups of people as "dead in law" can be traced from the "black codes" of
the Caribbean and the American South to the Thirteenth Amendment and the
constitutional language of containment to recent Supreme Court decisions
regarding conditions of confinement, punishment, classification, and capital
crime. How the mobilization of history is used to trump arguments about justice matters a great deal. If narratives of the past get constructed in and by law,
we might well say, then, as Austin Sarat put it, "law's history is a turn of respect.
Law always lives in the past. No horrors can awaken it."

The language of the law, amid the current spectacle of chain gangs, control
units, prison labor, and execution, delineates a tradition of deterrence and retribution that preserves the memory of slavery. What is remarkable in reading
these past slave codes together with the contemporary law of corrections and

confinement is the divorce between intention, law, and reality. As a set of legal acts that have their own history, the law articulates how material considerations, a concern for public security, and the force of racial prejudice produce the juridical nonexistence of the person through degrees of deprivation. What allowed the subtle conversion of slave into prisoner? I want to briefly turn to the Thirteenth Amendment to the Constitution: the directive that perpetuated the institution of slavery through a rationale of containment. In December 1865, the ratification of the Thirteenth Amendment was announced. It abolished slavery and involuntary servitude "except as punishment of crime whereof the party shall have been duly convicted." The legal exception became the means for terminological slippage: those who were once slaves were now criminals, and "forced labor" in the form of the "convict lease" system ensured continued degradation. The parenthetical expression guaranteed enclosure, a bracketing of servitude that revived slavery under cover of removing it. Such an amendment literally amounted to an escape clause, a corrective loophole that left the vestige of enslavement intact.

During the second session of the Thirty-ninth Congress (December 12, 1866–January 8, 1867), debates centered on the meaning of the exemption in the antislavery amendment, since punishment for crime found fit locale not only within the walls of prisons and jails but also on the auction block. In the very sentence abolishing slavery, provision had been made for its revival under another form and through the action of the courts of the United States. Those declared free by this clause of the Constitution found themselves returned to slavery. Senator Charles Sumner presented to Congress a notice posted by William Bryan, the sheriff of Anne Arundel County in Maryland: "Public Sale.—The undersigned will sell at the court-house door, in the city Annapolis, at twelve o'clock m., on Saturday, 8th December, 1866, a negro man named Richard Harris, for six months, convicted at the October term, 1866, of the Anne Arundel county circuit court for larceny, and sentenced by the court to be sold as a slave. Terms of sale, cash."[3] During this same session of Congress, other cases were presented to demonstrate that these sales were nothing less than lingering relics of the Black Code. In Georgia, an "old negro man, between seventy and eighty years old, a much-respected preacher of the Gospel," was arrested for vagrancy and put to work in chains for twelve months. In Maryland, twenty-five-year-old Harriet Purdy was to be sold for a term of one year in the state, and Dilby Harris, aged thirty, was to be sold for a term of two years in the state. No crime was mentioned in either of these advertisements for sale.[4]

Sumner emphasized what the language of the amendment allowed, objecting to its phraseology as "an unhappy deference . . . to an original legislative precedent at an earlier period of our history." Fearing what he saw as the congressional sanction of servitude, he had still hoped that the words "involuntary servitude, except for crime" applied only to "ordinary imprisonment." Noting, however, that what had seemed "exclusively applicable" had been "extended so as to cover some form of slavery," he asked that Congress "go farther and expurgate the phraseology from the text of the Constitution itself."[5] Throughout the recently disbanded Confederacy leased prisoners maintained plantations and rebuilt public places. Slave codes shaped the language of contracts for convict labor, and plantations turned into prisons.[6]

Contemporary exercises in servitude endorsed by state legislatures from New York to Florida are transmitted to a public, apparently eager to revisit scenes of hard labor and humiliation. Most often, this labor is nothing more than a costly performance that could be argued to be the most extreme violence that could be inflicted on a people: state-implemented imitation that assumes the agreement and the pleasure of a mimetic society. Fashionable calls for the tags of race and class are decimated in those places where historically nuanced processes of stigmatization assure that the poor and the powerless will be converted into so much material exposed to institutional degradation: the kind of precise and repeated rituals of domination that produce what Orlando Patterson calls "social death": the original, transforming violence of transforming human into thing.[7]

Terminology and changing definitions matter a great deal, since the assessment of criminality and control of the confined is in large part a rhetorical endeavor. Discursive obfuscation spares one the need to confront the extreme, even unspeakable, practices subsumed under the name of "corrections": for example, when "solitary confinement" is retermed "special management" or when those who carry out executions are known as "the special operations team." Words like *security, person, pain,* and *punishment* must be redefined, since the delimitation of liberty required, in what one officer described to me as "this other world," produces an environment of language unlike any other. This linguistic surround is enabled by judicial rhetoric that turns to the form of law as the rule of action: a judge's self-justification through what Robert Cover calls "law language," the rules of which "are arrived at primarily by examining the way language is spoken in the past."[8]

Whether in state prison or county jail, the remnants of past methods of incarceration and punishment are now systematized in laws and regulations that

promote the requisite images of vagrants, social outcasts, and misfits to a public receptive to the categorical embodiment of denigration. Here, for a moment, I turn to Ian Hacking's emphasis on "dynamic nominalism" as productive of the possibilities of action. "What is curious about human action is that
by and large what I am deliberately doing depends on the possibilities of description . . . all intentional acts are acts under a description. Hence if new
modes of description come into being, new possibilities for action come into
being in consequence." [9] Making taxonomies in the twentieth-century United
States is somewhat different from the conjuring of bodies of color and caste in
eighteenth-century Saint-Domingue. For we are not busy inventing numerous
categories and labeling individuals in the manner of a Buffon or Moreau de
Saint-Méry, who were conscious of the need to define something as indefinable
as blood quanta and the taxonomies applicable to the products of colonial mixing. Instead, definition is assumed. Divestment and subordination need no
complex method of gradations. The generality of the criminal type is all that
matters: the broad stroke of exclusion that can fit as many different types of a
certain kind of people under the category of criminal.

The projection of something called "criminality" inevitably returns us to
the idiom of racial difference as necessitating places of containment. W. E. B.
Du Bois's equation between formal emancipation and legal bondage in *The
Souls of Black Folk* urges us to consider how the curse of color was utilized to
consolidate the claims of capital: "when the Negroes were freed and the whole
South was convinced of the impossibility of free Negro labor, the first and almost universal device was to use the courts as a means of reenslaving the
blacks. It was not then a question of crime, but rather one of color." [10]

In contemporary rituals of incarceration, African-American men are imprisoned at a rate six times that of white men. Although these African Americans make up less than 7 percent of the U.S. population, they constitute almost
half of the prison and jail population. In Arizona, African Americans are over-
represented in the prison population (16.3 percent) compared to their percentage of the state's general population (2.9 percent), as are Hispanics in
prison (31.1 percent) compared to the general population (18.8 percent). [11] And
now, as an increasing number of citizens, redefined as criminals, are imagina-
tively recolored to match or, more precisely, to embody retrospectively the figure of the slave, the legal status of inmates matters more than ever. [12]

What constitutes the idea of the person in jails and prisons? And what is necessary to maintain that personal identity? Finally, what are the legitimate rights
of the county or state over the interests of the incarcerated? I move through a

few scenes of redefinition. Taking the county jail system in Phoenix, Arizona, as my example, I turn to spectacles where divestment and subordination are enabled, where those incarcerated—no matter for what reason—become indistinguishable, where words like *nature, security,* or *crime* reconstruct a system of dominance that remembers the substance of slavery.

DOING CHAIN

Nowhere is the slick packaging of spectacles of punishment as apparent as in Sheriff Joe Arpaio's Maricopa County Jail Chain Gangs. Arpaio calls the inmates in his jails his "extras," part of his "film crew," for unlike the chain programs in the state prison system, Arpaio's local reforms—tent cities, posses, "last chance" chain gangs—have been aired on *Hard Copy, Sixty Minutes, Donahue,* and *20/20,* have been covered on French, English, German, and Australian television, and have been discussed in a wide range of newspapers and magazines.[13] Sometime in July 1995, I turned on *A Current Affair,* which began: "We go behind the bars with the toughest Sheriff in America." The hyperbole drew attention not to the condition of the inmates, their chains, or their compulsory participation in Arpaio's spectacle, but to Arpaio's heroics: "this is one old-fashioned Wild West cop," "the making of frontier legend," "a real Wild West hero." The program ended with a tribute: "In the end he just might do what all good lawmen do in the movies, walk into the sunset."

Unlike inmates in prisons, those in the county jails either have not been sentenced and await trial or they have been sentenced for a year or less. Recognized as one of the top undercover agents in drug enforcement history, Arpaio promises to bring "law and order" to Maricopa County, and he has made a ritual of incarceration, treating inmates as objects of scorn, to be taunted, humiliated, and tested. Arpaio's presentation of crime and punishment draws on images deep in the psyche of the American Dream: a fantasy so at risk that the transport of post-emancipation criminal codes and convict labor from the New South to the contemporary southwest has made Arpaio the most popular politician in the state.

On September 19, 1996, fifteen women—ten of them African American— wearing bright orange jumpsuits and chained together, picked up trash along a Phoenix street. Arpaio calls himself an "equal opportunity incarcerator" and boasts that women in his jails can take the hundred-degree heat as well as men.[14] The solicitude for gender that cost Alabama corrections commissioner Ron

Jones his job—when he envisioned putting women inmates to work in leg irons—bites the dust in Arizona. One of these women, who called herself Princess, said she had put on makeup for the event, glad to "do publicity for Joe." Another woman in her early twenties had been arrested for prostitution—on the street she now walked in chains—by Arpaio's posse in their crusade "Operation Zero Tolerance" or "Operation Adopt a Whore," more popularly known as the "Pussy Patrol." Turning away from the cameras, she asked me if I would like to change places with her. "This is bullshit," she said, "nothing but a publicity stunt. The chains, makeup, and video cameras get all the attention, not the showers with worms, the stun guns, hog-tying, and rotten food." The show matters less for what it accomplishes in terms of correction, than for how it works as performance. Arpaio, intent that the degradation be a recuperation of chains past, has recently outfitted his chain crews in white pants and trousers with horizontal black stripes. They are accompanied by dogs.

Arpaio thrives on publicity, and during our first interview, he demonstrated how much he likes to shock those who wonder about his methods: "See anybody dying?" he asks, when I wonder about the tents, where over a thousand prisoners live in summer temperatures that go up to 130 degrees.[15] He had, after all, already summed up his criminal treatment program: "My whole philosophy is, put more people in jail. We've got a vicious crime problem out there, and the answer is to take them off the streets and educate them through punishment." For Arpaio, this recasting of education as chastisement summons a new definition of success: "I got guys in jail that have come back thirteen times."

Arpaio's "Sheriff's Posse" (twenty-five hundred members, of whom eight hundred are armed) arrest prostitutes on Van Buren Street, assist deputies in drug busts and vagrancy cleanups, chase down graffiti in "Operation T.A.G." ("Operation Take Away Graffiti"), and seek out "deadbeat dads" in "Operation Pay-Back," which Arpaio has described as a "Happy Mother's Day Gift from the Maricopa County Sheriff's Office." Arpaio has also introduced the "Scared Straight" program, which uses his chain crews to bury the poor at the county cemeteries. "I'm not trying to scare anyone stiff," Arpaio claims. "This is a tough program and teaches a serious lesson to these inmates about how life could end up for any one of them if they don't turn things around and straighten up." The Ecumenical Chaplaincy for the Homeless, which supplies clergy for burials in two cemeteries for the poor and the homeless, has refused to preside over these interments. The Reverend Gerald Roseberry, founder of the group, objected to manacled inmates in bright orange jumpsuits shoveling dirt over coffins and to Arpaio's characterization of the dead as "crack addicts, criminals, people whose lives have come to nothing."

Those incarcerated in the Maricopa County jail system have two choices: either a regeneration that must be arduous, if not impossible, given the over-determined world of criminal (substitute *sinful*) nature or else reprobation, condemned to a state of relentless repetition. If they are soiled and infected with criminality, a corruption of "nature" so deep that they keep defiling themselves, then all that can be done for this majority—which Arpaio puts at almost 70 percent—is to incarcerate them as befits their nature. As Arpaio commented to me, "I have more people in jail than in the whole history of Maricopa County. Almost 6,000, which makes me the fourth, almost the third, largest jail system in the country. I tell every police officer and every judge, don't tell me you don't put people in jail because there's no room. This sheriff will always have room in his hotel. My jail system should hold 3,900 people, and I'm up to 6,000."

Crime and punishment is another, more popular version of sin and retribution. "Incapacitation," which means quite simply the restraint on criminals' ability to commit crime, can be seen as a secular analogue of excommunication. Cloaking individuals in the categories of castaways, aliens, or reprobates becomes a persuasive strategy in Arpaio's new book, *America's Toughest Sheriff: How to Win the War against Crime.*[16] Along with the tough-talking, mean-strutting persona of the solitary lawman of the Old West (claimed by Arpaio when he recalls his childhood love of cowboy fictions of Tom Mix, Gene Autry, and Roy Rogers), comes the voice of a zealous minister or proslavery advocate who knows how to recognize the fiendish glance of the brute, who warns his community of felons bent on turning Maricopa County into a pit of darkness. Though perhaps not as pronounced as his tone of hearty common sense— "sound management practices and a rational penal philosophy"—these resonant images form the dramatic plot of Arpaio's reflections.

America's Toughest Sheriff reclaims the fable of a spanking new Canaan played out in the desert: God's country, virgin land, and peoples evacuated and renamed. This fantastic underside of our heritage, often masked by the bracing call to plain truth, is the backdrop to Arpaio's innovations in Maricopa County: the cordoning off of those branded by a certain kind of hyperbolic fix. For the assumptions that ring clear and true are made possible by the privilege of the populist who wields the terms of denigration. Arpaio turns a night spent in the tents with the inmates (accompanied by a reporter) into a journey to the underworld, or more precisely, he recalls the experience in terms reminiscent of an Edward Long, taking his readers to his vision of darkest pseudo-Africa: "This was new, uncharted territory for me. . . . Criminals are basically a cowardly and brutish bunch, and brutish cowards are most dangerous in the shadows, in the dark. . . . And as I lay on that thin mattress on that cold, black night . . . I couldn't help but think about all the other cold, black nights I had spent in strange places, distant lands, waiting for drug dealers, murderers, human vermin of all kind, bluffing and dealing and duping the bad guys, making them crawl out of their hidden holes into the light." [17]

Although prison officials in Arizona mock Arpaio and contrast their "public display of chain" with the sheriff's publicity-seeking antics, Arpaio's message has been influential beyond state lines. Since most Americans do not know the difference between state prisons and county jails—none other than Senator Phil Gramm praised Arpaio's practices as the model for prison reform in this country—Arpaio's methods, popularized in such catchy sound bites as "posse-mania," "proud his jail is a living hell," "get tough with lowlifes," are playing to a public quite comfortable with cruel and unusual punishment. No doubt his call for "discipline" and "a total absence of frills" seem as much a cause for celebration in our America as a rousing game of baseball, a piece of mom's apple pie, or a good fight in Iraq. Arpaio likes to compare his tents in the desert for "sentenced convicts" to the tents used in "Operation Desert Storm" for the "heroic young men and women" in the Saudi desert. If these soldiers sacrificed their comfort for their country, Arpaio declares, "I think the very least we can ask of our criminals is to sacrifice a little for the taxpayers."

Arpaio patterned Tent City after the army. Not only were the tents military surplus, dating from the Persian Gulf War, the Korean War, and even World War I, but, as he explained to me in a rapid-fire sequence of images and staccato beat: "I only have two officers guarding a thousand, twenty criminals in each tent, double bunks, military, my sergeants and lieutenants, the Korean War, First World War tents. I just put up a sixty-foot tower. When you see it, you say, gee, I'm back in the army again. This is a division, a division of troops here. I have more than a thousand in the desert. I'll have room in three months for three thousand in the desert."

These locales for punishment make use of tactics of humiliation that turn inmates into outsiders, superfluous human beings. The unconstitutional conditions of Tent City—plagued by unbearable heat, overcrowding, rodents, dust, and violence—become the material for Arpaio's bouts of derisive sport and gratuitous cruelty. Arpaio brags about meals of unmarketable "green" bologna, forcing criminals to wear pink underwear (and then putting autographed pink boxer shorts like "those criminals wear, only better" on sale at Wal-Mart), and restricting television to Newt Gingrich's ten-part video series, *Renewing American Civilization,* and the Weather Channel, so "they'll know how cool it is in Buffalo while they're boiling in their tents in Phoenix."

The prisoners in the first of the tent units—"In Tents" (Arpaio laughed, and repeated to me, "*intense,* right?") followed by "Con-Tents" (he joked, "Con . . . Convicts, Contents, Table of Contents")—are, Arpaio claims, convicted felons. Though Arpaio's critics have argued that those detained in the tents have been convicted for minor crimes such as lapsed license plates, shoplifting, technical probation violations, petty theft, and drugs, Arpaio insists that he's detaining murderers, rapists, and child molesters. Tent City 3 is called "Pre-Tents" (and again, he signaled the cleverness of the pun, "pretense, pre-tents, pre"), which will house pretrial detainees.

Who are these people called criminals who must be in jail, how are they classified, and what kind of education are those convicted and put in tents getting? Further, what are the mechanisms of control, the codification of inmates that assures their exclusion from the realm of human relations? Arpaio's chain gang operation, what one officer called "the public display of chain," more blatantly than any of his other correctional antics, marks the passage from considered correctional philosophy to the visualization of domination and duress. Inmates are chained together six feet apart at the left ankle by quarter-inch proof coil, about five to six feet long. They work six days a week, breaking rocks or clearing rubbish. They are not paid. Arpaio talks about his chain gang with familiarity. They are his dependents; in the worst of cases, they are naughty children who need to be taught a lesson, and the more insulting the means of teaching, the better. Our interview ended with his claims of a peculiar relation with his inmates. "Now, the inmates have my number now. They know I love it when they say they hate it, now they're starting to say they like it. I get very angry when they say that. Today they won't say they like it out there, it's 120 degrees."

According to Arpaio, for those who have misbehaved and are in lockdown, it's their "last chance" to prove themselves and regain their privileges, but he then added, "Yeah, whatever privileges they have left." In August 1995, the first of the sheriff's "Last Chance" chain gangs asked for a graduation ceremony. After their thirty-day assignment was completed, each member was given a specially designed graduation certificate, with the heading: "Certificate of Achievement." Arpaio described the event: "I graduated them last week. I gave them a nice certificate. . . . I'll make you a copy. They get hooked together on chains for thirty days. They're out there every day, hot, cleaning up the street, the bushes, and all that, all over the county. I got them in downtown Phoenix. When I gave them their graduation certificate, it was down where all the hookers are. They were cleaning up a church, around the church and all that."

Inmates who want to be part of the chain gang program fill out a form called "Last Chance," requesting, as explained by Captain David Wilson, commander of the Special Projects Division under Sheriff Arpaio, the opportunity "to voluntarily participate in the Last Chance Program." [18] Wilson explains his own philosophy of chain: "It's what I call 'involuntary compliance,' a little behavior modification. Compliance means that you agree to do what you can't help but do, because the alternative is unbearable."

Behavior becomes a fluid category that allows for various quasi-articulated diagnostic features of classification. You become a problem and are assigned to lockdown or disciplinary segregation for thirty days if you refuse to cut your hair, will not work, get caught with contraband, or talk back to an officer. If these inmates want to take part in the chain gang program, they fill out the form "requesting to voluntarily participate in the Last Chance Program." Then, besides Tent City rules, they must agree to and also memorize the following orders, which Captain Wilson calls "the promise list":

1. I will be a model inmate.

2. I understand profanity or insolent language or comments will not be tolerated.

3. I will remain in "lock-down" while in this program and will undergo a daily personal and cell inspection.

4. I will maintain a "military style" haircut, with no facial hair.

5. Possession of any contraband, refusal to comply with staff's instructions, or violation of rules will result in permanent no-work status.

6. I will be required to work on a labor detail, six days per week, in leg chains, while in the program.

7. I understand I am to address all staff members with the appropriate "Officer," "Sir," "Ma'am" at all times.

8. I will maintain all property in the provided property boxes.

9. I will be issued two sets of uniforms (one set of blues and one jumpsuit) and one hat. I will not alter the items.

10. I will wear the jumpsuit only on work details; blues will be worn in the facility.

There are more volunteers than can be accommodated, so those inmates who are not accepted on the chain gang could remain in lockdown for an indefinite time, depending on Captain Wilson's judgment of the behavior problem and the necessary punishment. It is not surprising that thirty days on Arpaio's "Jail Inmate Chain Detail"—what one inmate described as his "Kiddie Show"—remains a popular alternative to long-term deprivation.

CLASSIFYING CODES

On June 1, 1996, Scott Norberg, detained in the Madison Street Jail, died of asphyxia after deputies shocked him with an electronic stun device and restrained him in a position that, according to the county medical examiner, kept him from getting air. He had been tackled by fourteen detention officers and placed in a restraint chair with a towel over his face. In July, after months of investigating whether the civil rights of county inmates had been violated in Arpaio's jails, the U.S. Justice Department issued a two-hundred-page preliminary report that addresses allegations of abuse, inadequate medical care, overcrowding, use of excessive force, and conditions in the tents: too hot, not enough water, worms, bugs, snakes, and garbage.[19] One inmate described the tent city locale to me: "a dog pound on one side, where dogs burn all night; the city dump on the other side; and a little down the road, a factory where dog food is made."

Arpaio called the report "outrageous," but I remember an earlier incident that had been captured on the jail's video equipment. An inmate who had been arrested on a traffic warrant called an officer a name; he was yanked from his cell and thrown against the wall by three officers. His arm broke at the elbow. When asked in an interview with *CBS News* whether he knew how the inmate's arm was broken, Arpaio answered, "No, I don't, but so what? I'm sure that my officers had a reason to slam him against the cellblock."

Amnesty International is now investigating Arpaio's cruel, inhuman, and degrading treatment of inmates in the Maricopa County jails, both in the hard facilities and the tents.[20] Given Arpaio's glee in discussing his methods, these recent findings make the claim of "education through punishment" sound more like depersonalization through terror: evidence of faces slammed into concrete walls, bones broken, and teeth smashed; four-point restraint chairs, which international law prohibits from being used as punishment, except as an absolutely last resort, but which have been used about six hundred times from January to early June 1997; the abusive use of stun guns, including repeated gratuitous shocks to inmates; no exercise in the open air; and male guards' unrestricted access to female quarters.

What Peter Linebaugh in *The London Hanged* has called the "denaturing" of "men and women who fell foul of law" in eighteenth-century England is handily accomplished in Arpaio's tents.[21] The men and women in tents, whether they've committed a felony or misdemeanor, are, to use Arpaio's words, "dumped in together." Thus, categorization of inmates according to crime goes by the board in the novel strategy of incarceration made possible in Arpaio's Tent City. As Captain Wilson explained to me: "They're all the same risk. They're all convicted." The generality of the criminal type is all that matters.

There is a legal history to the new social order of divestment. In 1977 inmates Damian Hart, Michael G. McKane, and Bartholomew L. Trumble, pretrial detainees in the county jail, brought a civil rights action against Jerry Hill, at that time sheriff of Maricopa County, "for the purpose of eliminating and remedying the degrading, inhuman, punitive, unhealthy and dangerous conditions . . . which violate rights secured to them by the First, Fourth, Fifth, Sixth, Eighth and Fourteenth Amendments to the Constitution of the United States." The 1981 U.S. District Court decision *Hart v. Hill* mandated that inmates be "promptly classified, managed and housed."[22] The objective classification system identified three classification levels: maximum, medium, and minimum, which ensure the safety of inmates and staff. A maximum-security inmate, because of a high risk of violence, would require higher internal security than medium-security inmates, presumed to be a moderate risk, and minimum-security inmates, who present a low risk. After this ruling, the individual jails in Maricopa County established rigorous divisions between inmate populations.

But the tents, praised for their low-cost construction and operating budget, permit the abolishment of the programs and opportunities instituted after *Hart v. Hill.* Violations recorded at the time of the case included:

1. books, magazines, and newspapers could not be received in the mail by plaintiffs;
2. no telephones were available for use in the county jail;
3. no library was available, and detainees were not allowed to read newspapers;
4. no access to law books or a law library;
5. detainees are never allowed to visit with their children or friends under the age of eighteen, and no conjugal visits were permitted;

6. overcrowding in cells (four beds on each of the two sides of the cell) required that detainees were confined to their beds nineteen hours a day;

7. no cleaning implements were provided to clean the walls, sink, toilet, beds, or bars, and these surfaces were not cleaned by defendants;

8. no exercise or recreation program.

By instituting the various phases of Tent City, Arpaio has ensured that all those convicted do not necessarily have minimal civil rights. They are exempt from the 1981 judgment mandated by the U.S. District Court in *Hart v. Hill*.

The tents provide a place where nonclassification can be instituted. On January 10, 1995, the Amended Judgment to *Hart v. Hill* judged it no longer necessary for defendants—the sheriff's office—to "provide periodic reports to the United States District Court for the District of Arizona regarding the operation of the Maricopa County jail system." As evident from Amnesty International's findings of brutality and excessive force, this amendment has allowed the sequence of humiliation and violence to proceed unchecked and unpunished.

Now that sentenced inmates are no longer scattered in the various hard facilities (a centralization instituted by Arpaio), what some deem serious abuses can be more easily carried out: no library (how can you have a library in tents?); no drug rehabilitation (there's no room in the tents, and as many inmates told me, contraband is everywhere); and then there are the innovative changes that made Arpaio famous, no longer actionable in light of this "hands-off" policy: no coffee, no "girlie" magazines, no movies, random drug testing, no "rewards" for "good behavior" (words deemed "fraudulent" by Arpaio), no hot lunches.

In my final contacts with Captain Wilson and Sheriff Arpaio, I was preoccupied with the nonclassification of inmates and the broad stroke of exclusion it allowed. Whatever happens to sentenced inmates inhabiting Tent City is judged fit punishment for ubiquitous criminality. (Note that barracks are being built in the desert for pretrial detainees.) "A guy out in the tents could be put in lockdown for eleven months for having carried two cigarettes," Captain Wilson explained. "He's a fine candidate for the chain gang. But others, whether a child molester or a person with a suspended license, are all the same." The philosophy behind this neutralizing of differences is clarified in an official letter I received from Arpaio.[23]

The letter is direct in its logic. The convicted criminal is a person without honor, rights, or distinction. Indeed, Linebaugh's "history of misappropriated things" provides a chilling background to the new social order founded on the detention of those considered unfit or stigmatized.[24] The legal fiction implied by Captain Wilson is that anyone who commits a crime, whatever it is, has forfeited all claims to an identity that might protect or validate the request for protection. After all, as Wilson put it, "They're all the same once they're sentenced." Arpaio's letter uses the familiar language of budget constraints and public protection. Sentenced inmates do not need "specialized housing," nor do they deserve any "criteria" of placement. Such concerns demand too much money and too much space. Sentenced inmates "*can* be considered classified according to whether they are working or non-working." And division commanders (like Wilson) "have the authority to administratively place any sentenced inmate into non-work status (e.g. disciplinary segregation or lockdown) as circumstances dictate." Since many of the inmates in Tent City will be released into the community when their terms of incarceration expire (an average of sixty to ninety days), this short time in jail allows them to be classified the same way, "regardless of the crime for which they were convicted."

What remained unsaid in the letter was set forth by Captain Wilson during one of our phone conversations. As usual, he was direct. "The sheriff wants it done." The case of *Hart v. Hill* "involved living conditions for inmates—unsentenced inmates. Hart won the case, but it applies only to pretrial detainees. So, in the case of sentenced inmates, we pack them all in the tents, and the federal mandate doesn't apply. 'We don't have to do it, so let's not do it.' That's how the figuring goes." He identifies only one out of five inmates who have a tendency to "victimize" and adds, "Of the one thousand inmates who are out there, at least two hundred should not be there, but then the sheriff would answer, 'Sorry, we don't have the beds in the hard facilities.'"

For Captain Wilson, what matters is society, not the criminal nor the gender of the criminal. "Our criterion is simple: male sentenced to the county jail. That is their classification. We stopped our tradition of classifying, since the traditional categories of medium and maximum change when you consider the sentencing context. We can't separate those hardened criminals from society once they're out, so how hardened are they? To me, it's worse putting the guy next door to you than next door in the same tent with another guy who's sentenced." Since liberal sentencing mechanisms let the guy out soon, why put him in maximum security? To be "sentenced" becomes a condition of being. "If the judge can put those in maximum security on work furlough, why can't we put them in tents?" Wilson's approach is pragmatic:

If you have a person that is a maximum-security inmate, arrested for first-degree murder, he goes through the jail system and during the trial process does a plea bargain. So, he gets one year in county jail on work furlough and four years probation. He gets a job as a welder. Now, look, you've got a maximum-security prisoner in the community during the day, so where's the threat? The guy housed in the tent with him or the coworker in the welding shop? I'm more worried about the coworker. It seems ludicrous to treat someone as maximum security when in a year the guy can be out, if he's getting out anyway soon.

In arguing for what he calls "the realistic approach," Wilson says, "I think we have a better mouse trap." Tax money is wasted in the jails, since everyone will be out in a year, probably 80 percent in the next six months. "I'm turning the people loose on society, so why waste money now? We'll do it in the tents with minimum cost, two officers for a thousand inmates. We're just kind of baby-sitting them until they get out again. It's a holding place—detention." To detain a particular class of individuals, as Wilson suggested toward the end of our phone conversation, can be understood as acting for the public good. And it makes sense, especially if you accept an effective typology based on those who have and work and those who do neither: "After all, who are we incarcerating? The largest percentage of our inmates are lower-income or un-employed individuals. We're not incarcerating the people who are hard work-ers in Paradise Valley."

A critical change has occurred within the cultural domain of corrections: an end to the belief that an incarcerated individual should have the opportunity for things that might be lacking outside. Nothing can be done to help or change the inmate, so the implicit reasoning goes, for they are, after all, "lower-income or unemployed." Though many of those incarcerated in Arpaio's tents are not violent offenders, they are exposed to the most visible degradation. These in-novations in civil society, not the least of which is the belief in "warehousing" criminals, reveal that criminality does not explain the treatment of criminals; rather, the treatment of criminals exposes society in the act of inventing crim-inality. The paradigm is nonrelation. Crime is not the issue, but the creation of a new class of condemned.

NOTES

1. Joan Dayan, *Haiti, History, and the Gods* (Berkeley: U of California P, 1995), 203–12; 224–37.

2. Orlando Patterson, *Slavery and Social Death: A Comparative Study* (Cambridge:

Harvard UP, 1982), 5. See Joan Dayan, "Held in the Body of the State," in *History, Memory, and the Law,* ed. Austin Sarat and R. Thomas Kearns (Ann Arbor: U of Michigan P, 1999).

3. Alfred Avins, ed., *The Reconstruction Amendments' Debates* (Richmond: Virginia Commission on Constitutional Government, 1967), 258.

4. Avins, *Reconstruction,* 258.

5. Avins, *Reconstruction,* 258.

6. As David M. Oshinsky argues in *"Worse than Slavery": Parchman Farm and the Ordeal of Jim Crow Justice* (New York: Free Press, 1996), the post-emancipation criminal code was thus established as a vehicle of racial subordination. See also Alex Lichtenstein, *Twice the Work of Free Labor: The Political Economy of Convict Labor in the New South* (London: Verso, 1996).

7. The most chilling fantasy of reification is evoked by the much celebrated conversion of servile bodies into commodities or, more precisely, stock shares. The Real Estate Investment Trust, more commonly known as REIT, allows private property to go public. Nowhere are investments more assured than in the private prison industry. See "They Want Out; Do You Want In? Fast Growth Attracts Investors to Prison Stocks," *Barron's,* October 13, 1997, 44. Admitting that some investors might balk at buying stock in prisons—where profit depends on bodies incapacitated—the article reminds readers: "Stock prices will be largely immune to news of inflation, currency fluctuations, Mideast jitters. . . . Paradoxically, and almost perversely, bad news, like a rise in the crime rate, will goose this industry's stocks. And a recession, which typically increases crime, would not be bad for these stocks, either." The new regime of turning "dross into gold" amounts to nothing less than a consummate disposal system that makes money for those buying into a REIT, trusting that the corporation will run the prisons, as long as new laws like mandatory sentencing, "three strikes and you're out," and juvenile incarceration ensure the continuous flow of prisoners, not only convicted but detained for longer periods of time.

8. Robert Cover, *Justice Accused: Antislavery and the Judicial Process* (New Haven: Yale UP, 1975), 126.

9. Ian Hacking, "Making Up People," in *Reconstructing Individualism: Autonomy, Individuality, and the Self in Western Thought,* ed. Thomas C. Heller, Morton Sosna, and David E. Wellerby (Stanford: Stanford UP, 1966), 231.

10. W. E. B. Du Bois, *The Souls of Black Folk* (New York: Library of America, 1986), 130.

11. For a discussion of "the darkening of jail and prison populations during the past twenty years" and the increased "terrors of incarceration," see Randall Kennedy, *Race, Crime, and the Law* (New York: Pantheon, 1997), 128–35.

12. Mumia Abu-Jamal describes the legal apparatus necessary to ensure "dehumanization by design." See especially the chapter titled "Teetering on the Brink between Life and Death" for his discussion of *McClesky v. Kemp* (1987), which documented how

the race of the victim and the race of the defendant determined whether the convicted would live or die. Mumia Abu-Jamal, *Live from Death Row* (Reading, Penn.: Addison-Wesley, 1995).

13. Mark Fisk, "Modern Wild West Sheriff Packs Prisoners into Tents in the Scorching Desert," *National Enquirer*, October 25, 1994, 1; Marc Cooper, "Law of the Future: Meet the Phoenix Posse," *Village Voice*, January 18–24, 1995, 30; Richard Grant, "The Mean Machine: Meet America's Toughest Cop—and Don't the Voters Love Him," *Sidney (Australia) Morning Herald*, June 10, 1995, 8–9; Seth Mydans, "Taking No Prisoners, in a Manner of Speaking," *New York Times*, March 4, 1995, 1; William Neuman, "America's Toughest Sheriff: Proud His Jail Is a Living Hell," *New York Post*, May 30, 1995, 8–9; Bob Ford, "America's Most Wanted: A Guy Who'll Get Tough with Lowlifes," *Philadelphia Inquirer Magazine*, June 18, 1995, 18–27; Carol J. Castaneda, "Arizona Sheriff Walking Tall, But Some Don't Like His Style," *USA Today*, May 26–29, 1995, 7; Jonathan Freedland, "Pride and Prejudice of Sheriff Joe, the Meanest, Cheapest, Harshest Jailer in America," *Manchester Guardian*, May 23, 1995.

14. Eun-Kyung Kim, "Maricopa County Sheriff Plans 1st Female Chain Gang," *Arizona Daily Star*, August 26, 1996, 1.

15. My first interview with Arpaio on June 8, 1995, was followed by numerous phone calls during the course of that summer.

16. Joe Arpaio with Len Sherman, *America's Toughest Sheriff: How to Win the War against Crime* (Arlington, Va.: Summit, 1996).

17. Arpaio, *America's Toughest*, 67.

18. On July 10, 1995, I arrived at Tent City at 5:00 a.m., in order to meet Captain Wilson and to observe the inmates line up, have a military check, and march to the place where they would be chained for their work, which on this day involved cutting a firebreak between the desert and a cluster of new homes. I was allowed to talk to and take photographs of the chain crew, also called "Sheriff's Jail Inmate Labor Detail." Note that in the state prison system, photographs are not allowed of prisoners, which would be a violation of their privacy.

19. U.S. Department of Justice, Civil Rights Division, March 25, 1996.

20. Amnesty International, *Ill-Treatment of Inmates in Maricopa County Jails—Arizona* (New York: Amnesty International, August 1997). See also "Indecent Enclosure: County Jails Deny Human Dignity," *Arizona Republic*, September 28, 1997, H1–2.

21. Peter Linebaugh, *The London Hanged: Crime and Civil Society in the Eighteenth Century* (Cambridge: Cambridge UP, 1992), xviii.

22. *Hart v. Hart*, No. CIV 77–479 PHX-EHC-MS.

23. The letter is dated August 3, 1995. Wilson later informed me that he had drafted the letter and sent it on to the sheriff for his signature.

24. Linebaugh, *London Hanged*, xxiv.

Maryse Condé and Slavery

DORIS Y. KADISH

Reflections on slavery in the Francophone world have appeared in the writings of the Guadeloupian novelist and playwright Maryse Condé over the last three decades. Some of those reflections appear in her widely acclaimed two-volume novel *Ségou* (1984–85), a saga of African history from the seventeenth through the twentieth centuries; and in her celebrated novel *Moi, Tituba, sorcière . . . noire de Salem* (1986), the story of the female West Indian slave who was at the center of the infamous Salem witch trials.[1] Other observations on the subject of slavery occur in two volumes of historical and literary essays from the late 1970s—*La Civilisation du bossale* (1978) and *La Parole des femmes* (1979)—as well as numerous other published essays and interviews.[2] On all of these diverse occasions, she has focused on the distant voices and forgotten acts of the people, including slaves and women. Consistently she has asserted the importance of going beyond the notion of the black, which she considers a European invention, and beyond victimization, which she maintains fails to take into account the active role that blacks themselves played in the history of slavery in Africa. Regarding *Ségou*, in which she depicts African involvement in the slave trade, she has stated: "I wrote it so that African people will know who they are . . . and why they were defeated, and that Africa's decline is not due to a lack of energy, or personality, or dynamism on the part of Africans." Showing that some Africans were complicitous in the slave trade at least recognizes individual identity and agency, as opposed to erasing differences among blacks in the name of some common, mythologized essence of negritude. At its worst, she argues, essentializing black identity has led to totalitarian regimes like Duvalier's in Haiti: "Black people have already suffered too much from myths: those created in Europe, those created by certain blacks. Thus we see the sorry results of negritude when it is realized and built upon as a system of government."[3]

Whether her intended audience has been African, Caribbean, French, or American, Condé's interest has always focused on the significance of the subject of slavery for the present and the ways in which people today can draw upon the past to forge identities as free and independent citizens for the future. An important occasion for the expression of her views about slavery arose at the time of the bicentennial of the French Revolution when Condé was commissioned to write the play *An Tan revolysion* (*In the Time of the Revolution*), which was performed at the Fort Fleur d'Epée in Gosier, Guadeloupe, on November 11, 1989. Although thousands of Guadeloupians flocked to the two outdoor performances that were held on that occasion, the play was not performed again, either in France or the Caribbean, until its first English-language performance during the conference on Slavery in the Francophone World at the University of Georgia in October 1997. That performance was directed by Freda Scott Giles, with a cast of American, African, and African-American students and with the participation of local groups of Haitian musicians and dancers.[4] Condé expressed special satisfaction in seeing the play performed in English because the French performances that she had hoped for never materialized. As she stated at the second of two roundtable discussions that were held during the conference:

> We performed it in November, and we were expecting to be invited to the other islands of the Caribbean, certainly Martinique; somewhere in France, maybe in Paris; and to be on TV one evening, to have a certain publicity for the play in Guadeloupe and eventually in France. But I suppose that for many reasons the play was perceived as not convenient for the celebration of the French Revolution, and there was a complete sort of blackout about it. All of us were totally frustrated because we were expecting a life for the play, and there was no life. After two performances it was totally dead. So, it is one of the reasons why we were so happy yesterday and so moved, because we had the feeling that the play was born again in English on American soil.[5]

In an interview with Frank Thompson Nesbitt in April 1997 she expressed similar frustration about the play's fate in the Caribbean and her satisfaction at its performance in the United States: "Although we couldn't bring the play to Jamaica, Trinidad, Barbados, even Martinique, the way we wanted to, the fact that it's being taken up now by Americans and an African-American troupe is performing it proves that it has succeeded in fulfilling its mission."[6] Especially noteworthy in this regard was the tremendous enthusiasm of the student performers in the Georgia production, which Condé compared to the similar spirit among the young actors, dancers, and musicians in Guadeloupe.

This essay looks at three of the main themes related to slavery in the play — demystifying heroism, highlighting women's roles, and the legacy of slavery — and attempts to place them in the context of Condé's other works.[7] It closes with transcriptions of some of the most noteworthy remarks that Condé made at the 1997 conference concerning the significance of remembering slavery for future generations in the Caribbean, France, and the United States. All three themes are marked by a rejection of essentialist, nationalist, or authoritarian definitions of Caribbean identity and culture. From the deconstruction of the notion of the return to African roots in her early writings in the 1970s to critical statements in the 1990s regarding the ideological imperatives of Edouard Glissant, Patrick Chamoiseau, and Raphaël Confiant, Condé has consistently called into question the definitive, canonical status of the words or acts of male figures in Caribbean history and cultural life. According to her, using those figures as models for giving meaning to the past or the present can only lead to the kind of mythic, epic definitions of Caribbean identity that she rejects. Focusing instead on obscure figures of resistance, often women or little-known slaves, Condé elaborates a particularist vision based on local conditions for political and cultural change. As Françoise Lionnet states, her characters "singularize and concretize the real."[8]

Deflating traditional heroism emerges as one of the key themes of *An Tan revolysion,* as can be seen from its nontraditional dramatic structure. Unlike most plays, constructed through a linear plot and fully developed characters, *An Tan revolysion* deploys a broad historical saga in which the traditional figures of the French, Haitian, and Guadeloupian Revolutions appear briefly on the stage, stereotypes resurrected from schoolbook histories. By making traditional heroes into stereotypes, Condé undermines their privileged role in history. Meanwhile, slaves and women rise up from the forgotten recesses of history to emerge as the true heroes who fought in the battles for Haitian and Guadeloupian independence and freedom.

The play is divided into three parts corresponding to three historical moments: 1789, when news of the outbreak of revolution in France fuels the fires of the slaves' discontent and will to revolt; 1794, when emancipation in the French colonies is declared, and the slaves in Saint-Domingue achieve some degree of power under the leadership of Toussaint Louverture; and 1802, when Toussaint is arrested, slavery is restored in Guadeloupe, and the hope of ever achieving meaningful independence and liberty in the French colonies becomes increasingly dim. The play contains some sixty different characters, who were played by different actors in the original performance but were depicted by a cast of fifteen in the small-scale Georgia production, with each actor playing a variety of different parts.

By thus reducing historical figures to episodic and stereotypical roles, Condé adopts a deconstructive stance in which she calls into question the heroism and transcendent significance of key historical figures and events. In contrast, for example, Henri Bangou, a leading Guadeloupian politician and member of the Communist Party, also writing at the time of the bicentennial of the French Revolution in 1989, argues that the period from 1794 to 1802 should be seen as exemplary, for Guadeloupe and Saint-Domingue at that time were the only places in the Caribbean and the Americas in which slaves acquired equality with their former owners and in which the two groups lived productively and responsibly together. Bangou thus echoes the seminal writings of a precursor of negritude in the 1920s, the Guadeloupian historian of color Oruno Lara, who, although admitting the injustices to which slaves were subjected after slavery was abolished in 1794, extols the period of emancipation during the French Revolution as "the most glorious and interesting that we have ever known." In a similar vein Lara considers the slave Ignace, denounced by most other historians as especially violent and irrational, to be the foremost member of the Guadeloupian pantheon of heroes: "Ignace is ours: a child of our people, he arose through his own efforts. He knows our soil, our race, our sufferings of yesterday, and our hopes for tomorrow." [9] This is the kind of pious, reverential treatment of Guadeloupian history that Condé rejects.

Her contestatory treatment of revolutionary figures finds a privileged target in Toussaint Louverture, often hailed as the savior of Haiti and the founder of Haitian independence. Condé's point is that the hero worship surrounding Toussaint not only has the negative effect of reinforcing the male dominance and phallocentrism that mark Caribbean society; she also perceives a direct and pernicious link between his authoritarian rule, which existed during the revolutionary period, and such rule in the modern period, especially in Africa. At the second roundtable session she stated:

> The play was conceived as making fun of what we can call hero worship. You could see that all the heroes were either ridiculed or treated very lightly. For example, I had some problems with a historian of Guadeloupe who confronted me because of my treatment of Toussaint Louverture. I don't know, I don't care: maybe Toussaint was a great man; but when

I studied his actions in the history books, I could see that he was not far, at the time, from being a dictator. Of course, maybe it is true that it is necessary to be a dictator when you bring a nation to life again. I am not commenting on that. I wanted to sort of make fun of Toussaint Louverture and compare him to many African dictators; that is why we call him Osagyefo, which was the name for Kwame Nkrumah. And I was especially pleased to see that Freda had chosen an African actor to be Toussaint Louverture, because it seems to me that she had guessed what I wanted to portray through the character Toussaint. And if you look at all the males—Dessalines, Ignace, and all that—you can see after all that there is a kind of derision about that male authority and virility and that, in fact, they don't bring anything positive to their people.

An example of Condé's demystifying strategies in the play consists of dwelling on Toussaint's tyrannical tendencies and his indifference to the will of disenfranchised women and former slaves. When soldiers report to him that the people are demanding ownership of the lands that they have been farming and that have now passed from the white plantation owners to Toussaint's generals, he replies, "What insolence! give them a lashing!" When women ask to be heard, he proclaims, "Silence. I'll hear nothing more from them."[10] In contrast, Condé finds nonverbal, theatrical ways of giving a voice to those condemned to silence, both by Toussaint and later by historians. Thus, for example, the staging of military victories is followed by stage directions that bring on scene the women who must suffer the tragic aftermath of war: "(Shots, smoke, shouts. Darkness on both stages. Silence). (The left stage slowly lights up, without ever being fully lit. You can see bodies spread out on the ground. In complete silence, women dressed in white arrive from staircases leading to the different corners of the stage. They crowd onto the stage, kneel next to the dead men, place lit candles at their feet and sing a capella)" (8). By repeating the exact same scene later in the play, Condé reinforces its significance as a way to articulate the suffering of slave women in the past and to make their voices resonate along with the voices of heroic men that echo more audibly in historical accounts of Haiti's past.

Deflating traditional heroism goes hand in hand with a second key theme in *An Tan revolysion*, highlighting the distant voices and forgotten acts of women. As the title of the earlier work *Parole des femmes* indicates, Condé's work consistently aims at calling attention to the often neglected works of Caribbean women writers and bringing visibility to the many courageous stories of survival, resistance, and even military heroism in the lives of obscure Caribbean women of the past. One of Condé's most notable achievements in this regard is *Moi, Tituba, sorcière . . . noire de Salem*. As the first-person title indicates, Condé's Tituba protests her omission from history and succeeds in creating her own myth, which will be sung by slaves in her native Caribbean home of Trinidad after her death in their revolt against oppression. As Kathleen Balutansky has said, "In telling her own story, Tituba has created her own myth, thus generating for women an alternative to the images of Toussaint, Dessalines, Christophe, and of Césaire's Caliban as revolutionary symbols for the Francophone Caribbean." And as Angela Davis has observed in the foreword to *Tituba*, that myth lives on in the twentieth century because of Maryse Condé: "Tituba's revenge consists in having persuaded one of her descendants to rewrite her moment in history in her own African oral tradition. . . . Tituba's voice is infused with the historically complex and imaginative voice of her creator. It is therefore not rigidly anchored in the social issues of Tituba's times." But at the same time, Condé resists the temptation to mythologize Tituba, deploying a narrative strategy that oscillates between epic and parodic. As Michèle Praeger observes, "Condé's initial enthusiasm and indignation are tempered by an iconoclastic and postmodern desire to attack the image of the strong black woman."[11]

Condé's observations about *An Tan revolysion* provide important clarifications of her treatment of women characters in the play. In response to a question that I asked her at the second roundtable discussion, she denied having "feminist" intentions in the sense of promoting the role of female warriors; but she then went on to articulate a clear sense of the importance of highlighting the role of women during the period of the revolution:

It was a very hard time when people were dying, suffering, starving, and so on; and we wanted a sort of feminine presence. So you have that repetition of women dressed in white with candles coming three or four times during the play just to look after the dead and the suffering people. It was very important to have that female procession of women coming; really, it was hard to express the kind of love and tenderness and power to heal, power to cure, that you have in the feminine presence. So I don't know whether you can look for feminist views in that play. But we wanted to show Solitude, who is a very important character in Guadeloupian historiography. We wanted to show her pregnant and saying to everybody that

she knew she was expecting a girl. Because normally you are always expected to have a boy, and we wanted to refuse that: we wanted Solitude to
be the mother of a girl. So, for us, it was the only feminist part in that play.

Condé's version of the story of the Guadeloupian heroine Solitude, pregnant
at the time of her participation in the slave uprisings, thus differs significantly
from André Schwarz-Bart's version in his well-known novel *La Mulâtresse
Solitude* (1972), in which nothing is said about the gender or fate of Solitude's
child and that culminates in Solitude's defeat. Condé instead focuses on a Solitude who names and passes on freedom to her daughter Aimée, as she states in
the play: "It's my belly that gives me strength and courage! (She touches her
belly) I don't want her to live through what we've endured. For the child will
be a girl. That's how I want it to be. I'll call her Aimée . . . for Aimée, everything will be different. The world will change. . . . No more masters, no more
slaves ever again!" (40, 41).[12]

Instead of André Schwarz-Bart, Condé seems here to echo his wife, the celebrated Guadeloupian writer Simone Schwarz-Bart, who imagined a maternal
heritage for Solitude in *Un Plat de porc aux bananes vertes*, written in 1967,
some five years before her husband's novel.[13] The following words used by
critic Clarisse Zimra to describe Simone Schwarz-Bart could apply to Maryse
Condé as well: "the individual self can only be grasped through the mythical
genealogy of many past selves. And those selves are all female. . . . Woman has
thus no need for *négritude*, no desire to go back to her roots, to search for the
lost father. She is her own genitrix." [14]

Condé also calls into question the negative stereotypes of women in standard historical accounts of Francophone slavery. In the first part of the play, for
example, she uses the storyteller, who introduces and explains the action
throughout the play, to express the following sarcastic description of revolution: "Revolution is like a woman: you do whatever you want with her. Soldiers of fortune sodomize her, poets read her poetry, the middle class makes her
cough up the cash. In the kingdom of France, revolution aborted the baby that
had turned its womb into a mountain of justice. All that remains is a stinking
pile of coagulated blood lying in the gutter" (13). In the second part, the storyteller corrects himself, stating this time: "Revolution isn't a woman. It's a witch.
She feeds on fresh blood. She smears it all over her jowls. She licks it off her
fingers. And then, in the colorless hours before dawn, she gives birth to monsters"(24). Condé warns against the tendency throughout history to thus use

gendered images for political ends. For women and for Caribbeans generally to construct their racial and political identity necessitates deconstructing these narratives of the past.

Regarding the third theme, the legacy of slavery, from a strictly political viewpoint Condé appears to view the past, present, and future in pessimistic terms. Consistently the play leads to the conclusion that the violence and loss of life that occurred during the revolution ultimately produced nothing positive for the people of Guadeloupe and Martinique. For Condé, as for many Francophone writers, the departmental status of the French islands and their continued control by France signify that they have failed to this day to achieve freedom and independence and thus that there is an important sense in which neither slavery nor colonialism ever really ended in the French Caribbean. Near the end of the play the storyteller, whom Condé identified in the second roundtable session as her spokesperson, states: "What do you want me to say? That I've invented a happy ending like in American movies? This time will be like all the others. Death, which never has its fill, will have a belly full; and those who love freedom will end up in mass graves. Sometimes I say to myself that if the earth is so red in Guadeloupe it's because she's seen so much blood flowing!" (41). Admittedly one might say that the pessimism expressed here by the narrator is mitigated by the fact that *An Tan revolysion* ends with the arrival of the Guadeloupian refugees on the shores of Saint-Domingue in 1804 and with cries of "Liberté!" "Indépendance!" emanating from the assembled crowd of slaves. When asked in the Nesbitt interview which of the two views she shared—the storyteller's bleak vision as opposed to the people's hopes for the future—Condé replied: "I'm more on the side of the storyteller. I don't see anything positive coming out of 1989 in terms of dynamism or understanding. . . . It seems to me that in Guadeloupe things are getting worse. The situation is becoming more serious. . . . As for the ideal of independence, we're not even thinking about it any more because now we're in the post Maestricht era. Now everyone is worrying about how we'll deal with Brussels, how we're going to get help and money from Europe. Already France is withdrawing tremendously. So as for me, I see the future of the French Caribbean as gloomy." In that same interview she stated that her goal in writing the play was to make the people of Guadeloupe understand that they, who had been denied privileges and re-enslaved following the events of 1789, had nothing to celebrate for the bicentennial of the French Revolution.

Despite her pessimistic assessment of the political situation in the French Caribbean, Condé has an optimistic view of the possibility and the significance of understanding the past. As she stated to Nesbitt, "To understand the past thoroughly, to dominate it, to know its reality without making it into an object of nostalgic veneration is one of the conditions of freedom . . . to know the past with lucidity, to know what is positive and what is negative, what needs to be retained and what needs to be forgotten is a way first of all of knowing how to conduct oneself in the present and also perhaps a way of avoiding the errors that have already been committed, and to go forward." And as she stressed in the first roundtable discussion, there is an urgent need to remember and understand the past, not only in the Caribbean but also in France and the United States, all of which suffer from forms of cultural amnesia regarding slavery for a variety of reasons:

I'm going to ask myself whether the people of Guadeloupe and Haiti are forgetful of their own past. And I'm going to take the example of my family. Nobody ever told me anything about slavery, and you could believe that maybe it is something totally forgotten or eradicated from the memory of the people. But in fact, I think there is a different explanation. People believed, my family for example, that it was a kind of starting point, and they were proud of what happened before. After that, they had climbed up the social ladder. They had become literary, they had gone to universities, to school, and all that. So they were more ready to emphasize their achievement, and they did not want to talk so much about, you know, where they were coming from. Not that they were forgetful or ashamed, but it was more important to show how they had progressed since those very dark days. As far as the French are concerned, it seems to me that they don't like to talk about slavery just because they never liked to look straight at the dark sides of their own history. Look, for example, at their attitude toward Vichy and when they believed and they wanted us to believe that all of the French people, men and women, had been for the resistance along with de Gaulle; and it is only now that they had to face the fact that the majority of the French people were in fact collaborationists. Now we have the trial of Maurice Papon, so we know exactly what is going on. So I don't believe that they are forgetful, but they don't want to face it when it is so tragic and difficult. But anyway, next year we are going to have a huge celebration of the 150th anniversary of the abolition of slavery. So after they did so much wrong to people, they are going to celebrate the time when they suddenly became, let's say, more reasonable. So you see, they are going to celebrate the triumph of good sense and reason, which is bizarre. They forget about the time when they were totally mad and cruel, and they are going to celebrate the time when they see clearly. You see, that is a kind of attitude which is very typical with the French people. I don't know whether the U.S.A. remembers more about its own past because when I teach my classes, the kids don't know anything about their past, about slavery. It seems to me that for them it is a kind of story—not history, story—that they are not very much aware of. I have the feeling that apart from the intellectual circles in the U.S.A., people are just like the French. They don't like to have to face the dark side of their past and they tend to overlook what happened before.

At the same time that Condé articulates the need for new generations to remember slavery, she has expressed her own need to put an end to the remembering and the need to move beyond a subject that she has treated in one form or another for over twenty-five years. At the first roundtable session she stated: "I have decided sometimes in my life to stop remembering slavery. I have often decided: I am not going to write even one line about slavery any longer, and let's go forward. As long as you keep looking at the past you cannot go forward." She went on to explain what it means for her as an author to go forward in the following terms:

Sometimes we have a tendency to see ourselves all the time as victims and to dwell on the memory of the sufferings of the ancestors. For example, when I write a play, even the play that you are going to see tonight [In the Time of the Revolution], when you think of the blood, the people dying, the pregnant women, you know, beaten to death, and so on, you have a kind of sinister background in your mind and you have a kind of masochism. You like to think about that, to see how much the race you belong to suffered. And it seems to me that it's wrong because, after all, it is the past. The past is the past. Let's go ahead. And we have integrated that. We know that it happened. We have, we should have, the memory of it somewhere. But, especially for a writer, you should go on writing about things which are totally different. For example, in my last novel,[15] I made an effort never to mention the past, I tried to think of the problems of today; that is to say, migration, people with new problems of identity, people with new places of origin, people who don't know about their ethnicity, about their language, people who really don't know who they are exactly. So, I mean, it is what I am trying to do: to integrate the memories of the past into my consciousness, to go forward, and to produce different stories where we are going to deal with the new, and maybe even more complex, issues. I'm afraid that while we are thinking of slavery where everything is in black and white (without *un jeu de mots*) that maybe we forget what is going on around ourselves in the world today, in the country where we are living today, and maybe it is a kind of easy—not easy, but often said, often described—way out.

Integrating memories of the past under slavery into the consciousness of those living in the present and using those memories in attempting to deal with the new and complex issues in the present: this articulation of the legacy of slavery in the Francophone world corresponds closely to the conceptual framework underlying all of the essays included in this book. Although the subjects span several centuries, from the late eighteenth century to the present time, and several geographical settings, in France, the United States, and the French Caribbean, the authors all focus in one way or another on the issues that appear in Condé's formulation: "people with new problems of identity, people with new places of origin, people who don't know about their ethnicity, about their language, people who really don't know who they are exactly." For those people, and for us all who are part of their new societies, understanding slavery is a vital component of understanding ourselves in the present and for the future.

NOTES

1. Jean-Christophe Deberre, "*Ségou, les murailles de terre,*" *Notre Librairie* 75–76 (July–October 1984): 226–28; Marie Clotilde Jacquey et Monique Hugon, "'Ségou' est-il un roman malien? Entretien avec Maryse Condé," *Notre Librairie* 84 (1986): 56–60; Anne-Marie Jeay, "*Ségou, les murailles de terre:* Lecture anthropologique d'un roman d'aventure," *Novelles du Sud* 4 (1986): 115–37. For recent critical analyses of *Tituba,* see the following articles in *Callaloo* 18, 3 (1995): Michelle Smith, "Reading in Circles: Sexuality and/as History in *I, Tituba, Black Witch of Salem,*" 602–7, and Michelle Smith, "*Moi, Tituba, sorcière . . . noire de Salem* as a Tale of *Petite Marronne,*" 608–15; see in *World Literature Today* 67, 4 (1993): Elisabeth Mudimbe-Boyi, "Giving a Voice to Tituba: The Death of the Author?" 751–56, and Lillian Manzor-Coats, "Of Witches and Other Things: Maryse Condé's Challenges to Feminist Discourse," 737–44; see also Jeanne Snitgen, "History, Identity and the Constitution of the Female Subject: Maryse Condé's *Tituba,*" *Matatu: Journal of African Culture and Society* 3, 6 (1989): 55–73.

2. See my chapter titled "Tituba et sa traduction," in *L'Oeuvre de Maryse Condé: Questions et réponses à propos d'une écrivaine politiquement incorrecte* (Paris: L'Harmattan, 1996): 231–47.

3. Kathy Koch, "Storyteller Traces Route of African Culture's Decline," *Christian Science Monitor* (December 13, 1988), 10; Maryse Condé, "Propos sur l'identité culturelle," in *Négritude: Tradition et développement* (Paris: PU de France, 1978), 77.

4. The Georgia production took place on October 16, 17, 19, and 20, 1997; approximately 200–250 people attended each performance. Costume design was provided by Constance Campell. Choreography was directed by Ellen Bleier. The role of Zéphyr was played by Mario Chandler.

5. In addition to Maryse Condé and to her husband and translator, Richard Philcox, other participants at the Georgia conference were two Guadeloupians responsible for the original production: José Jernidier, assistant director, and Micheline Damico, costume designer.

6. Maryse Condé, interview by Frank Thompson Nesbitt at Columbia University on April 12, 1997, in Nesbitt, "Revolution in Discourse" (Ph.D. diss., Harvard University, 1997), appendix.

7. For an analysis of this and other plays by Condé, see Christiane P. Makward, "Reading Maryse Condé's Theater," in *Callaloo* 18, 3 (1995): 681–89.

8. Chris Bongie, *Islands and Exiles: The Creole Identities of Post/Colonial Literature* (Stanford: Stanford UP, 1998), 122, 143; Françoise Lionnet, *Postcolonial Representations: Women, Literature, Identity* (Ithaca: Cornell UP, 1995), 76–77.

9. Henri Bangou, *La Révolution en l'esclavage à la Guadeloupe, 1789–1802: Epopée noire et génocide* (Paris: Messidor/Editions Sociales, 1989), 91; Oruno Lara, *La Guadeloupe dans l'histoire* (Paris: L'Harmattan, 1979), 98, 149.

10. Maryse Condé, *An Tan revolysion: Elle court, elle court la liberté* (Pointe-à-Pitre: Conseil Régional de la Guadeloupe, 1989), 23, 24. The translation used in this essay and the Georgia production was written by Doris Y. Kadish and Jean-Pierre Piriou.

11. Kathleen L. Balutansky, "Creating Her Own Image: Female Genesis in *Mémoire d'une amnésique* and *Moi, Tituba, sorcière*," in *L'Héritage de Caliban*, ed. Maryse Condé (Pointe-à-Pitre, Guadeloupe: Editions Jasor, 1992), 45; Maryse Condé, *I, Tituba, Black Witch of Salem*, trans. Richard Philcox (Charlottesville: UP of Virginia, 1992), xii, 201, 212; Michèle Praeger, "Maryse Condé: Mythes et contre-mythes," in *L'Oeuvre de Maryse Condé*, 210–11.

12. Similarly *Tituba* depicts Tituba living on through her adopted daughter Samantha.

13. Charlotte H. Bruner contends that *La Mulâtresse Solitude* was jointly authored, an argument that seems plausible inasmuch as Solitude's story belongs to the cultural tradition of Simone, not André, Schwarz-Bart. See Bruner, "A Caribbean Madness: Half Slave and Half Free," *Canadian Review of Comparative Literature/Revue Canadienne de Littérature Comparée* 11, 2 (1984): 236–48. When I asked Maryse Condé about

the question of joint authorship of this novel, she dismissed Bruner's assertion as unfounded.

14. Clarisse Zimra, "Négritude in the Feminine Mode: The Case of Martinique and Guadeloupe," *Journal of Ethnic Studies* 12, 1 (1984): 69, 70.

15. At the time of these remarks, Condé's most recently published works were *Desirada* and *Pays mêlé* (Paris: Robert Laffont, 1997).

Selected Bibliography

Adelaïde-Merlande, Jacques. *Delgrès: La Guadeloupe en 1802*. Paris: Karthala, 1986.

Adrien, Claude. "The Forgotten Heroes of Savannah." *Americas* 30 (1978): 55–57.

Alibar, France, and Pierrette Lembeyre-Boy. *Le Couteau seul: La Condition féminine aux Antilles*. Paris: Editions Caribéennes, 1981.

Alleyne, Mervyn C. "Acculturation and the Cultural Matrix of Creolization." In *Pidginization and Creolization of Languages*, ed. Dell Hymes, 169–86. Cambridge: Cambridge UP, 1971.

———. *Syntaxe historique créole*. Paris: Karthala, 1996.

Arendt, Hannah. *Essai sur la révolution*. Paris: Gallimard, 1967.

Arnold, A. James. "*Créolité:* Cultural Nation-Building or Cultural Dependence?" In *(Un)Writing Empire*, ed. Theo D'haen, 37–48. Amsterdam: Rodopi, 1998.

———. "The Erotics of Colonialism in Contemporary French West Indian Literary Culture." *New West Indian Guide* 68, 1–2 (1994): 5–22.

———. "Poétique forcée et identité dans la littérature des Antilles francophones." In *L'Héritage de Caliban*, ed. Maryse Condé, 19–27. Pointe-à-Pitre, Guadeloupe: Jasor, 1992.

Baade, Hans W. "The Law of Slavery in Spanish Luisiana, 1769–1803." In *Louisiana's Legal Heritage*, ed. Edward F. Haas, 50–55. Pensacola, Fla.: Perdido Bay Press for the Louisiana State Museum, 1983.

Babb, Winston C. "French Refugees from Saint-Domingue to the Southern United States: 1791–1810." Ph.D. diss., University of Virginia, 1954.

Balch, Thomas. *The French in America during the War of Independence of the United States, 1777–1783*, trans. E. S. and E. W. Balch. Philadelphia, 1895.

Bangou, Henri. *La Révolution et l'esclavage à la Guadeloupe, 1789–1802: Epopée noire et génocide*. Paris: Messidor / Editions Sociales, 1989.

Bébel-Gisler, Dany. *Léonora: L'Histoire enfouie de la Guadeloupe*. Paris: Seghers, 1985.

Bell, Caryn Cossé. *Revolution, Romanticism, and the Afro-Creole Protest Tradition in Louisiana, 1718–1868*. Baton Rouge: Louisiana State UP, 1997.

Bell, Madison Smart. *All Souls' Rising*. New York: Pantheon, 1995.

Bénot, Yves. "La Chaîne des insurrections d'esclaves aux Caraïbes de 1789 à 1791." In *Les Abolitions de l'esclavage de L. F. Sonthonax à V. Schoelcher, 1793–1794–1848*, ed. Marcel Dorigny, 179–86. Paris: PU de Vincennes, 1995.

———. *La Révolution française et la fin des colonies*. Paris: Edition de la Découverte, 1989.

Berchtold, Alfred. "Sismondi et le Groupe de Coppet face à l'esclavage et au colonialisme." In *Sismondi européen*. Geneva: Slatkine, 1976.

Berlin, Ira. *Slaves without Masters: The Free Negro in the Antebellum South*. New York: Pantheon, 1974.

Bernabé, Jean, Patrick Chamoiseau, and Raphaël Confiant. *Eloge de la créolité*. Bilingual ed. trans. Mohammed B. Taleb-Khyar. Paris: Gallimard, 1993.

Bogger, Tommy L. *Free Blacks in Norfolk, Virginia, 1790–1860: The Darker Side of Freedom*. Charlottesville: UP of Virginia, 1997.

Bongie, Chris. *Islands and Exiles: The Creole Identities of Post/Colonial Literature*. Stanford: Stanford UP, 1998.

Bowser, Frederick P. "Colonial Spanish America." In *Neither Slave nor Free: The Freedmen of African Descent in the Slave Societies of the New World*, ed. David W. Cohen and Jack P. Greene, 19–58. Baltimore: Johns Hopkins UP, 1972.

Bradley, Patricia. *Slavery, Propaganda and the American Revolution*. Oxford: U of Mississippi P, 1998.

Brasseaux, Carl A. *Denis-Nicolas Foucault and the New Orleans Rebellion of 1768*. Ruston, La.: McGinty, 1987.

Burton, Richard D. E. *La Famille coloniale: La Martinique et la mère-patrie, 1789–1992*. Paris: L'Harmattan, 1994.

———. *Le Roman marron: Études sur la littérature martiniquaise contemporaine*. Paris: L'Harmattan, 1997.

Césaire, Aimé. *Discourse on Colonialism*. Trans. Joan Pinkham. New York: Monthly Review Press, 1972.

———. "Et Les Chiens se taisaient." In *Les Armes miraculeuses*. Paris: Gallimard, 1970.

———. *Toussaint Louverture: La Révolution française et le problème colonial*. Paris: Présence Africaine, 1962.

Chamoiseau, Patrick. *Antan d'enfance, haute enfance*. Paris: Gallimard, 1993.

———. *L'Esclave Vieil Homme et le molosse*. Paris: Gallimard, 1997.

———. *Texaco*. Paris: Gallimard, 1990.

Chanlatte, Juste, Comte de Rosiers. *L'Entrée du roi en sa capitale en janvier 1818.* Cap Haïtien, Haiti, 1818. Reprinted in *Le Nouveau Monde: Supplément du dimanche* (Port-au-Prince, Haiti), August 19, 1970.

Chaudenson, Robert. *Des Isles, des hommes, des langues: Langues créoles, cultures créoles.* Paris: L'Harmattan, 1992.

Clark, George P. "The Role of the Haitian Volunteers at Savannah in 1779: An Attempt at an Objective View." *Phylon: The Atlanta University Review of Race and Culture* 41 (1980): 356–66.

Cobb, Martha K. "The Slave Narrative and the Black Literary Tradition." In *The Art of Slave Narrative: Original Essays in Criticism and Theory,* ed. John Sekora and Darwin T. Turner, 36–44. Macomb: Western Illinois University, 1982.

Cohen, William B. *The French Encounter with Africans: White Response to Blacks, 1530–1880.* Bloomington: Indiana UP, 1980.

Cohn, Bernard S. *Colonialism and Its Forms of Knowledge: The British in India.* Princeton: Princeton UP, 1996.

Comhaire-Sylvain, Suzanne. *Le Créole haïtien: Morphologie et syntaxe.* Wetteren, Belgium: DeMeester, 1936.

Condé, Maryse. *An Tan revolysion: Elle court, elle court la liberté.* Pointe-à-Pitre: Conseil Régional de la Guadeloupe, 1989.

———. *La Civilisation du bossale.* Paris: L'Harmattan, 1978.

———. *Moi, Tituba, sorcière . . . noire de Salem.* Paris: Mercure de France, 1986.

———. *La Parole des femmes: Essai sur des romancières des Antilles de langue française.* Paris: L'Harmattan, 1979.

———. "Propos sur l'identité culturelle." In *Négritude: Tradition et développement,* 77–84. Paris: PU de France, 1978.

Confiant, Raphaël. *Eau de café.* Paris: Livre de Poche, 1993.

———. *Ravines du devant-jour, haute enfance.* Paris: Gallimard, 1993.

Cornevin, Robert. *Haïti, que sais-je?* Paris: PU de France, 1982.

Curtin, Philip. *The Atlantic Slave Trade.* Madison: U of Wisconsin P, 1969.

Daget, Serge. "France, Suppression of the Illegal trade, and England, 1817–1850." In *The Abolition of the Atlantic Slave Trade: Origins and Effects in Europe, Africa and the Americas,* ed. David Eltis and James Walvin, 193–217. Madison: U of Wisconsin P, 1981.

Dash, J. Michael. *Edouard Glissant.* Cambridge: Cambridge UP, 1995.

Davis, Cyprian. *The History of Black Catholics in the United States.* New York: Crossroad, 1990.

Davis, David Brion. *The Problem of Slavery in Western Culture.* Ithaca: Cornell UP, 1966.

————. *Revolutions: Reflections on American Equality and Foreign Liberations*. Cambridge: Harvard UP, 1990.

————. *Slavery and Human Progress*. New York: Oxford UP, 1984.

Dayan, Joan. *Haiti, History, and the Gods*. Berkeley: U of California P, 1995.

Debbash, Yves. "Le Marronage: Essai sur la désertion de l'esclavage antillais." *Année sociologique* 3 (1961): 1–195.

Debien, Gabriel. *Plantations et esclaves à Saint-Domingue*. Dakar, Senegal: Université de Dakar, 1962.

Dessalles, Pierre F. R. *Historique des troubles survenus à la Martinique pendant la Révolution, 1794–1800*, ed. Henri de Fremont. Fort-de-France: Société d'histoire de la Martinique, 1982.

Du Bois, W. E. B. *The Souls of Black Folk*. New York: Library of America, 1986.

Egerton, Douglas R. *Gabriel's Rebellion: The Virginia Slave Conspiracies of 1800 and 1802*. Chapel Hill: U of North Carolina P, 1993.

————. *He Shall Go Out Free: The Lives of Denmark Vesey*. Madison, Wis.: Madison House, 1998.

Elisabeth, Léo. "Saint-Pierre, août 1789." *Compte rendu des travaux du colloque de Saint-Pierre* (Centre Universitaire Antilles Guyane). December, 1973.

————. "La Société martiniquaise aux XVIIe et XVIIIe siècles, 1664–1789." State doctoral thesis, Université de Paris I, 1988.

Ferguson, Moira. *Subject to Others: British Women Writers and Colonial Slavery*. New York: Routledge, 1992.

Fick, Carolyn. *The Making of Haiti: The Saint-Domingue Revolution from Below*. Knoxville: U of Tennessee P, 1990.

Fiehrer, Thomas Marc. "The African Presence in Colonial Louisiana: An Essay on the Continuity of Caribbean Culture." In *Louisiana's Black Heritage*, ed. Robert R. Macdonald, John R. Kemp, and Edward F. Haas, 3–31. New Orleans: Louisiana State Museum, 1979.

Foner, Laura. "The Free People of Color in Louisiana and St. Domingue: A Comparative Portrait of Two Three-Caste Slave Societies." *Journal of Social History* 3, 4 (1970): 406–30.

Fordham, Monroe. "Nineteenth-Century Black Thought in the United States: Some Influence of the Santo Domingo Revolution." *Journal of Black Studies* 6 (1975): 115–26.

Fouchard, Jean. *Les Marrons de la liberté*. Paris: Editions de l'Ecole, 1972.

————. *Les Marrons du syllabaire: Quelques aspects du problème de l'instruction et de l'éducation des esclaves et affranchis de Saint-Domingue*. Port-au-Prince, Haiti: Editions Henri Deschamps, 1988.

Frey, Sylvia. *Water from the Rock: Black Resistance in a Revolutionary Age.* Princeton: Princeton UP, 1991.

Garrigus, John D. "Catalyst or Catastrophe? Saint-Domingue's Free Men of Color and the Battle of Savannah, 1779–1782." *Revista/Review Interamericana* 22 (1992): 109–25.

Gaspar, David Barry, and David Patrick Geggus. *A Turbulent Time: The French Revolution and the Greater Caribbean.* Bloomington: Indiana UP, 1997.

Gautier, Arlette. "Le Rôle des femmes dans l'abolition de l'esclavage." In *Les Femmes et la révolution française,* ed. Marie-France Brive, 153–61. Toulouse, France: PU du Mirail, 1990.

———. *Les Soeurs de Solitude.* Paris: Editions Caribéennes, 1985.

———. "Women from Guadeloupe and Martinique." In *French and West Indian: Martinique, Guadeloupe, and French Guiana Today,* ed. Richard D. E. Burton and Fred Reno. Charlottesville: UP of Virginia, 1994.

Geggus, David P. "Racial Equality, Slavery, and Colonial Secession during the Constituent Assembly." *American Historical Review* 94, 5 (1989): 1290–1308.

———. *Slavery, War, and Revolution: The British Occupation of Saint-Domingue, 1793–1798.* New York: Oxford UP, 1982.

———. "The Slaves and Free Coloreds of Martinique during the Age of the French and Haitian Revolutions." In *The Lesser Antilles in the Age of European Expansion,* ed. Robert L. Paquette and Stanley L. Engermann, 282–85. Gainesville: UP of Florida, 1996.

Genovese, Eugene D. *From Rebellion to Revolution: Afro-American Slave Revolts in the Making of the Modern World.* Baton Rouge: Louisiana State UP, 1979.

Gillard, John T. *The Catholic Church and the American Negro.* New York: Johnson Reprint, 1968.

———. *Colored Catholics in the United States.* Baltimore: Josephite Press, 1941.

Girod-Chantrans, Justin. *Voyage d'un Suisse dans les diverses colonies d'Amérique pendant la dernière guerre.* Neuchâtel, Switzerland: Imprimerie de la Société Typographique, 1795.

———. *Idylles et chansons ou essais de poésie créole, par un habitant d'Hayti.* Philadelphia: J. Edwards, 1818.

Glissant, Edouard. *Le Discours antillais.* Paris: Seuil, 1981.

———. *Le Quatrième siècle.* Paris: Seuil, 1964.

Goodman, M. F. *A Comparative Study of Creole French Dialects.* The Hague: Mouton, 1964.

Gouges, Olympe de. *Théâtre politique,* ed. Gisela Thiele-Knobloch. Paris: Côté-Femmes, 1970.

Gregory, Clarence K. "The Education of Blacks in Maryland: An Historical Survey." Ed.D. diss., Columbia University Teachers College, 1976.

Griffith, Louis Turner, and John Erwin Talmadge. *Georgia Journalism, 1763–1950.* Athens: U of Georgia P, 1951.

Guibert, Jacques Antoine. *Zulmé,* ed. John Isbell. *Cahiers staëliens* 47 (1996).

Hall, Gwendolyn Midlo. *Africans in Colonial Louisiana: The Development of Afro-Creole Culture in the Eighteenth Century.* Baton Rouge: Louisiana State UP, 1992.

Hanger, Kimberly S. *Bounded Lives, Bounded Places: Free Black Society in Colonial New Orleans, 1769–1803.* Durham: Duke UP, 1997.

Harris, M. Roy. "Cofè 'pourquoi,' un africanisme parmi d'autres en créole louisianais." *Revue de Louisiane/Louisiana Review* 2, 2 (1973): 88–102.

Hatin, Eugène. *Bibliographie historique de la presse périodique française.* Paris: Editions Anthrops, 1965.

Hegel, George Wilhelm Friedrich. *The Philosophy of History,* trans. J. Sibree. New York: Dover, 1956.

Heinl, Robert Debs, and Nancy Gordon Heinl. *Written in Blood: The Story of the Haitian People, 1492–1971.* Boston: Houghton Mifflin, 1978.

Hennesey, James. *American Catholics: A History of the Roman Catholic Community in the United States.* New York: Oxford UP, 1981.

Hickey, Donald R. "America's Response to the Slave Revolt in Haiti, 1791–1806." *Journal of the Early Republic* 2 (1982): 361–79.

Hoffmann, Léon-François. *Le Nègre romantique, personnage littéraire et obsession collective.* Paris: Payot, 1973.

Holm, John A. *Pidgins and Creoles.* Cambridge: Cambridge UP, 1988.

Hough, Franklin B. *The Siege of Savannah by the Combined American and French Forces under the Command of General Lincoln and the Count d'Estaing in the Autumn of 1779.* Spartanburg, S.C.: Reprint Company, 1975.

Hudson, Frederic. *Journalism in the United States, from 1690–1873.* New York: Harper and Brothers, 1873.

Hunt, Alfred N. *Haiti's Influence on Antebellum America: Slumbering Volcano in the Caribbean.* Baton Rouge: Louisiana State UP, 1988.

James, C. L. R. *The Black Jacobins.* New York: Vintage, 1963.

Jones, Charles, C. Jr. *The Siege of Savannah in 1779 as Described in Two Contemporaneous Journals of French Offices in the Fleet of Count d'Estaing.* Albany, N.Y.: J. Munsell, 1874.

Jordan, Winthrop D. *White over Black: American Attitudes toward the Negro, 1550–1812.* Chapel Hill: U of North Carolina P, 1968.

Jourdain, Elodie. *Du Français aux parlers créoles.* Paris: Klincksieck, 1956.

Kadish, Doris Y. "The Black Terror: Women's Responses to Slave Revolts in Haiti." *French Review* 68, 4 (1995): 668–80.

———. "Tituba et sa traduction." In *L'Oeuvre de Maryse Condé: Questions et réponses à propos d'une écrivaine politiquement incorrecte*, 231–47. Paris: L'Harmattan, 1996.

Kadish, Doris Y., and Françoise Massardier-Kenney. *Translating Slavery: Gender and Race in French Women's Writing, 1783–1823*, ed. Doris Y. Kadish and Françoise Massardier-Kenney. Kent, Ohio: Kent State UP, 1994.

Kauffman, Christopher. *Tradition and Transformation in Catholic Culture: The Priests of Saint Sulpice in the United States from 1791 to the Present*. New York: Macmillan, 1988.

Kerr, Derek Noel. *Petty Felony, Slave Defiance, and Frontier Villainy: Crime and Criminal Justice in Spanish Louisiana, 1770–1803*. New York: Garland, 1993.

Klein, Herbert S. *African Slavery in Latin America and the Caribbean*. New York: Oxford UP, 1986.

Kobre, Sidney. *The Development of the Colonial Newspaper*. Gloucester, G.B.: Peter Smith, 1960.

Labat, Jean Baptiste. *Nouveau Voyage aux isles de l'Amérique*. Fort-de-France, Martinique: Editions des Horizons Caraïbes, 1972.

Laborie, P. J. *Réflexions sommaires adressées à la France et à la colonie de Saint-Domingue*. Paris: Imprimerie de Chardon, n.d.

Lachance, Paul F. "The 1809 Immigration of Saint-Domingue Refugees to New Orleans: Reception, Integration and Impact." *Louisiana History* 29, 2 (1988): 109–41.

———. "The Politics of Fear: French Louisianians and the Slave Trade, 1786–1809." *Plantation Society in the Americas* 1, 2 (1979): 162–97.

Langley, Lester D. *The Americas in the Age of Revolution, 1750–1850*. New Haven: Yale UP, 1996.

Lara, Oruno. *La Guadeloupe dans l'histoire*. Paris: L'Harmattan, 1979.

Laurent, Gérard. *Haiti et l'indépendence américaine*. Port-au-Prince, Haiti, 1976.

Lawrence, Alexander A. *Storm over Savannah*. Athens: U of Georgia P, 1951.

Leconte, Vergniaud. *Henri Christophe dans l'Histoire d'Haiti*. Paris, 1931.

Lefebvre, Claire. "Relexification in Creole Genesis: The Case of Haitian Creole." In *Substrata versus Universals in Creole Genesis*, ed. Peter Muysken and Norval Smith, 279–300. Amsterdam: John Benjamin, 1986.

Liljegrin, Ernest R. "Jacobinism in Spanish Louisiana, 1792–1797." *Louisiana Historical Quarterly* 22, 1 (1939): 47–97.

Lionnet, Françoise. *Postcolonial Representations: Women, Literature, Identity*. Ithaca: Cornell UP, 1995.

Lofton, John. *Insurrection in South Carolina: The Turbulent World of Denmark Vesey.* Yellow Springs, Ohio: Antioch Press, 1964.

Lucas, Edith. *La Littérature antiesclavagiste au XIXe siècle.* Paris: Boccard, 1930.

Makward, Christiane P. "Reading Maryse Condé's Theater." *Callaloo* 18, 3 (1995): 681–89.

Manessy, Gabriel. *Créoles, pidgins, variétés véhiculaires.* Paris: CNRS Editions, 1995.

———. "Réflexions sur les contraintes anthropologiques de la créolisation: De l'improbabilité du métissage linguistique dans les créoles atlantiques exogènes." *Etudes créoles* 19, 1 (1996): 61–71.

Martin, Gaston. *Histoire de l'esclavage dans les colonies françaises.* Paris, 1948.

Martin, Jean. "Esclavage." In *Dictionnaire Napoléon,* ed. Jean Tulard. Paris: Fayard, 1989.

Maximin, Daniel. *L'Isolé Soleil.* Paris: Seuil, 1981.

McCloy, Shelby. *The Negro in France.* Lexington: U of Kentucky P, 1961.

McColley, Robert. *Slavery and Jeffersonian Virginia.* Urbana: U of Illinois P, 1973.

McGowan, James Thomas. "Creation of a Slave Society: Louisiana Plantations in the Eighteenth Century." Ph.D. diss., University of Rochester, 1976.

McWhorter, John. "It Happened at Coromantin: Locating the Origin of the Atlantic-Based English Creoles," *Journal of Pidgin and Creole Languages* 12, 1 (1997): 59–102.

Meier, August, and Elliott M. Rudwick. *From Plantation to Ghetto.* 3d ed. New York: Hill and Wang, 1976.

Misner, Barbara. *"Highly Respectable and Accomplished Ladies": Catholic Women Religious in America, 1790–1850.* New York: Garland, 1988.

Moreau de Saint-Méry, Médéric Louis Elie. *Considérations présentées aux vrais amis du repos et du bonheur de la France.* Paris: Hachette, 1972.

———. *Description topographique, physique, civile, politique et historique de la partie française de l'île de Saint-Domingue.* Paris: Société française d'histoire d'outre-mer, 1984.

Mott, Frank Luther. *American Journalism: A History, 1690–1960.* New York: Macmillan, 1962.

Mullin, Michael. *Africa in America: Slave Acculturation and Resistance in the American South and the British Caribbean, 1736–1831.* Urbana: U of Illinois P, 1992.

Nash, Gary B. *Forging Freedom: The Formation of Philadelphia's Black Community, 1720–1840.* Cambridge: Harvard UP, 1988.

Nemours, General Alfred. *Haiti et la Guerre de l'Indépendance Américaine.* Port-au-Prince, Haiti, 1950.

Nesbitt, Frank Thompson. "Revolution in Discourse." Ph.D. diss., Harvard University, 1997.

O'Brien, Conor Cruise. *The Long Affair: Thomas Jefferson and the French Revolution.* Chicago: U of Chicago P, 1996.

Ormerod, Beverly. *Introduction to the French Caribbean Novel*. London: Heinemann, 1985.

Ott, Thomas O. *The Haitian Revolution, 1789–1804*. Knoxville: U of Tennessee P, 1973.

Pange, Comtesse Jean de. "Madame de Staël et les nègres." *Revue de France* 5 (1934): 425–43.

Patterson, Orlando. *Slavery and Social Death: A Comparative Study*. Cambridge: Harvard UP, 1982.

Peabody, Sue. *"There Are No Slaves in France": The Political Culture of Race and Slavery in the Ancien Régime*. Oxford: Oxford UP, 1996.

Pensey, P. Henrion de. *Mémoire pour le nommé Roc, nègre, contre le sieur Poupet, négotiant*. Paris: Imprimerie de J. Th. Hérissant, Imprimeur du Cabinet du Roi, 1770.

Pérotin-Dumon, Anne. *Etre Patriote sous les tropiques: La Guadeloupe, la colonisation et la révolution*. Basse-Terre: Société d'Histoire de la Guadeloupe, 1985.

Perroud, Claude. "La Société française des Amis des Noirs." *La Révolution Française* 69 (1916): 122–47.

Phillips, Christopher. "'Negroes and Other Slaves': The African-American Community of Baltimore, 1790–1860." Ph.D. diss., University of Georgia, 1993.

Phillips, Glenn O. "Maryland and the Caribbean, 1634–1984: Some Highlights." *Maryland Historical Magazine* 83, 3 (1988): 199–214.

Pluchon, Pierre. "Introduction." In Général Pamphile de Lacroix, *La Révolution de Haïti*. Paris: Karthala, 1995.

———. *Nègres et juifs au 18e siècle: Le Racisme au siècle des lumières*. Paris: Tallendier, 1984.

Pouliquen, Monique. *Doléances des peuples coloniaux à l'Assemblée Nationale Constituante, 1789–1790*. Paris: Archives Nationales, 1989.

Praeger, Michèle. "Maryse Condé: Mythes et contre-mythes." In *L'Oeuvre de Maryse Condé: Questions et réponses à propos d'une écrivaine politiquement incorrecte*, 205–15. Paris: L'Harmattan, 1996.

Reed, Revon. *Lâche Pas La Patate: Portrait des Acadiens de la Louisiane*. Montréal: Editions Partis Pris, 1976.

Rémusat, Charles de. *L'Habitation de Saint-Domingue ou l'insurrection, 1825*. Paris: Editions du CNRS, 1977.

Resnick, Daniel P. "The *Société des Amis des Noirs* and the Abolition of Slavery." *French Historical Studies* 7 (1972): 558–69.

La Révolution française et l'abolition de l'esclavage. Paris: EDHIS, 1968.

Ros, Martin. *Night of Fire: The Black Napoleon and the Battle for Haiti*. New York: Sarpedon, 1994.

Rouse, Michael F. *A Study of the Development of Negro Education under Catholic Auspices in Maryland and Washington, D.C*. Baltimore: Johns Hopkins UP, 1935.

Saint-Ruf, Germain. *L'Epopée Delgrès: La Guadeloupe sous la Révolution française.* Paris: L'Harmattan, 1977.

Sand, George. "Le Poème de Myrza." *Revue des Deux Mondes,* March 1, 1835.

Schafer, Judith Kelleher. *Slavery, the Civil Law, and the Supreme Court of Louisiana.* Baton Rouge: Louisiana State UP, 1994.

Schwarz-Bart, Simone. *Pluie et vent sur Telumée miracle.* Paris: Seuil, 1972.

Scott, Julius S. "The Common Wind: Currents of Afro-American Communication in the Era of the Haitian Revolution." Ph.D. diss., Duke University, 1986.

Seeber, Edward D. *Anti-Slavery Opinion in France during the Second Half of the Eighteenth Century.* Baltimore: Johns Hopkins UP, 1937.

———. "*Oroonoko* in France in the Eighteenth Century." *PMLA* 51, 1 (1936): 953–59.

Segal, Ronald. *The Black Diaspora.* London: Faber and Faber, 1995.

Sidbury, James. "Saint-Domingue in Virginia: Ideology, Local Meanings, and Resistance to Slavery, 1790–1800." *Journal of Southern History* 63 (1997): 531–52.

Singler, John V. "African Influence upon Afro-American Language Varieties," in *Africanisms in Afro-American Language Varieties,* ed. Salikoko Mufwene, 235–53. Athens: U of Georgia P, 1992.

Sobel, Mechal. *The World They Made Together: Black and White Values in Eighteenth-Century Virginia.* Princeton: Princeton UP, 1987.

Spalding, Thomas. *The Premier See: A History of the Archdiocese of Baltimore, 1789–1989.* Baltimore: Johns Hopkins UP, 1989.

Steward, Theophilus G. "How the Black St. Domingo Legion Saved the Patriot Army in the Siege of Savannah, 1779." In *Occasional Papers No. 5.* Washington, D.C.: American Negro Academy, 1899.

Sypher, Wylie. *Guinea's Captive Kings.* Chapel Hill: U of North Carolina P, 1942.

Trouillot, Michel-Rolph. *Silencing the Past: Power and the Production of History.* Boston: Beacon Press, 1995.

Valdman, Albert. "Les Créoles français entre l'oral et l'écrit." In *Proceedings of the Freiburg Symposium on Creole Literacy,* ed. Ralph Ludwig, 43–63. Tübingen, Germany: Gunter Narr Verlag, 1989.

Vandercook, John W. *Black Majesty: The Life of Christophe King of Haiti.* New York: Harper and Brothers, 1928.

Vidalenc, Jean. "La Traite des nègres en France au début de la Révolution française." *Annales historiques de la Révolution française* (1957).

Walvin, James. *Slavery and British Society, 1776–1846.* Baton Rouge: Louisiana State UP, 1982.

Watson, Alan. *Slave Law in the Americas.* Athens: U of Georgia P, 1989.

Webb, Barbara J. *Myth and History in Caribbean Fiction: Alejo Carpentier, Wilson Harris, and Edouard Glissant.* Amherst: U of Massachusetts P, 1992.

Weld, Isaac. *Travels through the States of North America*. 1807. Reprint, New York: Augustus Kelley, 1968.

Williams-Myers, Albert James. "Slavery, Rebellion, and Revolution in the Americas: A Historiographical Scenario on the Theses of Genovese and Others." *Journal of Black Studies* 26, 4 (1996): 381–400.

Wish, Harvey. "American Slave Insurrections before 1861." In *American Slavery: The Quest of Resistance*, ed. John H. Bracey Jr., August Meier, and Elliott M. Rudwick, 21–36. Belmont, Calif.: Wadsworth, 1971.

Zimra, Clarisse. Introduction to *Lone Sun*, by Daniel Maximin. Charlottesville: UP of Virginia, 1989.

———. "Négritude in the Feminine Mode: The Case of Martinique and Guadeloupe." *Journal of Ethnic Studies* 12, 1 (1984): 53–77.

Contributors

A. JAMES ARNOLD is Professor of French at the University of Virginia. He has written widely on French Caribbean studies, including *Modernism and Negritude: The Poetry and Poetics of Aimé Césaire* (1981), *A History of Literature in the Caribbean* (Vol. 1, 1994; Vol. 3, 1997), and *Monsters, Tricksters, and Sacred Cows: Animal Tales and American Identities* (1996). He is series editor of New World Studies at the University Press of Virginia.

JOAN DAYAN is Regents Professor of English at the University of Arizona. Her most recent book is *Haiti, History, and the Gods* (1995). Her current book project is titled *Held in the Body of the State: Chain, Classification, and the Death Penalty in an Arizona Prison.*

DOUGLAS R. EGERTON is Professor of History at Le Moyne College. He is the author of books on Denmark Vesey and Charles Fenton Mercer. *Gabriel's Rebellion: The Virginia Slave Conspiracies of 1800 and 1802* was a History Book Club selection and winner of the SHEAR Annual Book Prize in 1994. His articles have appeared in *Journal of Southern History, The Historian, Civil War History, Journal of the Early Republic,* and *North Carolina Historical Review.*

Before her death, KIMBERLY S. HANGER was Assistant Professor of History at the University of Tulsa. Her book *Bounded Lives, Bounded Places: Free Black Society in Colonial New Orleans, 1769–1803* (1997) was awarded the Kemper and Leila Williams Prize for the best book in Louisiana history published in that year. She also wrote *A Medley of Cultures: Louisiana History at the Cabildo* (1996) and several articles published in *Colonial Latin American Historical Review, Louisiana History, Revista/Review Interamericana,* and *Military History of the Southwest.*

JOHN CLAIBORNE ISBELL is Assistant Professor of French at Indiana University. His published works on Romantic world civilization from 1776 to 1848 focus on Germaine de Staël, including *The Birth of European Romanticism: Truth and Propaganda in Staël's De l'Allemagne* (1994), *Madame de Staël: Ecrits retrouvés* (1995), and *Madame de Staël: Oeuvres de jeunesse* (1997).

DORIS Y. KADISH is Professor of French and Women's Studies at the University of Georgia. She has written widely on women writers and slavery in French nineteenth-century literature, including *Translating Slavery: Gender and Race in French Women's Writing, 1783–1823* (1994), *Politicizing Gender: Narrative Strategies in the Aftermath of the French Revolution* (1991), and *The Literature of Images: Narrative Landscape from* Julie *to* Jane Eyre (1987).

DIANE BATTS MORROW is Assistant Professor of History and African American Studies at the University of Georgia. Her current work focuses on the Oblate Sisters of Providence, the first Roman Catholic African-American sisterhood, which was established in Baltimore in 1828 and cofounded by members of the Francophone diaspora fleeing the San Domingan slave revolution.

GABRIEL LOUIS MOYAL is Associate Professor of French at McMaster University, Hamilton, Ontario, Canada. He is the author of *La Trace du somnambule: Maître Cornélius de Balzac* (1985) and *Traduction et textualité* (1986). He has published widely on topics in nineteenth-century French literature and history, translation, psychoanalysis, and literary theory. His current projects include a study of Balzac's *Le Cousin Pons*.

MARIE-JOSÉ N'ZENGOU-TAYO is Associate Professor of French at the University of the West Indies, Mona, Kingston, Jamaica. Her publications on Haitian popular migration and its literary representation have appeared in *Journal of Haitian Studies, Espace Caraïbe, Journal of West Indian Literature, TTR: Traduction, Terminologie, Rédaction, Moving beyond Boundaries: Black Women's Diaspora*, and *The Bordering of Culture: Latin America, the Caribbean, and Canada*.

CATHERINE REINHARDT is a lecturer at the University of Memphis. Her areas of research include slavery in Martinique, Guadeloupe, and Saint-Domingue during the eighteenth century and contemporary Francophone and comparative Caribbean literatures.

LEARA RHODES is Assistant Professor of Journalism at the University of Georgia. Her works on Caribbean mass communication have appeared in *Journalism Quarterly, Caribbean Affairs Journal, Journal of Development Communication*, and others. Her journalistic activities and research have been conducted in Haiti, Trinidad, and Dominica.

ALBERT VALDMAN is Rudy Professor of French and Italian and Director of the Creole Institute, Indiana University. He is past president of the American Association of Teachers of French and author of numerous works on linguistics, language teaching, and creole studies. His works in creole studies include *Pidgin and Creole Linguistics* (1977), *Le Créole: Structure, statut et origine* (1978), and *Haitian Creole-English-French Dictionary* (1981). His recent research includes works on creole languages in Louisiana as well as the Caribbean: *Ann pale kreyòl: An Introductory Course in Haitian Creole* (1988), *A Learner's Dictionary of Haitian Creole* (1996), and *Dictionary of Louisiana Creole* (1998).

Index

abolition, 11, 49–50, 53, 67, 219; arguments against, by planters, 30–34; arguments for, by slaves, 26–30; in Saint-Domingue, 34, 98. See also *Le Constitutionnel;* emancipation; *Société des Amis des Noirs*

abolitionists, xii–xiii, xiv, xvi; Clarkson, xv, 4, 21, 40, 46; Condorcet, xvi, 2, 21, 34; Genet, 94; Hugo, xvi; Lamartine, xvi; Raynal, xvi, 2, 40; Schoelcher, xiv, 182; Staël, xvi, 39–50; Warville, 21, 40, 95. See also *Société des Amis des Noirs;* Wilberforce, William

Adam, Lucien, 280, 281

Adams, John, 99, 100

Addison, Joseph, 41

Adrien, Claude, 80, 82

African languages: comparisons among, 150–52; and Creole, 147, 149–52, 158–60, 160 (n. 4); Ewe, 149, 151–53, 155; Igbo, 151, 161 (n. 8); Kwa, 149, 152, 153; maintenance of, 154–56, 181; Yoruba, 151, 152, 155

Africans: and authoritarian rule, 214–15; different nations of, 155; religious argument for enslavement of, 5, 29; and slave trade, 63–70, 156, 211

agency, xv–xviii; by blacks, xvii–xviii, 5, 6, 25–27, 35, 181–82; by Europeans, xvi–xvii

Ailhaud, Jean Antoine, 6

alienation, 54, 176, 183

Alleyne, Mervyn, 157

Amiens, Treaty of, 10, 43, 102

Amis des Noirs. See *Société des Amis des Noirs*

Arendt, Hannah, 22, 28

Arizona, xxi, 191, 192, 197–208

Arpaio, Joe, 192, 204–8

Assemblée Nationale, 22, 31–33

Balas, Marie, 122–24, 130–31

Balch, Thomas, 82

Baltimore, 122–35

Balutansky, Kathleen, 216

Balzac, Honoré de, 119–23

Bangou, Henri, 214

Baum, Joan, 49

Beauvais, Louis Jacques, 80, 84

Bébel-Gisler, Dany, xxii, 157, 167; and education, 172; and gender, 172–74; *Léonora: L'Histoire enfouie de la Guadeloupe,* 171–74; and social action, 173–74

Beddenhurst, Alexander, 102

Behn, Aphra, 41, 45